Just Another Lost Boy

Stewart Brown

The Author asserts the moral right to be identified as the author of this work.

All rights reserved. No part of this publication may be reproduced or transmitted, in any form or otherwise, without the copyright owner's prior permission.
The cover art used belongs to the Publisher.

Copyright © 2025 **Stewart Brown**
Published in the UK by Greystone Consultancy LTD
ISBN: 978-1-0683590-2-6

Content Warning

This book includes references to child sexual abuse and its aftermath. The material is handled with care and does not glorify or sensationalise abuse, but may still be distressing for some readers.

Disclaimer

This is a work of fiction. While inspired by the author's experiences and observations during his work with young people in London, the characters, names, and many settings have been changed. Any resemblance to actual persons, living or dead, or to real events or places, is entirely coincidental.

DEDICATION

In memory of Pauline, who I know would have loved this book

I would like to thank Carolyn Brown for her continued patience, editing skills and support.
My nephew, Paul Offord, for his observations and initial editing suggestions.
The fellow author, Anka B. Troitsky, for her book cover and production skills.
Encouragement from friends and colleagues to get this very important story out there.

The following are part sections of my book reviews:

Phil Jones: Journalist and former BBC Editor of the Jeremy Vine Radio Show.
This is a book that Stewart needed to write, and the rest of us need to read. Whether or not you're familiar with the world it describes, the stories of these boys, their lives, their struggles, and their humanity deserve to be heard and understood by everyone.

Fergus (Gus) Cairns: Oxford Graduate, Volunteer at Gay Switchboard and Centrepoint Soho in the 1980's. Psychotherapist and HIV survivor. Editor of 'Positive Nation'.
I loved this novel. It's so close to the spirit of the times. It wasn't easy, or safe, being a gay teenager in the 1970's, has it ever been? But at least, there was the beginnings, in the 1980's in London, of a slow relaxation of the laws against gay sex. A commercial clubbing scene was being develop where men could meet and hang out and gay specific help services began to exist, starting with Gay Switchboard, where I'd also been a volunteer, and found that I was quite good at talking to people even more bewildered than I. Stewart portrays this in the book which is a real tale of survival. One of the most impressive aspects of Stewart's story is, that it may dive into the darkest depths of abuse and paedophilia, but it never loses sight of the humanity of its victims, whose misadventures are fuelled by hope, a hope that, somewhere out there on the mean streets, lies a world of fulfilment that will take them away from the grey misery of childhood.

Malcom Stow: Senior Social Worker. Independent Chair of Local Authority Child Care Case Reviews in the UK.
I read this to the end in one sitting. It is a very compelling piece of character personalised necessary social history. It is authentic, true and is a difficult read from the start.

Introduction:

Two sexually abused young boys, with different backgrounds, families, and life experiences, who were drawn into London's rent boy scene.

I met so many like them through 'Centrepoint Night Shelter'. Support services for homeless kids in Central London during the 1980's.

I will never forget.

This story is about the seemingly endless stream of 'Lost Boys' their survival instincts, short life experiences, profound sadness, and a hope that emanates from the aspirations and the natural yearnings of youth.

As a youth worker in the late 1970's and 1980's specifically as a full-time Night Shelter Worker at 'Centrepoint', I witnessed a trail of boys and girls who got sucked into the sleazier side of Piccadilly and Soho.

Picked up by pimps who would do anything they could to take control of any young person considered to have some street value. They used charm, gifts, drugs, adult persuasion and threats to influence and inflict power and control, usually on well-chosen youths who were vulnerable and susceptible to those who were well practised at grooming young people, and in some cases had experienced similar levels of abuse in their own lifetimes.

While working at 'Centrepoint' during the early 1980's we were constantly challenged by, how little could be done for underage children at the night shelter, even with the associated support agencies in the West End. It often felt like we were leaving 'lambs for the slaughter', right outside on the streets of London, as there was no provision by Law at the time, to legally take an under 16-year-old child off the street and provide them with accommodation.

We were being told that as an organisation and as individuals, we could be sued and closed down for taking this action. Children were being sent back home or to care by the police or social services departments against their will and going out of the back door and returning to London, but this time avoiding the helping agencies for fear of being returned.

Chapter 1

Stephen four days ago, countdown - Saturday 22-01-1983.

I

I felt like shit, it was after 10.00pm, I was cold, and January is the worst month to be out and about on the streets in London.

I had just wanked and sucked off a punter in the small park behind the 'Centrepoint' homeless place, in St Anne's gardens, off Wardour Street where it meets with Shaftesbury Avenue, and made £20. It was a good place to take someone in a busy part of the West End for a quick earner, in the corner of the church garden, where there is some tree and bush cover from passersby.

I was finding it more difficult these days picking them up, as there were always younger boys, who were the preferred kind, a safer option sort after as demand dictated. We'd all been easily accessible to passing trade on the chicken run, at Piccadilly Circus. I had been doing it for years, since I was 15. We were the 'chickens'... young and willing to do most things for a price, rent boys ready and able for fun and perversions.

That last punter was an older guy, about 50 something. He looked okay. He was nervous but was excited and stimulated because of what he was paying me for and knew what to expect as he'd done it before.
I told him the price for a hand job with extras, but I didn't give a fuck as I was desperate for the money and needed to find Dougie.

I had started using again after months off the stuff. St Ann's Garden was a good place to do what you needed to, and doss down if you were desperate.

The only problem was that you had to often share the small park with the dosser alcoholics, who were not the easiest people to be near, as they would rob you as soon as look at you, awake or in your sleep, if you gave them a chance by leaving a bag or coat within easy reach for them to rummage through. They rarely were aggressive but at odd times you got the ones who were drunk, angry, or mental, and they were scary beings that you just needed to avoid.

Anyway, this punter handed over the £20 and we found a corner of the garden where he started by putting his arms around me, as they do, pulling me close and caressing my back and wanting to kiss me, I told him not on the lips, so he kissed my neck and cheeks.

I could feel his erection filling his trousers and I started to undo his belt and zipper, which allowed his trousers to fall to the floor. I wanted to get it over as quick as possible. I detested what I was doing but had to play it nicely to get through. He was excited and all I had to do was touch and suck to gain his trust.

I had a good feel in his pockets while his trousers were around his feet, but they only contained a crumpled tissue, "ugh I hated that." He was happy enough to let this whole process happen and when he had 'come', he thanked me and I told him that it was OK and I thanked him, sponging my hand with his tissue. He zipped up without wiping up and wanted to kiss and caress me some more, but really, he just needed to get away and so did I.

I often wondered what their stories were. Were they married and denying their sexuality? Were they bisexual or just into male prostitutes and quick sex? Whatever their reasons, I was left with twenty pounds in my pocket and nowhere to sleep tonight and in need of something to make me feel better.

I could have gone back to Piccadilly Circus and hang around to see what and who were still there. I could try to get into 'Centrepoint' but knew that someone would recognise me and send me off.

Bed and breakfast at Kings Cross would have cost £14 or waiting it out in the all-night café down by the Embankment was another option, but that was a real dive, and I always felt terrible the following day with lack of sleep.

I wanted to find Dougie most of all. I tried the Wimpy Bar by the "Dilly" but drew a blank. That was where we used to meet in the old days. He'd been as bad as me, sometimes taking more of the stuff than he sold, but had moved on in some respects and found a way through. Whatever happened, I knew I would need to keep £5.00 back to take the edge off and distract me from what was running through my head.

II

Dougie had been renting and ducking and dodging in London from 14 years old. He was three years older than me but looked young for his age. People often took us as brothers, and we used to sometimes team up when group time was required.

He was a manipulative greedy bugger who always got

what he wanted and was great at making you feel good and important. If he could see an angle or a way to make money or take advantage of a situation he would do it with little regard for others.

He was a cool gay who was able to entertain and draw people into his circle. People liked him, he made me laugh, and he was a great dancer oozing confidence. He had loads of funny stories and the ability to talk as though he had a world of experience. I was drawn to him and felt special when I was there with him. Believing briefly that I was his chosen one and best friend.

Yeah, I'd slowly learnt not to trust him, but he was still my best mate. There was a vulnerable damaged side to Dougie too. Like the rest of us, he had more stories than he would ever want to remember or disclose.

III

I walked around to Dean Street towards Shaftesbury Avenue in the hope I would get picked up by someone I know from my time here in this big shitty City called London. I now see it as a place that eats up innocents, and spits it out, once it has taken all the sustenance that it can consume from one person, my youth, and it has had the best of me I can tell you, it took me too long to learn.

It was now Saturday night, and I am 20 years old going on 30, and feel like I am not worth anything, I have done it all and got nothing, just this £20 and the clothes on my back. Where are those people who promised that they would look after me?

I went into the Golden Lion pub in Dean Street and spent £4.10 on two double whiskies and cokes to help anaesthetise the taste and fear of infection at the back of my throat, knowing that there was no chance of Bed and breakfast now.

This was a strange pub with a mixture of clients ranging from the odd tourists, local West End residents and gay older men, who always gave you that look, half questioning why you were there. They probably wanted to make contact, but most were too withdrawn to introduce themselves.

I recognised a couple of them from before, but I did not think that they knew me. One was particularly obvious with his tall thin looks. He shot me long glances as he talked with his friends.

This guy was mid 40's with thick black hair, combed to one side, wearing wire-framed glasses. He spoke with a Scottish accent, like me, but I couldn't shake an uncomfortable feeling. I kept my eye focus mainly on my drink, occasionally looking up as Save Your Love by Renee and Renato played on the pub jukebox, followed by You can't hurry love by Phil Collins, which I liked the best. It had a good beat, and you could dance to it.

I always felt awkward in pubs on my own and did not particularly like the smell of beer and smoking. It was a good place to get warm and participate in some alcohol, but all I really wanted was to find Dougie. At least the whisky helped me feel better and a little pissed, as I had not eaten anything since this morning.

I left the pub and turned right onto Shaftsbury

Avenue, past McDonalds and decided to go back and get myself a Big Mac dinner and Coke, more money but it was a place to sit for a while.

Walking down Shaftesbury Avenue, I saw the Centrepoint workers interviewing some youths at the gate. I popped my head in to see Linda and said half joking: "is there any chance of a bed tonight?" I knew the answer, as they had told me many times that I had used up all my stays at the emergency night shelter.

They were always friendly, though, and asked me how I was getting on. I reminded myself of the many chances that they and the 'Soho Project 'had given me, how many times they had warned me about the West End and helped me to get back to Scotland.

Too late now. I walked onto the Dilly as I had so many times before.

Centrepoint log: Stephen Addair. DOB: 10.06.1962. 22-01-1983

Stephen came past the gates tonight about 11.00pm and said hello.
He seemed in reasonable good spirit but was on his own and looked a little grubby. He walked down Shaftesbury Avenue in a hurry. Need to inform Soho Project on Monday.

Linda.

Chapter 2

I

I was 15 years old when I first came to London. I was so innocent and thought the big city was magic. I loved the sense of freedom excitement, and fun that seemed to be going on all around and wanted to be part of it.

I wanted to live here and make my life, future, fame, and fortune away from Scotland. No more Edinburgh, no more mum, and that children's home.

It was Monday, May 1978, two weeks before my 16th birthday. I had decided to run away from Glenallan children's home, it was boring and Edinburgh was too quiet.

I didn't want to take my exams either. I don't think my school was that worried. I had always struggled to keep up because I used to bunk off so much.

The Bee Gees 'Staying Alive was playing on my mini radio. I liked funky dance sounds and had seen the film last year, which had made me feel like I was missing out on something. I wanted to be free to do what I wanted, like Tony Manero (John Travolta) and loved to do the bounce walk to the music.

I was good at dancing, and when I danced at home and in discos, I felt like people looked at me, kind of watching, which made me feel special, like I was important.

I took the train from Edinburgh Waverley to Kings Cross. It was a fast one that only stopped at York and lasted just over six hours. I had saved some money from my allowance at the children's home and what I'd got from my street encounters, and from Travis.

Travis was my key worker at Glenallan. He had been a good person to talk to when I was confused and angry. They called it running away from home, but I never felt like I had a home. It was a place where I could keep my clothes, get my pocket money allowance, eat hot food, wash, and hang out until something better came along.

In the early days, I would try to get back with my mum, the trouble was that it took me a long time to realise, by talking to Travis, that my mum was not that good at being a mum.

When I used to turn up unexpected, she would mostly be drunk and with some complete loser.

II

I felt angrier than ever that she did not learn by her mistakes, care about her-self or me.

Her home was mostly pretty scruffy and filled with cigarette smoke and she would be half dressed with a stranger, and out of her head most of the time, but there was nothing I could do or say that I had not done or said already, she was my mum. I felt like I should be helping her as I did think about her a lot but knew she would continue hurting herself over and over again.

I kind of remember that I used to have regular short visits with her when I was seven and eight years old. She seemed to make the effort to not be drunk when the social worker took me over to visit.

We would sometimes go out to the shops, but she would always end up in a pub and sit me by a table with some crisps, with the blue salt wraps and Pepsi Cola or Irn-Bru, but I liked Pepsi best.

My social worker, Peggy, said that my mum loved me but was not able to be the kind of mum she would like to be because she would get distracted by people and other stuff.

My mum would whisper to me, "don't tell Peggy", when she was going out, "they will not let you visit me anymore if you do".

After the visits, just as I was being collected by Peggy, she would always give me some money as I was leaving and tell me to spend it wisely, then she would place her finger to her mouth like we had a secret.

Stephen Addair aged 7. Lothian and Boarders Children's Services. DOB: 10.06.1962. Monday 16th March 1970. 10.30am.

First supervised visit with Stephen to Barbara Addair's flat in Craigshill, Almond Road, Livingstone.
Barbara was sober and alone and seemed happy to see Stephen. She was welcoming and asked Stephen how he was and were they looking after him.
There was very little physical contact, and Stephen went straight to the television and switched it on. The flat was tidy but smelt heavily of cigarette smoke. I was offered a cup of tea and looked into the kitchen, where there was a cup left on the drainer with a saucer leaning against it but no

evidence of alcohol on the premises. We drank our tea, and I explained that this was the first supervised visit and that if it went well that there would be a second two hour visit next month, that could be unsupervised.

Barbara seemed slightly agitated. She talked about how hard it was bringing a child up on her own on this fucking estate and lit a cigarette.

She told me that her mum had done the same with her, stating 'that woman could smoke for Scotland' and that she never really knew her dad. She remembered him but could not say that she knew him, and her mum had died when she was 17 from, she said, 'I think cancer, or a broken heart, she was only 42 when she died, same age as me now'.

Barbara told me that she had one other bairn, a girl, but lost her years ago.

I explained that I would talk to the alcohol support group about bereavement counselling. When we left. Barbara gave Stephen a £2.00 telling him to spend it on what he wanted.

Peggy Smith. Social Worker.

Stephen Addair, age 7. Lothian and Boarders Children's Services. DOB: 10.06.1962.
Thursday 17th of May 1970

This was the second, two-hour, unsupervised visit.
Stephen seemed happy and willing to be there, knowing that they would be left alone for a couple of hours.

The stay would be from 10.30am, and that I would collect him at 12.30pm. I asked Barbara how she was feeling and what she was going to do with Stephen today. I suggested a walk to the park, but she said she was not feeling one hundred percent and they would probably watch some TV together.

I collected Stephen at 12.30pm and he walked out with me without saying anything to his mother other then "bye." Barbara said it had gone well, but she seemed distracted and eager to close the door behind us.

Stephen said it was Ok, and that his mum had given him two pounds this time.

Peggy Smith. Social Worker.

III

I was so excited that first time my train pulled into Kings Cross Station. I ran up the platform, almost forgetting to show my ticket at the barrier.

I gazed up at the big clock as it moved to 5.30pm exactly and looked for the exit sign. London was bright and sunny and warmer than Scotland.

The sun was glimmering through the glass roof at the station, and I felt excited and alive.

I wanted to see the sights of this big city but had not really planned anything. I had £35, which seemed like a lot of money back home. It didn't last long.

Kings Cross Station was big and imposing inside, but the outside was not that nice a place, with loud car and bus noises that bustled, beeped and boomed with the stench smell of dust and engine oil. I stepped out of the station onto a fume filled road running along the entrance to the station with two junctions to the left, where black cabs jockeyed for first spot in a queue directly in front.

I decided to walk up the Euston Road past St Pancras station, which was a beautiful but dirty building next to King Cross station. I felt that I looked smart in my Ben Sherman shirt, baggies and brogue style platform shoes.

I had a sling bag with a change of clothes and carried my bomber jacket under my arm linked through the drawstring of the sack. People seemed to be rushing past and London was so different to what I was used to. I felt a little lost and started to get scared as to what I had done and worried about where I would stay that night.

I got to the Capital Radio building, Euston Tower, and the big London hospital on the junction of Tottenham Court Road and Euston Road.

I walked along Tottenham Court Road and saw a road sign giving directions to Oxford Street, a place I remembered from playing monopoly. The road seemed fun and lively, with music playing from various music sales outlets.

The shops and food places were buzzing with people, I felt better and excited again. I went into a really good shop that sold music systems. I remember going in, and the radio was playing the 'Commodores', 'Three times a lady', and I started thinking that I could get one of those, as the sound seemed to surround you and it felt like I was in the middle of something smooth and special.

One of the salespeople approached me and asked if they could help. I pretended that I wanted to buy a record player and had practiced my speech about being 17 years old. I was born in 1960, if anyone asked, and would turn 18 this June. He showed me the latest stereo system with dual tape decks and explained every aspect of it. I asked about something more portable. He showed me a radio and tape mini boom box that I really liked, but it was £39.99.

He also showed me pictures of the new portable compact size Sony Walkman coming to stores soon. It looked brilliant, light blue-and-silver, and I thought that I would love to have one of those.

I carried on walking along Tottenham Court Road eventually arriving at Oxford Street and saw this very tall building called CENTREPOINT. The name was written across the top in capital letters.

Standing on the pavement at the front of the structure was a group of punk rockers by the fountains. They seemed so vibrant, proudly looking like the classic Punks with multi coloured Mohican hairstyles, wearing tartan trousers, tartan skirts, and black T-Shirts. Great slashes of the clothing were being held together with safety pins, of varying sizes, fastening fragments of fabrics around the torso.

They were a bit drunk, shouting and pushing against each other, like they needed to keep moving and making contact by falling about, but also looked like they were having a whole lot of fun together on that Monday evening in late May.

They appeared to be on show, performing, and loving every bit of interest they were receiving from people around them. Photographs were being taken while well-practiced two fingered poses were positioned in the direction of the cameras in an attempt to fully shock tourists and spectators.

I saw money being handed over from Chinese tourists who smiled, as the punks made half-hearted angry gestures and expressions, while having their pictures taken with them. Their hair was amazing, raised bright plumes standing tall with faces daubed with black lipstick. I was not into punk music, The Clash, The Sex Pistols, Jonny Rotten, and Sid Vicious. I didn't like that look, it was scruffy and too stuck together with the safety pins and sticky looking hair.

My mate Dennis back in Edinburgh was a punk and used sugar water to hold up his Mohican. He tore holes in his T-shirt and trousers and used safety pins to hold the rips together. I was more like a soft Mod who liked chart music but also still had my tight Baggies, which I thought had gone out of fashion now, but who cares anyway. I could not do the Punk thing, as I wanted to feel smart and normal when out and about with my friends. That's why I did not want to hang out with Dennis anymore even though he was good fun to be with. He also knew his music and liked the loud rawness of the punk sound, while I liked what was in the charts especially if it had some disco and funk.

I walked onto Charing Cross Road where I bought a kebab and sat in a small park at the bottom of a narrow road to a place called Soho Square. It was starting to get late, and I suddenly felt anxious and very alone, looking around at all the people with friends, girlfriends, and boyfriends.

I sat there for some time, thinking how long it would take me to walk back to Kings Cross Station and could I catch a train home.

After a while, I noticed a boy who was about my age, maybe older, with thick black hair cut in a Rod Stewart style. He was dressed smart in a navy-blue V-neck wrap around jumper, flares, and suede platform shoes. There was a can of Coca cola in his hand, and he was sat on a bench.

He stared over, then slowly got up and started walking towards me, as I sat on my bench. He smiled and said: "Hi mate, how's it going?"

I told him I was fine, but I felt awkward, as he was kind of looking straight at me, into my face and eyes.

"What are you doing here?" he said, I told him I was visiting London and wanted to see Piccadilly Circus and Trafalgar Square. He said he would show me where it was, "it is very close."

He asked me where I was from and said his name was Dougie. He asked, "What's yours hen?" I told him it was Stephen and that "I'm not a lassie or queer".

He said: "Stevie that's good, nice to meet a fellow Scot".

Dougie talked a lot, telling me how he lived in London and knew loads of people. He had come to London from Glasgow to have fun when he was 14. It was great, good clubs.

He hated skins and punks, but the punks were OK if you kept away from them and left them alone to do their stupid glue-sniffing thing.

He asked me to guess his age, and said, "People always guess me as being younger than I am". So, I said "17".

He told me he was 18 but "good guess wee man, I am 19, this September".

Dougie admitted he had seen me walk across the square and thought I looked lonely, like I might need a friend. I was a little unsure at first, but he seemed a nice guy and quickly made me laugh by pointing to a fat man with a pot belly, saying: "Ha, I wonder when the wee bairn is due?"
We walked through the square, and I appreciated the friendly attention of a fellow Scot, who, seemed to like me. I felt a little safer and less anxious about being down south in the big city.

Chapter 3

Nine years earlier.
Stephen Addair aged 7. Lothian and Boarders Child Protection Services. DOB: 10.06.1962

28-11-1969. 9.30pm

I was called to Mr. and Mrs. Logan's flat to make an assessment of Stephen Addair who was a vulnerable child living with an alcoholic mother one flat down from them. We had some previous information on file, which I subsequently found, headed Craigs Hill school actions, which listed seven other families where concerns had been raised.

His school had flagged him up as vulnerable child who had poor attendance and there were concerns about how capable his mother was because of poor hygiene, some neglect, and a previous sibling fatality, but no home visit had been made to date.

The neighbours were concerned for his safety and had taken him in and called the police who contacted child protection. I went to his mother's flat at 10.34pm this evening and found her to be very drunk and in the company of an older man who was semi clothed and very abusive.

The Police supported me as I explained to Mrs. Addair that she was in no fit state to look after a child and that Stephen *was being taken to a safe place. Mrs Addair made some protest, but she was not capable or able to argue about the decision that I had made.*

We took Stephen to an emergency foster home in Edinburgh in the short term so that we could fully assess how best Stephen could be supported.

John Sissons. Emergency Social Worker. 00.10am. 29-11-1969.

November in Livingstone, Scotland is a cold and wet place to take a child away from his mother into an unfamiliar car with a Policeman and a strange man. Stephen was confused and frightened by what was happening to him, but was also concerned about his mum, worrying that Jocky might hurt her.

He was taken away from Mr. and Mrs. Logan and Jamie's home and led down the stairs by John Sissons, who held his hand as they left late at night, in the dark and rain. Stephen picked at his scratched left arm as he sat in the back of the social workers car not knowing where and to what he was being taken to.

Mary Logan had tried to reassure Stephen that everything would be fine, and that as soon as they found out where he was living that they would come and visit him.

His life was to change forever. He was put into foster care when he was 7 years old because it was decided that he was neglected, vulnerable and in an unsafe home.

Chapter 4

Stephen at 6 years had not been going to school and was playing out until late into the evening and night.

The truth was that he did not like being at home when mum was, out of it, angry, and with the men.

It was easy to stay out of their way and hide, as they did not see him as a person and he could do what he wanted to do.

He did worry about his mum as there were times when he had to help her up out of her bed, make her a cup of tea or some toast. They ate a lot of toast with jam, Marmite, fish paste spread, Kraft cheese segments, if there was no spread, Stephen would have sugar on buttered bread.

He liked the morning best, when the radio was on, as this was when his mum was quiet and gave him some attention.

She occasionally put her arm slowly on his shoulder and leaving it there to linger for a second or two. Or she would give him that look that seemed to tell Stephen he did matter, and she was in some way aware of him and his needs, before making a grab for her cigarettes and a glass of something.

She sometimes danced when Family choice played Elvis. 'Jail House Rock` was great and she liked it when Pete Murray made jokes. 'These Boots Are Made For Walking' and 'Roll Over Beethoven' by Nancy Sinatra and Chuck Berry were other favourites.

This was the best time of the day. She would ask Stephen to go to the shop and buy food and cigarettes, before getting more agitated as the day carried on. That's when she would leave him until later, mostly to do her cleaning job at the Tower Pub.

She would regularly come back with a man, who would stay the night. Then after two or more days they would argue, and it would go back to just Stephen and his mum, which was how Stephen preferred it.

Stephen did like one man called 'Billy' who stayed with his mum for a while, and he tried to keep the house clean and cooked hot food.

Barbara seemed fond of him for a short time and looked happy when he was around. Stephen was content with Billy, as he made him feel noticed and important. He would take Stephen to the park, swings, school, and tell him when he needed to go to bed, give him cuddles, bath and wash him and would tell Stephen a story, sometimes reading books to him. Stephen particularly remembered the stories about the Dragon and Gollum, and the one about Treasure Island.

When Stephen received a cake on his 7th birthday from Billy, something his mother would mostly not bother with, they sang 'Happy Birthday' and bought him a special present, a 'Spirograph' that was a pattern making drawing toy. Stephen loved it and played with it until the paper ran out.

Billy would stay with Stephen in the bedroom when it was time to go to bed. He would say he would look after him, and that he loved Stephen and that he would make sure nothing bad ever happened to him. He would kiss the boy in a special way on the lips, and in unusual places around his head, waist, back and legs, saying: "That's what daddies do".

He would tickle Stephen and laugh as he blew raspberries over his skin.

Stephen liked having his head stroked and Billy would run his fingers through his hair and caress his back, until he went to sleep. Sometimes Barbara would call out "what are you doing in there for so long?"

Billy would call out reading a story, but would say to Stephen, "It's our secret", and tell him not to say a thing to mum or anyone, or he may get into trouble and have to go away.

Stephen liked Billy, and wanted to call him daddy, and sometimes did. Billy would have let Stephen call him daddy, but his mum said he was only a friend not a dad.

He stayed with them and looked after Stephen and Barbara for nearly a year, even though she was drinking, and would sometimes get angry, and tell him to get out and piss off.

These were the times when Billy would cuddle Stephen close in his bedroom, saying it was their special time. Telling Stephen that he could call him Daddy when they were alone together, but not to tell his mum, or she would stop them seeing each other, as it was their secret. Billy would take his clothes off with Stephan and lie next to him on the bed, touch, and stroke Stephen all over, and put Stephen's hand on Billy's private part, which was hard, and Stephen knew Billy liked it and wanted to please him. Billy would tell Stephen that he loved him and the special things that they did together were what Daddies did when they loved their sons. Stephen wanted to make Billy happy and liked that feeling of closeness that he did not get from his mother.

Eventually Billy left after Stephen's mum came to his bedroom when Billy was sitting next to Stephen with his trousers off. He was watching Stephen dancing around naked, while pushing his 'willy' through his legs and saying, "look at me, look I am a girl". Billy laughed, and at that moment Barbara opened the door and started to shout and scream at Billy, pulling him out of the room. She called him a pervert and a fucking bastard and told him to get out and that if he came back, she would report him.

Billy never returned and Stephen did not see him again.

Barbara never really spoke to Stephen about what she had seen. In Stephen's eyes she was annoyed with him, he was frightened at first, but she just went back to going out and coming back angry and being scary drunk.

Stephen was confused, unhappy and felt hopeless when Billy left, and hated his mum for making him go. He did not want to show his mum that he had been crying, angrily pulling his fingernails across his left wrist again and again until he began to bleed, which helped to distract and absorb the pain.

Stephen always remembered Billy and felt like he had let him down by not going with him. He constantly looked for him when he was out.

Instinctively he knew that he just had to keep away from his mum when she was sad, thinking that he was to blame, hoping that Billy would come and visit on his next birthday and may be take him away.

Chapter 5

Stephen played with a boy in the flat above, called Jamie Logan who lived with his mum and dad in a nice home. They would ask Stephen to come into their flat and he would drink the best juice he had ever had, and eat the loveliest cooked food, chips, chicken, roasted tatties, short bread, and cakes. Jamie's mum Mary would ask Stephen about his mother and what she was doing, but Stephen did not like to talk about her that much, becoming agitated, and just said 'she's OK' or 'she is not feeling very well today'.

Stephen would play around the block with Jamie and as it started to get dark Mr. and Mrs. Logan would call out to Jamie from the window of their flat. Sometimes Stephen and Jamie hid out but then his parents would come and find Jamie by shouting, "Jamie where are you it's time to come inside" Stephen wanted Jamie to stay out longer but Jamie was scared that he would get in trouble with his parents and go to his mum. She would always say "Stephen you need to get off home as well" but he wouldn't and just messed around by himself until it was really dark, wondering if his mum would come looking for him.

When he got home, if it was calm, he would make something to eat. Check on his mum, sometimes helping her to be more comfortable or put a cover on her wherever she was, and then go to his bedroom. On a good day Stephen's mum would sometimes say Stephen where have you been?

But he could say anything, and she would hardly reply. The winters and dark cold nights in Scotland were the worst as not many children played out. They had to go inside their flats, as it was freezing and scary on the estate, particularly when the older boys and girls were about.

They had places where they would go, like the deserted garages, but that was a privilege of adolescent youth, not for the under 8-year-olds.

When some of the older boys and girls let Stephen into the group it was because he had some use, like when they were playing 'Kiss and Dare' and Stephen was used as the adjudicator, and his job was to watch, from a separate place, and report back, if they had done what was dared or kissed, and would call out, "done it" which gave Stephen a very good close up view of what boys and girls got up to in the game, and he quickly understood what sexed up meant when he watched the boys kiss and touch the girls, which he later realised was called fingering or wanking. He saw girls show boys their tits, nipples and one boy who showed his cock to a girl, who strangely screamed with a smile on her face, laughing at the semi hard piece standing forward from his trouser fly. He also saw girls hold and rub the boys off, like he had done to Billy and what Billy had tried to do to him.

Other than serving a purpose, Stephen and Jamie were too young, and if they did try to venture near one of the dens in another situation, the older boys would quickly shout and tell Stephen to go home to his fucking 'alco, prossi' mum, which meant very little, apart from the feeling that they hated his mum.

Those were the nights when Barbara used to stay out most of the time and come back with various men who also liked to drink. She was not always aware or worried that they would come into her flat, sometimes have a root around and steal anything that they thought would be worth a pound or two and piss all over the toilet seat and floor.

She used to buy and drink cheap strong cider and Special Brew, when her social was paid, or from the money she had made cleaning in the Tower Pub four afternoons a week, along with bread and spreads, so that she always had food in the house for Stephen. She was more aware of Stephen in the mornings and during these times would try to get Stephen to go to school and have a clean around once she felt up to it.

When the drinking hit its most extreme Barbara was oblivious to whom she brought home and Stephen was often confronted by one man he did not like, an older and ugly fat man called Jocky with grey spiky hair. Barbara did not always see him being mean, and abusive to Stephen, as he would push Stephen away and slap out shouting, "fuck off, you little bastard". Then he would take hold of Barbara and force himself onto her. Stephen tried to pull him away from his mum, by tugging at the man's soiled white string vest, because he was afraid that he was hurting her, and shouted at the mammoth form to, "leave her alone, you fucking fat pig". But he and also, she would tell Stephen to piss off and go away, striking out and just missing his head. It prompted the hulk to hunt him on unsteady feet. He was like a rabid large bear, frothing and dribbling from his mouth with flailing outstretched paws as he moved forward cornering the terrified boy in the angle of the room. With just enough space left for Stephen to nip under the unbalanced body of the pig, he would dodge his way to his room, hiding under his bed in an attempt to keep out of their way.

Stephen felt the most afraid that he had ever been that night as the man tried to grab him shouting "come here you little cunt", until his mum screamed in a drunken screech "leave him alone", but was not in any form of control as she would fall back shouting, "fuck off, you cunts, get out", and then look like she was going to fall asleep or collapse. Stephen had to hide and wait it out. Jocky was loud and mostly drunk, shouting a tirade of abuse, and fell over things, finally ending up sitting on the single lounge chair facing the hall, in an intoxicated stupor, only wearing his under vest and pants.

Jamie's mum and dad had heard the disturbance below them, and were concerned about the child's welfare, deciding to take a look before contacting the police. Coming down the communal stairwell to Barbara's flat, they could see the door was wide open and shouted, "hello Stephen, are you in there, are you OK wee hen"?

Jocky was sitting in the armchair facing the hall. When he spotted Mr. Logan walking through the front door, he stood up, quite rigid, standing staring at the couple, in his filthy under pants and vest, glaring at the invading pair, before sitting back down in a seemingly glazed stupefied state, while Barbara, semi dressed, was out of it on the couch in full view.

Stephen tentatively walked out to the hall, passing the ogre cautiously, as he made his way from his bedroom, relieved that Mr. and Mrs. Logan were there, and said, "I am here". Mrs. Logan held out a hand beckoning the boy to come to her, asking if he was hungry. Stephen said, "yes", so she encouragingly said, "come to us and have something to eat, come quickly".

Chapter 6

A man called John Sissons, and a Policeman came to Jamie's flat that night and told Stephen that he was going to take him to a nice house with other children, while he helped his mum sort herself out. Jamie's mum and dad told Stephen that everything would be OK and that they would come to see him at the new foster home. Stephen felt better when he heard them say that. Nervously scratching at his wrists as he was shown to the social workers car.

Stephen liked the man called John; he reminded him of one of his teachers. This was the first social worker Stephen had ever met, and he was very nice and saw Stephen two days later at the foster home.

The foster home was a big house with some other children who were being looked after. It was in Edinburgh and there were three children, all girls and they were friendly enough at first.

He stayed with Mr. and Mrs. Patterson who provided short-term fostering and also had children of their own. The youngest of the foster children was six years old, and her name was Sarah. Mr. and Mrs. Patterson's own girls were 7-year-old Zoe and 9-year-old Emma. They were friendly, welcoming and nice to play with. They were used to other children coming into their house.

Mr. and Mrs. Patterson were called Jeffrey and Jackie. Stephen was 7 years old and was made to go to bed early at

7.30pm at the same time as Sarah and Zoe and had to go to school every day. Stephen had to be a quick learner, as he had to sit at the table when they eat food throughout the day, even in the morning. He was expected to keep his room tidy and put dirty clothes in a special basket. Stephen followed what the family did and always took time to answer when he was asked a question, as he wanted to make sure, he said and did, what he thought was the right thing. He liked feeling looked after, safe and wanted, and even liked keeping his room tidy.

Stephen wondered what his mum was doing and was worried that she might not be well or that something bad might happen to her. He knew that Edinburgh was a long bus ride from his mum and that she would not know where he was but was secretly pleased knowing that Jocky could not come and get him.

After a long while he was taken to see his mum in a Family Centre with his social worker and was excited to be seeing her. Stephen had a new social worker called Peggy who was older than his mum but came to see him every two weeks. She would give him news about his mum and told him that she was trying really hard to get herself better and really wanted Stephen home with her. Peggy explained to Stephen that he could not go home until his mum was properly better and that Stephen would have lots of visits to see his mum.

Friday 12-12-69. Stephen Addair. DOB: 10.06.1962, aged 7. Lothian and Boarders Children's Services.
Child Protection Meeting with Senior Social Worker Gary Kemp, and team, to assess future needs.

Stephen to be allocated Peggy Smith as his immediate child protection social worker. Peggy will meet with Mrs. Addair, then the Patterson's, and school to fully assess Stephen's needs and report back to the team.

Gary Kemp, Senior Social Worker.

In the first meeting with his mum, Friday 30th January 1970 Stephen was taken to the Edinburgh Southwest Children's Centre, family room, where there were toys to play with and a relaxed place to talk. The radio was playing 'Two little boys' by Rolf Harris, as they waited for Barbara to arrive.

He was surprised to see that she was different and looked more awake and happier. She told them and Stephen that she was not going to drink anymore and had not been drinking for 10 days, and that she wanted Stephen to go back home with her, but the social worker explained that the plan was to see how mum got on and that Stephen would be able to visit regularly.

The second meeting with his mum was in the family room on Friday 27th February 1970. Barbara was again a little late, but asked Stephen "how he was? Did he like the food? Was he going to school?" Stephen was playing with the toys and said yes to everything. Peggy asked Stephen if he would like to visit his mum back in their old flat, in Craigshill next time, and Stephen said "yes" and paused, wanting to say, "as long as Jocky's not there", but said nothing, other than to take a deep intake of breath. 'Edison lighthouse' , 'love grows' was playing on the radio and he felt some pleasure at the thought of the familiarity that home evoked, but also the fear of what might happen again.

Stephen next saw his mum was on Monday 16th of March 1970. This was the first supervised visit to his old flat in Livingstone. Stephen was pleased to be seeing his mum and his old flat but was uncomfortable about being there and straight away remembered feeling scared and alone in his own home with his own mother and rubbed his wrists in anticipation. Barbara lit up a cigarette as they arrived had asked how he was, and what were the people like who looked after him. Stephen found himself feeling a kind of agitated happiness at being home, feeling the need to do something and asked if he could go and play with Jamie, but his mum said that Jamie had moved away from the flats.

Another planned visit was arranged for eight weeks later, and the strategy was that he would stay with Barbara for two hours unsupervised. He wanted it to be like when he talked to Peggy or Jackie Patterson, he wanted her to be different. His mum did ask him about what Mr. and Mrs. Patterson were like. Stephen told her about how early he had to go to bed and get to school on time, and that the girls were nice, but that they argued between themselves all the time. Stephen realised that his mum asked him these questions, but she was looking behind and through him, so he stopped talking and so did she.

Visits continued and he stayed longer each time. His mum always asked him about the Patterson's. He wanted to say Jackie was really nice; she made hot good food and talked to him after the girls had gone to bed and told him that she would look after him until he could return home to his mother. But as Stephen told his mum about Jackie Patterson, he felt that she did not like to talk about her and changed the subject and then said, "do you want to watch television", and Stephan switched it on not really paying attention to the program.

Stephen liked Jackie as she was kind and helped Stephen to understand how important it was to wash each morning and evening and to look after your teeth, Jackie would say, "if you look after your teeth, you get a big happy smile" and she would give him a reassuring shoulder hug, reinforced with a big happy smile. Stephen learnt that being clean felt right, along with having nice clothes to wear. In contrast each time Stephen visited his mother he got the feeling that she wanted to see him but did not know what things to talk about. The front room was always filled with a musky smoky smell, which evoked memories fear and anxiety that made him panicky at the thought that Jocky might turn up.

Stephen saw his mum on his 8th birthday, Tuesday 10th of June 1970. He was pleased and surprised that his mum had remembered his birthday, even though he had been given a card and present at the Patterson's. Barbara even told him "Happy birthday" and asked how he was getting on in his new school. She gave him a present in a plastic bag and when Stephen opened it he saw an action man figure dressed in Army clothes. He was so happy with this present as he had seen it in a comic and advertised on the television.

Barbara told Stephen that his older sister liked birthday presents, and Stephen asked, "Where is she?" "She died because of me", but she then stopped talking and paused, then looked at Stephen from where she sat with a vacant expression and started to light up another cigarette.

During his first overnight stay in October, Barbara seemed unhappy and told Stephen that she was going to the Craigshill shops, and that he needed to carry on watching the television and she would not be long. But she stayed away a long time, coming back late and angry with, two bottles, one opened and the other in a plastic bag. She did not want to talk to Stephen, instructing him to go to bed and out of her face. Stephen felt the same old emotional anxiety scratching his arms as he went to his room feeling unsafe, wanting to disappear and wishing he was back at the Patterson's.

By the time the social worker arrived the next morning to take him to the foster home he was pleased to be going. His mother was in bed and Stephen answered the door to Peggy, who immediately asked where his mother was.

Peggy went to talk to Barbara in her bedroom and after a short while left the flat with Stephen. Peggy asked Stephen how the night had gone and Stephen said, "I watched TV until late, waiting for mum to get home", she asked in clarification, "Did your mum go out"? And Stephen replied "yes" followed by, "mum forgot to give me my two pounds."

They never let Stephen go back to his mums to live, and cancelled his visits, telling Stephen that his mother was not very well, which made Stephen worry as he kind of wanted to see her.

Stephen Addair; DOB: 10.06.1962. Lothian and Boarders Children's Services.

30th October 1970.

Stephen has had regular meetings with his mum, and one overnight stay, since the initial meetings at the 'Family Meeting place'.

I have been monitoring Barbara's recovery from alcohol abuse and her ability to take charge and care of an 8-year-old. She initially appeared to be making progress, but I am concerned about her, in the long term, and Stephen's general welfare, as she is falling back into alcohol abuse and seems to be associating with her old acquaintances that have similar addictions as Barbara.
She did start well and attended the alcohol recovery group at St Peter's, culminating in home visits. I agreed that Stephen should have his first overnight stay, with his mother, on the 28th October 1970.
Unfortunately, Barbara stopped attending the group and on Stephen's overnight stay, was seen leaving the flat at night and went to 'The Tower', Pub, and left him on his own for most of the evening.
When I collected Stephen in the morning Barbara was still in bed and smelt of drink and two empty bottles of cider were left on the bedroom floor. I asked Barbara what had happened last night and she refused to tell me, only saying something about Stephen being better off without her and she told me to "go away."

I talked to Stephen in the morning, and he seemed fine, but he had said that he was pleased to be going back to the Patterson's as his mum scared him last night.
I will continue to visit Barbara but have cancelled home visits for the foreseeable future.
Peggy Smith. Social Worker.

Peggy Smith was Stephen's first proper social worker, and he thought she was really nice. Along with Jackie she made sure he had a whole new set of clothes, shoes, and an outdoor coat; She used to talk to Stephen about his mum and ask him how school was going. She sometimes brought him some sweets, a toy, a book, and presents at Christmas, he got a watch for his 9th birthday present and was so pleased as it made him feel more grown up.

He used to talk to Mrs. Patterson for a long time about friends at school, homework, and the girls in the house. He never liked talking about his mum or what it was like living with her, the men, or Billy, even though she would ask questions, but he did tell Jackie that he had an older sister, but she had died, and Jackie told Stephen "It must have been a difficult and sad time for your mum". Peggy did organise meetings with his mum at the family centre again, but Barbara failed to attend.

Chapter 7

Barbara was a war child in Edinburgh in 1940 where she felt the full force of the German bombing in Leith's Largo Place. Her dad Stephen Addair had died in the early part of the war aged 40 years old during June 1940. He had joined the army in 1936, mainly to find travel, adventure and to get a wage. He enrolled in the 'The Royal Scots Fusiliers', 15th Scottish Infantry Division. Barbara was 12 years old when her mother was given the telegraph stating that; 'he had died bravely in action and was a credit to his regiment'.

Her mother Stella struggled, always half expecting the worse once the war had started, but she coped with his passing by denial, believing that it was a mistake and that he would come back again. Latterly she would pretend that he would be coming home, along with her boys who had joined up after the news of their father's death. Stella was always fearful that her boys might also end up the same way as their dad.

Stella smoked as much tobacco that she could get hold of, saying; it helped her nerves and to get through another day. Stella's two boys were desperate to get involved in the war and signed up together at the early part of 1941, after the German Luftwaffe, at 8.30am, hit Leith on July 18th, 1940.

'The Scotsman' reported that a 'stray bomb' from a lone German raider demolished part of the tenement at 8, Gorgie Road, killing seven people, including 41-year-old

Cathie Redpath and her mother, who she had decided to visit that day. There had been no warning or sirens of an air raid. The plane flew out of the clouds and dropped a single bomb. John and Barbara had watched from Leith Walk frozen in time as the plane went back up circling before it released six more bombs. The first bomb fell, glancing down a roof, before exploding on the common stair of a tenement, causing the building to collapse and fall into an outburst of dust and flames. The other bombs fell short of their tenement hitting buildings and the common parkland. It was then that they ran back home to proclaim to their mother and older brother what they had seen.

Stella and Robbie were at home, well aware of the bombings and how close it was to their own tenement block worried and distressed as to how close it was to their own dwelling.

It was reported that 'The airplane was forced down over the river Forth by the RAF fighters, and the German pilot, who was slightly injured, was brought to The Western General Hospital.'

Robbie and John were convinced that this attack on Edinburgh was the affirmation that they needed to get involved and that they should follow their dad into action. Both boys were convinced that they could seek out some revenge for the death of their father but also knew that the war had to be taken to the Germans in Europe before it came knocking on their door again.

Barbara watched her mother give up on life after the news that Robbie had died.

When John came home in 1945, he seemed distant and distracted from Barbara and had lost that will to move on. He made the odd appearance when he was totally down on his luck and to attend his mother's funeral. But found him-self falling deeper into the seclusion of drink, drifting into town living as a vagrant until he eventually went away.

Stella died in January 1946 at the end of the war. Barbara found her in bed with a burnt down Woodbine cigarette between her fore finger and index finger in her right hand. It had scorched her skin, which were brown and discoloured anyway.

She had not been eating well and had taken to not getting up because of the cold. Her ration card had been used to swap food for tobacco on the black market.

Chapter 8

Barbara was left to fend for herself as the war ended and carried on living in her mother's tenement. She had friends who she could rely on, and their families understood and helped Barbara to move on with her life. Barbara was small and of a slight build at 4'11". She was attractive with light brown hair and fair coloured skin with some freckles on her cheeks, nose and down her arms. The end of the war brought parties in the early days, some drinking, when you could get it, and a general feeling of wellbeing and celebration.

Barbara and her friend Maggie would take full advantage of the good times and became confident 20-year-olds in 1948, who would make their way into town and dance halls where they made the most of the free drinks and attention from the men who were always willing to buy their attention. They would have no problems meeting desperate soldiers or returning Scotsman in need of some love, attention and good times. The girls had been spoilt with gifts from the many American sailors who were docked at Leith Harbour. When they were 16 and 17 in the early days, they were well used to get gifts of chocolate, and tinned goods. Then later, if they were lucky enough to see the same sailor twice would be given stockings. But that was beginning to end as the Americans were being posted to other places now.

1948 and 1949 were worrying times in Edinburgh, followed by a long period where there was very little hope of a job and the rude awakening that the hard times were not going away. Barbara had a job at Maggie's father's bakery and made enough money to pay the basic bills but was always a little short, which built up into debts mostly for the rent. She would meet men at the dances and was able to have a free night out knowing that, if she was friendly enough, her willing suitors would pay for everyting.

Maggie eventually met a Scottish 27-year-old ex-seaman, who she ended up spending more time with than Barbara, and in 1950, aged 22 years old, married him.

Barbara was quite fortunate to have her mother's tenement, and if she was careful not to bump into any of the other families in the block, she could take friends back without feeling guilty, but the tenement had a network of eyes and ears. Very little happened in secret. The men were more than happy with this arrangement and could see that Barbara was having a tough existence in her tenement dwelling. They could see from the upkeep, age and the general disheveled state of the two rooms that money was an issue. One soldier left her some money quietly on the table as he was leaving which Barbara momentarily questioned but secretly appreciated.

Her rent collector would turn up each week with a smile and the chat. Black leather bag hanging from his shoulder to deposit the coins collected from his round, along with the accounts book, which fitted comfortably into the front of the bag, where a record was kept of all his dealings throughout the tenements. Johnny Walsh cleverly avoided the draft during the war with a little bit of 'ducking and diving ' working as an air raid warden and special constable. He also missed conscription due to his age and ongoing voluntary police service, due to the chaotic conditions in the city.

When Johnny came to collect the rent, he would stop for a brew and a cigarette with the young Barbara. She felt flattered by the attention of the middle-aged rockabilly, as he was considered a good-looking man, but she knew what he was about.

During their time together he would make it clear that if she was short of money, she could make it up in other ways. He was a charmer of a man who thought he could get his way with most women. He had the banter and was funny and friendly.

Barbara resisted for years, knowing that he was interested in her. Eventually when she had really fallen behind with the rent and had come home 'worse for wear' with drink during the day, she gave in but also got him to agree to clearing the debt plus two weeks.

She allowed him to have sex with her, which she figured was the easiest way to deal with her immediate financial problems, while convincing herself that she had always fancied him anyway.

She realised that Johnny was a risk taker and a cheat who would always come back for more, but she kept control by reminding him that his wife could easily find out about the arrangement and he was happy with that. Johnny was a friendly chancer, who used his position and knowledge as rent collector to gain access and build up relationships in the tenements. He also liked Barbara and would sometimes bring her gifts like sugar; broken biscuits and the occasional packet of misshapen reject chocolates, which were cheaper than the perfect ones, but tasted just the same. He fancied himself as a bit of a ladies man and liked Frank Sinatra, and would comb his hair back in a similar style, always wearing matching jacket and trousers while on his rounds, and to get a laugh, would sing segments from Sinatra songs, with his favourite being "The Moon Belongs to Everyone, but the Best Things in Life are Free".

Chapter 9

Some years on Barbara met a man who she liked called Davey who wore his hair in the modern style like Elvis Presley. Davey had joined the Navy in 1942 when he was 18 years old to get near the action. He trained on war ships but applied to work on submarines becoming a Morse code operator. Even with the rum ration, it was a sobering and terrifying experience that was to affect the rest of his life, as memories of depth charges exploding at close quarters, with the fear of a hit as every upsurge rattled the submarine to its very core, would continually replay in his sleeping hours for the rest of his life. Barbara was now 26 and she had seen a job advertised in a local textiles factory, and with some basic training, was taught to sew buttons onto ladies' coats and hand stitch the linings and hems. This meant that she could give up the job at the bakery as sewing paid slightly better.

She spent more time with Davey, and he eventually moved into the tenement with her in on the 1st of February 1954, just when the North Sea floods had hit the coastland of Scotland hard, and had caused, devastation, deaths and logistical problems for shipping and boats docking in Leith harbour and around the United Kingdom. The news was full of doom and gloom and 'The Daily Herald' reported that 81 people had died in the UK from the floods. Scotland had its wettest winter in history and times were difficult and demanding for working people who depended on getting to their jobs to earn a living. Life was hard and ration books were still in use for specific products, although you could get most of what you needed on the black market if you could pay.

When Davey moved in, Barbara felt like her life was finally beginning and that she could plan a future. Danny Kaye was playing on the radio, "Wonderful Wonderful Copenhagen" and it felt like Davey was going to make a difference to her life and that she could be happy.

Davey struggled to find work after the war, as he had never really trained in anything except 'Morse code 'and used his wit and guile to make a living. He had contacts in the whisky business and was able to do some trading in odd bottles that were carefully removed from the local distilleries and delivery vans. Their room became a place to store and distribute the goods, and they both regularly sampled the scotch to the full.

It was a time of optimism in 1954; the radio was playing music that defined a new and exciting time and when 'Shake Rattle and Roll' by Bill Haley and the Comets played Barbara danced with the excitement of a teenager. Barbara was soon to find out that housewife's choice playing 'How much is that Doggy in the Window' and 'Que Sera-Sera' by Doris Day was as exciting as her life could get.

Davey used to wake up shouting and distressed, holding his head and ears with a fearful look of desperation, sweating, panicking, and crying out in sheer terror. Barbara would try to console him, but as time went on, she found it more and more difficult dealing with his mood swings and nasty outbursts, even though she knew it was because of the horror and fear of things he had been subjected to in the war and the drink. She had seen similar behaviors of despair when her brother Johnny returned from his time in that unforgiving conflict. Barbara and Davey became a regular couple, and were in general, happy to coexist together and found strength, support, and a quasi-happiness with each other for some years.

Davey had an old navy mate who after the war had been given a job working at a local whisky distilling plant and was able to do some trading with what his friend described as the knock off perks of the job. After the war a black market of illicit goods were available on most street corners. The theft of knocked off items were generally orchestrated by criminal gangs throughout Scotland and England. Having old mates who were in the forces was very helpful. Davey acted as the go between for various people and got to know some willing takers of the contraband, but it was short lived, and his friend was finding it more and more difficult and dangerous getting the bottles out. Eventually Davey did get a job working behind a bar in a pub called 'The Lioness of Leith 'in Duke Street from one of his landlord contacts. Barbara used to sit in the snug, ladies bar, three or four times a week while he worked. She liked the company, and she also got very used to having a drink to cheer herself up.

As the years went by Barbara often wondered why she had not fallen pregnant as she had never used anything to prevent a baby from happening, she just thought herself lucky, and they did it less and less these days anyway. They both liked to drink and smoke often going home feeling the worse for it and somehow stopped having sex, unless Davey woke in the morning with a stiffy on, and had a quick fumble from behind to relieve himself.

It was August 1956 and Housewives choice was playing 'Hound Dog' by Elvis, on the radio, at home. Barbara and Davey were spending less time together. Barbara was 28 years old and had met someone else called Jack who was older than Davey and who knew how to treat a woman, especially when she was drunk. Jack had seen Barbara sitting in the ladies' room at the 'The Lioness of Leith' and knew that Davey was her man. Jack considered Davey a waste of space and knew that he could get hold of Barbara if he chose the right moment.

He waited until she left the pub slightly drunk and strolled along side of her offering a cigarette and asked if he could walk her home. Barbara agreed and was flattered by the attention. They fell into her room and the relationship started with the drunken eagerness of a bungled fumble that both excited and alarmed Barbara and Jack, but they both knew that they wanted more. Jack Macleod continued to meet Barbara while Davey was working, and Barbara soon realised that she was pregnant and due to have his baby the following year.

Davey was becoming more difficult to live with. He was rarely physically aggressive but when he had taken on too much drink he started to talk in an abusive, hurtful, and insulting manner that demeaned and humiliated Barbara. But this time he hit out at Barbara, and the argument was heard from all sides of the tenement building. Barbara screamed at Davey telling him she was pregnant, and it was not his.

Davey was stunned to silence and left the room, storming out smashing and kicking doors as he left. When Davey came back home later, drunk, Barbara tried to lock him out but eventually let him in because of the embarrassment and what her neighbours were going through. He had started to cry along with kicking the door. Once inside he continued the abuse, telling Barbara what a whore she was and started pushing and damaging what little furniture she had, and hit Barbara across the chest with a frame of a broken chair, knocking her back across the floor. She hit her head on the fireplace surround, and in her semi consciousness she could hear other voices screaming and shouting at Davey to leave her alone. Davey panicked and left Barbara when he saw that she was bleeding from the head and pushed his way past Jen and Dan who had come to Barbara's rescue from across the corridor.

Barbara was taken to Western General Hospital and treated for a large laceration to the top of her head and bruising to the chest and arms. Davey was found by the police near the old docks and charged with actual bodily harm (ABH) during a domestic dispute. He appeared in court where his Royal Navy record was taken into consideration and was told to keep away from Barbara in the near future or face some time in prison. Barbara did not want to press the issue and felt sorry for what she had put him through still feeling some fleeting affection for a man who had made her happy in the early years.

A priest visited her from St Andrews and St George's West, who, finding out she was pregnant, questioned her about the father, and suggested that they could help with the adoption. Barbara had no intention of giving her baby up for adoption as she still had some vague hope that Jack might be more involved in their lives.

Her baby girl survived and was born on the 22nd of May 1957. She called her daughter Stella after her mum. Jack was around but really did not want to be involved as he was married with three children. He occasionally gave Barbara some money, but this was strictly on the basis that his wife never found out about them or Stella. Jack had been backing away from their relationship for some time and sex did not seem to be either wanted or looked for anymore. In reality, Jack had regretted the whole thing and if he could, he would have walked away from Barbara and the baby, but Barbara knew where he lived and used that information wisely to gain limited financial support.

The hospital maternity and care staff charity funding system helped Barbara with baby wear, goods and food parcels. She was informed that she would be able to apply for some financial help and support through a charity called 'The Scottish Benevolent Society 'that was started for the support of impoverished women in Scotland. Barbara survived by living, as frugally as possible and by entertaining Johnny Walsh, her rent collector, whenever times got tough. Johnny became someone who would take time to ask how she was and would be good at holding the baby and giving it a bottle when needed.

Barbara found some contentment through the love she felt for Stella and was able to find part time work in a local market selling clothes and shoes for Jen and Dan who lived on the same floor in her tenement block. Barbara would say that every little helped and she was able to afford the odd drink when the need called. Stella was given all that Barbara could afford but Stella had a low birth weight and was struggling to catch up. She also suffered from Colic and other chest related infections.

The Hogmanay of 1958 was a quiet time for Barbara. She could hear other families celebrating and felt a little lonely but was happy with her whisky and even put a tipple in Stella's milk and chinked it with her glass to bring in the New Year.

Chapter 10

Barbara continued to work at the market stall throughout 1958 and increased her hours but had to take Stella along in her secondhand pram while trying to manage Stella's growing needs to get out as she became more active. Looking after a baby on the stall was becoming more difficult, and distracted Barbara from the job of promoting and selling the clothes. Barbara was sometimes able to ask friends to help out minding Stella, even Johnny Walsh had found time to look after her, but 1958 was a difficult year for baby Stella as she struggled with colds that restricted her breathing and a bout of Pneumonia that left her weak, needing periods of hospitalisation, and the offers of help disappeared.

Feeling more isolated than ever in her life and the daily chore of having to look after a 2 year old in 1959 was taking its toll, she was drinking because she liked it, and to blot out the thought of having to feel responsible for this demanding, crying child that seemed to always be there, stopping her from doing things and being free. However, when she was sober, she understood that Stella was something that needed looking after. She made sure she was clean and had eaten some food and put her to bed as soon as she could.

Barbara felt inadequate, finding herself overwhelmed, desperate and exhausted, struggling to work and finding it easier seeking friendships with some financial reward, and used drink to blot much of it out. At the start she would sometimes leave Stella in her bed, when the urge to get out overwhelmed her, and the need for a drink and to get away drew her further from her reality. But later, getting out, would become much more habitual.

On a cold September evening in1960, Barbara had returned drunk with a male friend during the early hours, and even though she was in no fit state to do anything other than check on her daughter, she found her baby Stella curled up on top of her bed cold and silent. Instinctively she tried to cover her with the bedding and then to wake her by pushing and pulling on her arm not fully taking on that Stella was not just asleep. Barbara slid to her knees not wanting to, or able to understand, or accept what was going on, and fell half sleeping, vaguely rousing in a stupor of lethargy by Stella's bed until she passed out in a crumpled heap on the floor.

Wretchedly she faced the funeral in a semi-inebriated state, as she had become accustomed to drinking again, in an effort, to dull the pain for what she had done. The police had viewed the scene as accidental death, knowing that there had been neglect, but not having an appropriate procedure to charge Barbara with, as it was easier for the police to sweep it under the carpet of ignorance, blaming the poverty of the time, for a quieter life.

Johnny Walsh and some friends from the tenement came to the funeral. Jack Macleod was seen standing some distance from the place of burial but did not attempt to join them for fear of association, secretly walking away when he saw the group slowly move from the small simply marked grave. He later returned with a handmade wooden cross, that had been self-whittled, with a burnt and branded inscription stating her name, date of birth and death, and on the back the word 'SORRY'.

It caused Barbara to sink into a spiral of self-loathing, hating herself for Stella's death and using drink to block out and anaesthetise the pain she was feeling, as it dawned on her what she had done. She spent weeks alone, where the only person she had any kind of contact with was Johnny Walsh. Johnny supported her for some of the time, making sure her rent was paid and that she had some basic provisions. Eventually he had to inform Barbara that she had to pay her way and that her rent would be due next week.

Barbara became more aware in her sobriety that she had to do something to hold herself together. It was unthinkable that she could lose the family home, the place where she had been brought up and felt safe. She had nowhere else to go and understood that her drinking was the root of her difficulties, knowing that she had to do something about the problem.

She tried to tidy up and felt an overwhelming emotional panic to just get out. Blindly fumbling for her door keys, she made her way into Leith Walk. It felt good to feel the cool Scottish fresh air, with the Autumnal breeze and smell of the wood and coal burning stoves. She knew that very soon the winds from the north would bring in the colder winter weather, which often left her feeling that winter depression, but this time she would feel it blowing through her very sorrowful useless soul.

She walked onto the docks and could see that life was carrying on; tankers and large boats were being unloaded, men and women were going about their day. Barbara felt the need for a drink but battled hard not to get drawn into 'The Ship on The Shore 'but could not resist and ordered a strong stout with a whisky chaser.

Turning to view the occupants of the pub she could hear Elvis was singing 'Are You Lonesome Tonight'. It felt like he was speaking directly to her. Struggling to grasp her reality she became confused, with a visualisation from deep in her memory of her mother, cigarette in hand, dancing slowly around in circles to the music as if she was with someone. Walking forward Barbara held out her hand expecting her mother to acknowledge her, desperate for some love and the chance to find some solace in her mother's arms. Only to find herself being grabbed by some man who thought she was offering herself up to him. She found her-self violently tugging in an attempt to break away from her drunken suitor in the direction of the exit.

She left the tavern and walked around for some hours before it occurred to her that she did not have anything to drink if she went home. She decided to buy a bottle of cider, as it was cheap but as far as she was concerned it was not a proper drink. The fresh air and cheap cider helped her to push thoughts of baby Stella deeper into her subconscious where the next day life carried on, as it does.
Barbara was offered her old job back on the market and it felt good to be able to join in with real life, wanting in some ways to feel normal again, being able to pay her rent and still had

enough money to buy her bottles of cider and strong Tenant beer.

Chapter 11

It was 1961 and kids used coffee bars to hang out and listen to music. She could feel a wind of change taking hold around the smart areas of Edinburgh. Traditional Scottish music and 50's music was competing with rock and Roll. The radio would play Andy Stewart's 'A Scottish Soldier 'but the jukebox played Bobby Vee's 'Rubber Ball 'and Neil Sedaka's 'Calendar Girl'. She was drawn to the music and liked playing the radio, but was most comfortable in the pub.

Able to work more hours Barbara found that she could afford to go out. She developed a routine that allowed her to mask her hangovers, by taking aspirin and fronting it out when she was asked if she was unwell. There was a younger new world order that viewed having fun in the company of others necessary not only for males but also females after the misery of the war years. She met new friends in pubs where women were now accepted. In some public houses women were able to enter the main bar to drink, socialise and listen to the latest popular music on the jukebox.

Barbara was 34 years old and was missing adult company and the thought of a male relationship filled her with excitement. She was still a good-looking woman and had little problem attracting men who lit her cigarette and bought her drinks in the hope of something more than friendly conversation. Barbara would drink and find herself easy prey once outside, walking home or diverted down a side alley where male predatory sex was very clumsy, simple and quick. She had little consideration for her health and remembered fragments the following day. She soon realised that she was feeling sick in the mornings and had a low consistent pain around her pelvic area. She was pregnant but did not feel ready or able to have another baby and cried over and over. This was not what she wanted or could cope with again, at this time of her life.

It was late October 1961, the nights were drawing in and it was getting colder. Bobby Vee's 'Take good care of my baby' was playing on the radio and it made Barbara think about how she was not able to take good care of her baby Stella, and cried at the thought of having to go through with the whole thing again, but, something inside her, that voice that whispers from the other side of your mind said "you can do it this time, a baby" she wanted to make amends, atone and say sorry to Stella for not being what she should have been, 'a good mother.

Chapter 12

Stephen was born on a Sunday in The Western General Hospital, in the afternoon on the 10th of June 1962. It was a quick delivery and birth and held no fears for Barbara this time. He was a small underweight baby boy weighing 5 pounds and 10 ounces. He had arrived two days early and was a happy smiling child. Barbara took Stephen back to her Tenement, which she had prepared ready for a baby and had to remind herself that this is what she had done with Stella and grew fearful that she was not up for this again. Barbara felt a deepening sorrow as the memories of Stella flooded back. She wanted to be different this time around and was able to manage her childcare by accepting help from Jen and Dan who also offered her some work back at the market. Barbara was able to get started on the new birth control pill, even though she was not married, by virtue of the fact that this was her second child. Her female doctor had offered it to her, by suggesting that she helped with the trialing of the second-generation pill, provided by the NHS.

Barbara managed her dependency on alcohol by only drinking at home during the evenings but then found friendship with Mack who ran the fruit and vegetable stall next to hers. Mack was in his late fifties and was a casual friendship that allowed Barbara to be able to see someone as and when it suited her. Mack had been married and had four children, so he was good with baby Stephen in the early days.

Mack had worked the market all his life, six days a week rain or shine, and the 'Lord Kitchener 'pub was his go to place, which was where his friendships and social connections were. He was an important and well-liked man who drank steadily. He would always start with a whisky chaser followed by pints of 'Innis and Gunn' and was generous with those he liked and mixed with. He helped Barbara out with extra cash when she needed it and Barbara could take the baby in the 'Pusher 'to the pub, as Stephen in general was a restful child.

Over time, The Lord Kitchener felt comfortable and familiar to Barbara, and she would get angry when she had to attend to her child, particularly when the drink took hold. Mack would take the baby in an attempt to get Barbara to pay attention to her child, and as time progressed, he started to feel awkward when others looked on in judgment and some distain. Mack would go back to the tenement and try to explain the difficulty he had with the child in the pub and Barbara would say, "Fuck them, what am I supposed to do, not go out?" Eventually one morning he had gone, and she knew that it was over.

Stephen was 2 years old and wanted to run around and was not content to sit in the pusher pram. The next year was a mixture of a realisation that she was alone and tumbling back into the habits of a lifetime. For Barbara life was falling in around her, she struggled to get out and found herself penniless.

During the late nights, when Stephen was asleep, she would make her way down to Leith docks for a drink, and the short walk to Coburg Street, where she was able to make a few bob, by servicing one or two willing punters. She shared the streets with other girls and mostly could do it safely and get back to Stephen by the early hours. It was more difficult in the bitter winter cold nights, but the punters were always about, and a good drink and smoke helped her to get through. She also had her regulars, who liked Barbara, as she was young and still attractive at 37. They liked the familiarity and safeness of the same person, momentarily wanting to save her from this life of prostitution before scuttling off satisfied that they had relieved themselves until the next time.

When she was waiting, Barbara knew that her sideways glances were enough to get interest, and once they were close enough to talk, and the transactional contract was agreed, very soon the deed would be done, either in the park area opposite, or in the car, which was better, on bitterly cold nights. She felt safer in the trees, but knew there was always a risk, as some had turned nasty, particularly those who could not get it up, or struggled to even get started, would sometimes demand their money back. She would occasionally get abusive shouts from passing cars; 'dirty little whore', 'suck this you prossie tart'. Barbara hated what she was doing, and used drink, to anaesthetise and numb the impact of her reality, feeling this was her only way out, enabling her to pay her rent, save her home, and to get through.

Stephen was the child who coped, looked on, surviving the many lows that Barbara went through. Jen and Dan across the hall, tried to help Barbara with the ups and downs, attempting to be a friend but worrying about the child that they had become close to. Barbara always seemed to recover just as things were becoming impossible, falling into the next thing or being forced to make hard decisions.

Chapter 13

Barbara had been given notice that her Tenement building was going to be closed down, as it was unsafe; the tenements were a dilapidated eyesore, with communal toilets and no running hot water, wide concrete stairwells and a cramped reminder in Edinburgh and other Scottish cities, of the squalor of the previous half-century. All the residents were put onto a housing list for social rehousing and were offered a new home in the new towns, being developed around Livingstone, one of which was called 'Craigshill'. She felt that this was her way out of the mess she was in, a time for new beginnings, and a fresh start.

The housing estate was a good bus ride from Edinburgh and was situated in the country. Barbara was able to visit and look at the new development and view a show home flat, with two bedrooms similar to the one she was going to be given. It was described as a ground floor modern flat, with an inside private toilet of her own, and bathroom, and regular running hot water. It was wonderful, so clean, and new and she told people that, 'they give you a grant towards new furniture"! The main downside was that it would be a good hour bus ride from Edinburgh and all the people and places she knew.

Chapter 14

Barbara's 3-storey building in Craigshill had a shared entrance with adjoining flats, going up in the new Craigshill housing estate in Livingstone. Barbara was given a moving in date, as the 29th of October 1965, and was officially handed the keys to number 14, Almond Road, Craigshill, Livingstone. Barbara was an excited 38-year-old, who felt that this flat would give 3-year-old Stephen and herself a new start, and a chance to move ahead with opportunities and new beginnings.

The council estate was a brand-new brick and concrete island of houses, flats, and a small shopping Centre still being completed. It did not have the people, community, buzz of a city and the lifetime connections she was used to. The Tower pub was a modern lifeless structure that hid itself away in the concrete blocks that were unexciting analogous constructions, of what was described by the developers as modern homes for the future. The move soon began to feel like a big mistake as she started to become isolated, broke and lonely in her very modern flat. She missed the comings and goings of the tenement, the town and the people she had grown up with, which was all that she had ever known.

As Stephen approached the age of four, Barbara found life in her new home had soon closed in on her. She had to deal with the tedious, soul-destroying reality of poverty and lack of opportunities. She was lonely and would sometimes take the bus back to Edinburgh, but over time found the city less and less welcoming to a single mother. Her mood and thoughts would drift back to baby Stella, and when she could, would use drink as a method of suppressing any feelings of sadness, and mask her anger and loneliness, by picking up with anyone, who showed her any sympathy or attention. The Tower pub was the only social drinking place within walking distance to where she lived, which was predominantly occupied by men. Single women rarely visited for fear of being labeled. Barbara ignored the looks unashamedly using the Tavern, eventually getting to know various people who were mainly men. In the early days she found part-time employment in the Tavern as a cleaner, which helped with the bills.

The coming years saw Barbara steadily decline, while hanging onto whatever parenting values she had assumed and clung to from her own childhood experiences. Stephen had to learn fast, bringing himself up, particularly when he could not depend on his mother. The happiest months had been when he was 6 and 7 when Billy stayed and the most frightening times were when Jocky and the other men were around. But being fostered by the Patterson's provided Stephen with the knowledge and information about what a family should be, and he would always be grateful for that.

Chapter 15

After some time when Stephen was 9 years old, Peggy told Stephen that he was going to have another social worker, a man called David Williams. David was friendly and made time to meet with Stephen, but not as much as Peggy had.

Six months later David informed Stephen that he was going to be placed in permanent foster care with Lothian and Boarders regional Social Services Department and that his placement would be changed from the Patterson's to another foster home, in Colinton, Edinburgh, which meant another change of school and friends.

Lothian and Boarders Children's Services. Stephen Addair; DOB 10-06-1962.
Date: 14th September 1971.

This is my first meeting with Stephen since taking over from Peggy Smith. He seems to be happy and comfortable at the Patterson's, who originally took Stephen on as an emergency placement, but do not want to continue with full time fostering. I have liaised with Peggy and we have managed to find a family who will be prepared to take Stephen on as full time foster care providers.

I have visited Stephen's mother who I feel is not in a position to properly care for a 9 years old, and it is in the best interests of the child, that we continue to offer full time care to Stephen. I will meet with Barbara on a quarterly basis to monitor her general well-being, and mental state.

Initially I will visit Stephen and the Humphries each month and will inform and accompany Stephen to his new home.

David Williams.

Chapter 16

Stephen had liked being at the Patterson's as it felt like a family and he remembered feeling angry and sad at the thought of leaving them.

He decided to go and see his mum on his own, instead of going to school; he had some pocket money for his bus fare and knew the route and long bus ride to Craigshill. He got to the flat in Almond Road at 10.35 a.m. checking his new watch and knocked on the door. It took some time, but his mum came to the door in her bra and knickers and swiped her hair back with her left arm once, and then again, clumsily trying to sweep it back, exposing a large bloody graze on her forehead and cheek, while holding her right arm across her front in a sling. She asked with a look of surprise "what are you doing here"? Stephen did not feel welcomed but stood waiting to be asked in.

Barbara had just got out of bed, and the flat was smoky as usual. She quickly lit up a cigarette with the difficulty of a one-armed person and asked if he wanted some toast. Stephen told her that they were sending him to another family and then asked what had happened to his mum's arm. He waited for a response from his mum, but she looked kind of glazed and said that's good, maybe they will let you come and see me again. Stephen chewed on his toast and waited for a drink that never came so he made his own. Barbara had a cup of tea and also ate some toast and switched the television on.

Later that afternoon David Williams came to the door and asked Barbara if Stephen was there. She told him that she had fallen over and fractured the Ulnar bone in her right arm, but it was getting better. Stephen felt fine that David had come to find him, as he once again came to the realisation that his mum could hardly look after herself let alone himself.

Chapter 17

Stephen's next foster placement was with Mr. and Mrs. Humphries who were a bit older than the Patterson's. They had two teenage children, again girls, named Wendy and Natalie. Natalie had just finished school and was preparing to go to university and was often out. Wendy was 12 years, sociable in front of her parents but really wanted to be with her friends and not with her parents and Stephen. At first, she resented Stephen coming into their house, as she had to give up the box room and move into the big second bedroom with Natalie but was fascinated to have a boy living with them. Margaret Humphries went to work in a Bank and was out during the day and was tired when she got home. She was not as friendly as Jackie and left much of the parenting to her husband John.

He felt strange and uncomfortable with the Humphries. Mr. Humphries was very different to Jeff Patterson, a much more serious man. He tried to ask questions but to Stephen he seemed strict and a bit scary and less welcoming than Jeffrey.

Mr. Humphries made sure Stephen went to his bedroom at 7.00pm, he never liked him hanging around the living room and constantly suggested he should go to his room to do his homework and to get prepared for school the next day.

Stephen felt checked on, then he was told to lean over the bathroom sink when he cleaned his teeth and washed himself, as he was leaving drips on the floor. He constantly told Stephen to hold his knife and fork properly and lean over his plate when eating. Stephen quickly learnt to follow the house rules and did everything he could to fit in.

He was now 10 years old but was settling into his life with the Humphries. Stephen mostly tried to keep himself away from the family and was viewed as a loner by them. David Williams would occasionally do his social work visit at the foster home and would talk to John Humphries over a cup of tea. He would meet with Stephen and ask him if things were ok, and Stephen would just nod and say, "yes, it's fine".

David's Social Worker duties were to remember special dates and David bought Stephen a set of matchbox cars for his birthday, which he liked but it was not something he played with often. David always remembered his Christmas present and used to add a selection box full of chocolates.

Stephen used to talk to Wendy Humphries, if she talked to him first, but was a little frightened that she might laugh at him if he did the wrong thing and would make him feel like he was stupid when he did not know something, but eventually they grew to like and confide in each other.

Chapter 18

Stephen was preparing himself for his first year at big school now aged 11. Wendy was entering the third year and had told him about all the things that happened to first years.

He was worried that his head would be pushed into the toilet and flushed, or that he would get first year beats. She told him about the scary teachers and what they did if you did not do your homework. So, in his first year he was always on time with his homework, which he often struggled with, but did enough so that he did not get a detention with extras.

Wendy would tease him along with her friend Shauna, they would call him a gay little hen and say things like have you ever kissed a girl, or do you like boys better? Stephen would try to ignore them and hated when Shauna came around, as Wendy was worse when they were together. They would take pleasure in questioning him and would laugh and tease him about everyday things, like what kind of music he was into, and would dance around him like Pans People from Top of The Pops, and challenge him to dance, but Stephen refused saying he was no good. However, secretly Stephen liked the feeling of movement and rhythm, and when he was alone, felt like he could dance, particularly to soul and disco music, and would practice on his own, and even pretended to have a partner by holding the back of a chair.

As he grew older Stephen developed in confidence when he was with the girls and liked the attention that they seemed to always give him. Particularly because they were older than him, because they laughed, had fun and appeared to know so much about life.

Eventually they enticed Stephen to go into Wendy's bedroom and challenged him to play kiss or tell. Stephen felt awkward and a little trapped and was bullied into joining in, but knew how this game went, from his observations at the flats, with the older kids, in Craigshill. They took turns to flip a coin, heads was kiss, and tails was to tell something secret about yourself.

Shauna flipped heads and was supposed to kiss Wendy and they did, but secretly Shauna put her hand over her lips, so Wendy kissed the back of her hand. Wendy then flipped a tail and had to reveal her secret. She said that she had kissed a boy called Jack Lewis, one of the hunks at school in the year above. Shauna gave a look of amazement and disbelief when she heard this, but did say, "what was it like, did he use his tongue". Something Stephen remembered with Billy when he was 6.

He then flipped the coin and stared at it for some seconds. It had landed on heads, with the stark reality and realisation that he had to kiss Shauna was quickly dawning on him. He decided to do this reluctantly, but if he had to do it, he would do it well, as he had seen it being done behind the flats, on the films, and had done with Billy. Kissing on the lips gently with slightly opened mouth and then allowing his tongue to move softly against Shauna's tongue, because he guessed that was the correct way to do it. He continued kissing Shauna softly on the lips holding her head and then finding Shauna's tongue touching his, and softly sucked her tongue before pulling away, with a wet gentle kiss. It felt good, but he stopped kissing as Wendy shouted, "Stephen loves Shauna." Shauna was quite taken back with the confidence and forcefulness of the kiss and even quite liked it.

He seemed to get a lot more respect from the girls after this and his confidence with the lassies and kisses was greatly increased in the years to come.

Stephen was pleased to be able to hear and say, that he was not a queer, and the girls stopped calling him a gay lord, but he struggled to think the same, questioning some of his feelings of arousal, that were so random, that he could not clearly associate to one gender or another.

Stephen liked senior school better than primary as he felt more confident and grown up. He could keep himself to himself avoiding those children who he had very little in common with. Like those sporty loud kids, who always wanted to be aggressive and say hurtful things to each other. During year one he realised that he liked the creative subjects and geography. He loved the idea of travel and used to study world maps and got to know where continents and countries were on the school globe.

He was due to start the second year at school late August 1974 and could feel a difference in the way that Wendy talked to him. She was starting the fourth year, and he had noticed that she had developed boobs and was wearing a bra. Wendy was quite pretty, had braces on her teeth that made her feel self-conscious when she smiled, so she always covered her mouth when she laughed and talked. Stephen grew to really like Wendy, and he spent lots of time playing music and talking to her in her room, they even danced together to the Bay City Rollers, 'Remember (Sha-la-la-la)' and to many others of the tartan boy's hits. He felt safe with her and told her some things about his mum and Jocky. He never thought that he could talk to Margaret and John Humphries. Mostly he felt uneasy with them, sensing their discomfort with the amount of time that he was spending with Wendy, particularly when he was in her room. They sometimes played board games like Monopoly, but the best thing was playing music. She told Stephen that she did not like her dad either. Having a limited insight into what life had been like for Stephen, she tried to naively relate her own experience and situation to his.

Stephen lay on Wendy's bed as the music was playing. Her favourite band was 'The Bay City Rollers', and 'Shang-A-Lang 'blared out from Wendy's record player. Stephen felt safe and a happy in this place. Wendy asked Stephen "what was it like when you kissed Shauna?" and he tried to explain but said, "I would rather have kissed you" and she blushed and said, "Come on then". This was the second time Stephen had kissed a girl, but the first time he had touched a tit.

Wendy was someone Stephen really liked. He was nearly 13 years old, and she was 15. He leaned forward ineptly resting his body on Wendy and could feel her tummy heave and take a breath as the weight of his torso made close contact. She was open to his advances and allowed him to place his right hand under the waist of her blouse where he caressed her warm skin. Feeling curious, he reached further under her blouse where he touched her bra. But it was a struggle to go any further. He tried to force his fingers under the soft elastic, to find her left breast and maybe a nipple but it was too difficult, and he settled for a full gentle feel on top of her bra. Stephen felt Wendy take a deep breath, then pause as she accepted the touch while also providing consent to where his hand was travelling.

Not really knowing what she should do to him she clumsily stroked his back with her left hand, which was difficult. Her right arm lay squashed under his body. Stephen continued to move his right hand around the outside of her bra but as he lay there, he became aware of his extended left arm, which reached up to her head in an awkward fashion, finding that his fingers were limply hanging and doing very little.

Stephen persevered enjoying the closeness and started to get an erection, which had become a common response recently, when he had thoughts about naked bodies. He put his lips to hers and kissed with closed mouths and then open, placing wet tongues around each other. It seemed to last a while, and they both quietly smiled when it had finished. Stephen privately acknowledging the fact that he had touched Wendy's skin, breast and nipple, but also that she had probably felt a hard cock pushing against her for the first time.

After the kissing had stopped they quickly rearranged themselves and carried on listening to the music and talked about whom Wendy liked best in the whole world' Bay City

Rollers'. Once back into his own bedroom, feeling quite pleased with himself, Stephen felt the need to wank himself off, with the fantasy of Wendy's naked skin, and a weird memory of the closeness he remembered from his childhood. Billy flashed into his mind.

Wendy and Stephen never got that intimate again. Soon after, she had found a boyfriend, the same age or older, who she spent much of the next months with, often disappearing into her room with him for long periods of time which excluded Stephen. They were friends, and she would check on him and ask how he was. Stephen felt like he had a big sister, which was good, but a little distant at times.

Chapter 19

The summer was sunny and warm, with the long light nights that seemed to last forever but disappeared as quickly as they came. Stephen often found himself thinking about his mum and worrying that something had happened to her.

He decided to take the long bus ride to Craigshill and went to visit his mum but lingered at the door not really wanting to go in, he only wanted to know that she was well. He wandered into the small local shopping centre and waited around 'The Tower', which was his mum's local pub. He asked a man who came out if he had seen Barbara Addair, but he hadn't. Stephen went back to the flat, it was midday, and he could hear that the TV was on. He looked through the window and could see the cup and saucer on the stainless-steel drainer, and then saw his mum move between the kitchen, and living room. He felt relieved that she was up and about but did not want to make contact as seeing her was enough.

During the end of the second year at school, Stephen made friends with Frank Paulokofski, who was also a bit of a loner, and they started to hang out listening to music at Frank's house. 'The Trammps 'Hold Back The Nights'. Roxy Music' Love Is the Drug', David Bowie' Space Oddity', and 'Queen's' Bohemian Rhapsody' being their favourites. Stephen would call at Frank's house on the way to school, and they would call back at the end of school.

By the third school year Stephen was spending most weekends at Frank's, his mum and dad were a laid-back couple who had settled in Scotland from Poland after the war.

Frank would make Stephen laugh and talk about all kinds of things, but what most impressed Stephen was Franks record collection and record player as his dad gave him pocket money each week to buy chart singles and the occasional album. Franks mum would always offer a cup of tea, biscuits, and sometimes 'jaworki', that tasted like sweet crisp pastries that melted into your mouth with each bite, or 'mazurek' which was Stephen's favourite, a pastry fruit tart, when they got home from school. They would then start to sort through the records, before deciding on which one to play. They also watched television, played board games like 'Monopoly', 'Risk', and 'Cluedo', and were very competitive with each other.

Stephen never felt comfortable taking Frank around to the Humphries house as they at no time welcomed him or Frank, and Stephen felt that they did not approve of him bringing others into the house. He would hear them arguing about stuff, but was not really sure what, and often heard words like "we can't afford it" "It costs too much" and "go back to work if you need something different".

Stephen was allowed to sleep over at Frank's house, and they put a mattress on the floor of Frank's bedroom for Stephen to sleep on. This became a regular event during the warmer months of May to August 1976, and most of the time Frank slept on the mattress too. They were becoming more aware of girls, and both laughed and had a shared sense of understanding and erections when semi-nude images were found in magazines, mostly of sexy film star pictures and page three girls. They eventually were able to acquire a Mayfair Magazine and excitedly read each article together that described stories of sexual encounters, love, lust and images of fully naked women and men. Stephen and Frank would find it difficult to hide their physical reaction to the pictures and this night Frank showed Stephen his erection in his pants stating that it was pretty big, and he could see the same thing was happening to Stephen. They were both close to each other and openly held the erections in their hands comparing size and appearance. Stephen felt embarrassed but also interested and excited that he now knew that his was normal and so were erections. Frank invited Stephen to touch and then hold his, which Stephen did, feeling how hard and stiff it was, in a curious way, and Frank reciprocated and then got embarrassed and put his penis away inside his pants, as did Stephen, even though he wanted to make himself come, he resisted. They acted as if nothing had happened, but Stephen felt a tingle of excitement at what they had done, and Frank went back to his own bed and eventually went to sleep.

Stephen never had a sleepover at Frank's again once their new adventures had started. They had moved onto the thrill-seeking of petty crime buoyed by an adolescent adventure to try and steal and get away with it. A boy's own attitude with disregard to consequence made them feel like they were on an adventure, thrilled with the fact that they were getting away with it.

Frank and Stephen would go into a shop and Frank would rest his arm up against the sweet counter and take one or two when the shop person was not looking or was distracted. He also showed Stephen how to steel magazines by getting Stephen to divert the retailer's general view by pointing to something on a shelf or asking about the price, while Frank put a magazine under his coat.

Their biggest enterprise was when he told Stephen that there was a corner hobby shop, in a side street, with a cracked window, that would be an easy target. That they could break in and get hold of the air rifle that was clearly on display on the other side of the glass.

This was the 29[th of] July 1976, and the summer evening was still light until very late, a month and a few weeks after Stephen's 14th birthday. In the early hours, Stephen climbed out of his bedroom window, grabbed the drain down pipe, sliding feet against the wall until he reached the ground. He met up with Frank who was waiting in the side way of Mr. and Mrs. Humphries house, just after midnight as they had arranged. This was something Stephen had not done before but he liked that feeling of taking a risk, he felt exhilarated and free to do what he wanted to do. The thrill of the night and the anticipation of what lay ahead made him want more.

They wandered into town, carefully hiding in the shadows, making sure a random policeman did not spot them. It felt exciting, like a spy film an adventure. It was a warm and quiet night. The silence and stillness were palpable as they made their way through the Edinburgh streets on this summer evening. They could see seasonal flecks of light bouncing around the horizon where the darkness was battling to take control of the ambient light.

They arrived at the Hobby shop that Frank had told Stephen about, aware that the night was still and quiet. The corner shop sold air guns, rifles, knives, and other outdoor activity action type things. There was a side window down a connecting road with an air rifle on display with a large crack running through the window from top left to bottom right, with gaffer tape running along the splinter, and then, to Stephen's surprise Frank smashed the window with a brick, which took out a large piece of the glass pane. Somehow the rest of the window stayed in place. There was enough room for Frank to be able to reach in and take out the air rifle, which was on display. The rifle was wrapped in a poly packed cardboard back package, with the pellets included.

They ran scared but laughed as they realised that they had got away with it. Frank unpackaged the rifle and seemed to know what he was doing. He loaded the air rifle by folding it at a 45-degree angle across his knee and then placed a small lead pellet into the socket parallel to the gun barrel, closing it with an aggressive shunt and aiming it all around before starting to take a pot shot at a streetlight. Stephen had a go liking the feeling of the rifle in his hand shooting with a fixed aim at lights and signposts. They felt excited and full of mischief as if they were free and able to do what they wanted.

After some time, the exhilaration finally turned to fear as they just avoided a police car slowly driving along the suburban streets that lead to nowhere and eventually went back to their respective homes. Stephen climbed up the drainpipe to gain access; quietly creeping through his bedroom window before getting into bed reeling and breathless from the adrenalin rush he was feeling from the whole adventure. Frank kept the rifle and hid it in his house. They only used the rifle one more time when Frank snuck the rifle away from its hiding place under his bed. They went out to the countryside, to hunt for rabbits and birds, never really hitting anything. Most of the time not being very successful, mostly shooting at squirrels and missing because they could not find any rabbits, but it felt like they had the power to fight, or defend themselves if they were needed in a war, or a group of 'Red Indians' came at them from over the hill like in the movies.

John Humphries had changed his mind about wanting to foster long term and was happy that Stephen was spending more time out of the house and had found a friend. He never really wanted to foster, and only did it because he thought that fostering would help with paying the mortgage, as he was between jobs. But now that the girls were growing up and more independent, particularly Natalie who was going to university, he had decided that he might go back to work.

It was about this time that Frank's Dad turned up at John's door. He stated that he did not want Stephen coming to their house anymore and explained that he felt Stephen was a bad influence on Frank but did not say why. John asked what had happened, and Frank's Dad said something about stealing, but did not want to go into any specifics. He told John Humphries that he did not trust Stephen anymore and that was the end of it and walked away rather than go into any more detail.

Franks Dad had found the air rifle and a Mayfair magazine hidden in his shed and challenged Frank to tell him where they had come from. Frank had to think fast and said that they were Stephen's, and he had found them in a box at the back of a derelict big house at Eastcote Street. Frank's Dad was not prepared to accept this answer, he was intimidating and had smacked and used the belt on Frank before and pushed for the truth. Eventually Frank explained that they had met up because Stephen knew about a shop with a broken window and that Stephen had smashed the window and taken the rifle.

John Humpries did not want to confront Stephen and decided this was a good time to move Stephen out on the basis that Stephen could not be trusted, which was convenient. He informed social services that he wanted Stephen to be removed that evening. Wendy was not told that Stephen was leaving and was stunned when David Williams turned up to collect him. Wendy challenged her dad, but he never disclosed why Stephen had to leave their house, only to say that he could not be trusted. Stephen was not sure why he was being told that he had to leave the Humphries, he had no idea that it had anything to do with Frank and missed Wendy most of all. He asked David Williams why he was being moved so suddenly and David stated that Mr Humphries was no longer able to foster children and that he would be going to a children's home with other children his own age.

Stephen Addair. DOB 10.6.62. Lothian and Boarders, social services department.
August 10th, 1976

Mr. and Mrs. Humphries have decided that they cannot carry on with Stephen as they feel that they cannot trust him? I find this difficult to understand, because Stephen has never demonstrated any issues of dishonesty and he has a reasonable school report stating that he is a bright young person and in general progressing well. I will send a report to the fostering services and will ask them to try to get some information about why the sudden change from the Humphries. My feeling is that John Humphries was not very supportive or concerned about Stephens needs. Throughout my visits I felt that there was a growing reluctance to discuss Stephen's emotional requirements. Stephen seemed relatively happy and had just started to make new friends with other peers at school. Which is unfortunate, as Stephen will need to change his school to one nearer to Glenallan. I will need to set up a case review and inform his mother of the change in placement.

The only placement available for a teenager in an emergency is Glenallan Children's Home?

David Williams. Caseworker to Stephen Addair.

Chapter 20

Stephen found himself in a big building in the suburbs next to a large, green-grassed park surrounded with trees and housing. Glenallan Drive was a relatively new children's home, situated at the end of a cul-de-sac that could house up to 10 boys and 8 girls.

It was a wild place at times, compared to the relative tranquility of the Humphries and the Patterson's, with all kinds of characters. Most were aged between 11 to 15 years old.

When Stephen arrived at Glenallan he was placed in a room with the two older boys, Greg 14 and Bernie 15 years old, who were both in the 3rd year at school and attended the remedial education form (RE), which was widely thought of as the class for the thicko's, with learning problems.

There were five younger boys who slept in two other rooms on the male side of the house.

The girls had 4 double rooms, with the biggest reserved for the oldest. There was another room for a single boy, which was always kept empty and locked, and they were told that it had to be available, made up and clean, for emergency referrals. The youngest resident was an 11 year old, named Spanner, who was given the name because of the shape of his head. He was a complex person who would bang, tap or continually move about to get attention. There were 5 girls in total: two young ones 12 years old in one room, two

13- to 14-year-olds in the next, and the oldest 15, in the large double room, on the girl's side of the house.

The boy's area, toilet and showers were on one extreme side of the house, and the girl's area was on the other, with the staff office, reception, staff sleepover room, and medical room in the middle facing the entrance to 'Glenallan'. There was a dining room, kitchen, sitting room with TV, and a small quiet space for homework, reading and board games.

The staff was a mixed bunch too, who looked like they would rather be somewhere else. The worker in charge most of the time was called Brian McLennen and he was one of those who liked to be in control. He favoured, the girls, and often manipulated situations where he could be alone with whichever of the charges, he felt he could get something from. Stephen was a new and interesting referral that he needed to get to know. He started by getting friendly with him, by giving him special attention. Stephen did not know how to take him, yet he seemed to understand how Stephen was feeling and was able to hook into his vulnerable fears about his mum. He also asked Stephen about his foster home and friends and suggested that he could help Stephen meet up with Frank. He was the person who told Stephen that he had to have a medical examination on arrival.

At first McLennen seemed like a nice man who genuinely was concerned that Stephen got all he needed when he first arrived at 'Glenallan'. He showed Stephen to his room and around the children's home. He was funny and asked Stephen about girlfriends, what football team he supported and his favourite music.

Stephen was then led to the medical room where McLennen started to fill out a form. He told Stephen to take his shirt off and then his trousers, so that they could check for any cuts and bruising. McLennen took photos, noticing and inspecting Stephen's scarred left wrist. He held his hand at the scratched skin, saying very little other than to inform him that everything was fine and that he had a good clean body. He asked Stephen to take off his pants, but Stephen said no at first, as he was more self-aware of his body now that he had reached puberty. McLennen said that's Ok if you are shy and touched Stephen on his shoulder and slightly let his hand slide down his back saying, "if you want those under pants washed, they will have to come off eventually". Stephen felt uncomfortable but wanted to do the right thing as he had been informed that all the residents had to have a medical and reluctantly, he did as he was told. He asked if he could put his clothes on, quickly grabbing his trousers and shirt. McLennen said "I think we have covered everything for now, everybody has to have a medical when they arrive at Glenallan."

Stephen remembered that he was sitting in the TV room with the other residents when John Stringer first arrived as the single night worker. He walked toward Stephen pointing a long boney finger straight at his face and moved it from side to side in a wagging motion. "Hello, you must be Stephen, the new boy, we must get to know each other, my name is Mr. Stringer, but you can call me John". He then looked about the space casually reminding Stephen to follow the rules of the house and you will be just fine.

The others in the room went quiet as he arrived and they all seemed to listen attentively when he told Stephen what his expectations were: "Teeth, toilet, bed, be tidy, and quiet by lights out". Reminding them of his expectations particularly on school days.

He was a large, tall man with a beard and wanted to make it very clear to Stephen and the rest of the housemates that he was in charge tonight. He used his voice in a commanding manner to suggest to everyone that he was in charge and that they needed to follow the house rules. Which were bed at 9.00pm and lights out at 9.30pm.

McLennen was standing behind Stringer, and he called out to Spanner, gesturing to him to come to see him. Spanner reluctantly turned away, and Stringer shouted; "Spanner, get to it you heard your man", with that Spanner reluctantly walked to the door and into the sleep over room followed by McLennen.

Stephen was now aware that Stringer held power in this home and that the others were very compliant and submissive, particularly when Stringer expected something.

About three weeks after moving into Glenallen Stephen saw another young boy, he was 12, called Alex. Stringer summoned him to the medical room, because he had been late home by 40 minutes.

Later Stephen went to Alex's room where he was sitting with a face full of despair and when Stephen tried to talk casually about the staff, Alex put on a brave face, but was clearly upset. He told Stephen to fuck off. Stephen told him "OK, no need to be like that, I can be your friend". Alex was not really in the right frame of mind to talk so Stephen sat on the floor and tried to quiz him about his favourite music and asked him if he was a 'Roller'. He started to look up, and then replied that he was, but liked Glam rock better.

He gradually looked at Stephen and told him that "Stringer was weird", as he had pulled his pants down and had given him six smacks across his backside with a PE slipper for being late, "I can take the smacks but why did he pull my pants down. He then kissed my arse and said sorry and kind of, stroked my bum, McLennen was there, watching, and had his dick out".

Alex looked at Stephen in a pleading way, insisting that he must not tell anyone about anything. It confirmed all the initial feelings of Stephen's medical experience.

He then screwed up his face and said again that, "Stringer was a cunt and weird"

Stephen told Alex that he would not tell anyone and that he needed to be strong and think about good stuff to get through the bad times.

As he left the bedroom, he wished that he was back with the Patterson's or even the Humphries. Alex had stirred up all kinds of thoughts and memories.

Again, Stephen wondered what his mum was doing. He had some idea in his head that she had stopped drinking and had got back with Billy again and that they could live together as a family. He was old enough now to know that it was only a fleeting fantasy and memory, one of which left him confused as ever when he thought about Billy and the touching. He began to realise that Billy was someone who had given him some hope and comfort but left him confused. He was someone who did appear in dreams in various ways but was also still held dear. Somehow, he seemed to say that Stephen had to make his own dreams, and that his mum was never going to change.

Over time Stephen began to understand that Glenallen could be endured and found that if you kept quiet and minded your own business both in Glenallan and in school you could get through each day relatively intact. Stephen was approach by McLennen again, but by now he had realised by talking to Greg in his dormitory that McLennen was more interested in the girls and younger boys. Spanner was his favourite by far. Because he kept getting into trouble he was always in the medical room or the office.

Chapter 21

In September 1976 Stephen was also faced with having to attend a new local school. He only knew the children from Glenallan, who were seen by the others in the school as some kind of low life nutters. Liberton High School was a secondary school with a mixed group but in general most of the pupils had low expectations about what they could achieve in education and there was a high dropout rate of both sexes in the fifth year.

Stephen did become friendly with Dennis who was the only Punk in the school and also took a pounding of abuse from most others including the Glenallen crew who would consider him truly mad. Particularly with his torn trousers and vests he would wear in all weathers and always looked cold. Stephen thought that at least Dennis was interesting as an individual and liked a laugh. They were in most of the same classes together and spent their time out of class hanging out and avoiding the rest of the school.

Most of the classes were mad, with teachers who were not particularly bothered. History in particular was a free for all, where the teacher would insist that we opened a book at a particular page and write out 20 facts from the following text, while the rest of his time was spent avoiding eye contact by pretending to read a book. This allowed various members of the class to screw up paper balls and throw them across the room. They made up excuses to leave the classroom and would run around to the window on the outside. Then making faces to others in class sent the group into an even greater frenzy. Until finally Mr Fortune, who was a large black African with a thick, sometimes difficult accent to follow, would look up from his pretend state of reading a book, to shout, "that's enough, anymore and you will miss break" or he would smash his hand down on the desk slightly grimacing as he scowled across the room, only to return to his pretend reading as the chaos continued.

English was a little better and the nice American female teacher did try to run through the syllabus. Stephen was particularly interested in a good story and the one about 'Romeo and Juliet', written by William Shakespeare was his favourite. His understanding was that there were two warring families, star struck lovers from each family dreaming of a life together, the fun of boys goading and bantering with each other; dancing, fighting, revenge, death, passion and tragedy. Stephen was inspired to think that life was happening somewhere else, and that he needed to find it, wherever it was.

Winter in Edinburgh was cold and wet in 1977, with heavy sleet, and short daylight hours. There was a good snowy covering in January and February and Stephen managed to attend school most days, even though he felt that he was learning very little. Stephen had become wiser in his dealings with groups of kids; he was learning how to manage the bullies and growing in confidence from having to survive 'Glenallan'.

They called him names like; bender boy, poofter and queer boy, but he was able to smile, look right into their eyes, and tell them that, "he who calls it is it." He sometimes got pushed and threatened but could always rely on Greg from 'Glenallan' to deal with any real threat of violence as most of the bullies were afraid of him. There was an unwritten rule in 'Glenallen' that they looked after each other. Bernie was the boy who most people avoided, he was not that bright, but he had a reputation, and even Greg controlled his language when Bernie seemed to be a bit tetchy.

It was Friday the first of April, and everyone was trying to play April Fool tricks in school: Jump out and scare, false poo's, plastic flies in drinks from the joke shops were the usual, but Greg decided to ramp it up, with the jump out and scare prank, using a horror zombie mask. He waited at a corner of the school with Stephen and Bernie and jumped when Bernie gave him the signal. Greg gave a scream, and leapt, as Max and his friends were just arriving. The group jumped back shouting 'fucking hell man, you thick pricks' and started to gather around Greg who backed up to where Bernie and Stephen were standing.

Max confronted Greg, pushing his face closer and closer to him, in a slight head-butting action, with his chest stuck forward. While the rest of his group was pushing forward strategically surrounding Greg, who started to retaliate by shoving them away saying it was a joke.

Just as it was starting to kick off, Bernie moved in front of Max, and put a firm hand on his chest saying, 'leave him alone' while looking around at the others in an intimidating manner, which quieted them down and left Bernie and Max staring hard at each other.

There was a pause as each was waiting for the other to throw the first punch, but as they were sizing each other up, a voice from the end of the playground boomed, 'what do you think you lot are doing? There will be no fighting in this school'. It was Mr Wilkie, their PE teacher, who marched up to them demanding to know what was going on. The boys moved back pretending that there was nothing happening, collectively saying 'na sir, just a misunderstanding, everything fine'. Wilkie told them to move on, and get themselves home, and they slowly moved away, out of school in the direction of the local park.

There was an excited buzz on the Friday afternoon at the end of school, the words fight, fight, fight were reverberating. Groups of kids were walking towards the park, fight, fight. Max Dalglish had challenged Bernie, and the park was the venue. The groups were turning into a crowd baying for blood. Max was particularly agitated, building himself up and being egged on by his mates and followers. He was the first to stop and faced Bernie shouting, "come on then, I'll fucking kill yare".

He started to size up to Bernie for some time, walking about with his fists clenched, dangling by his sides, skipping and hopping, and then started holding out his fists, and swinging an arm and closed knuckle in thin air, followed by another. He ran at Bernie who moved purposely to avoid any of the flailing arms and Max continued to shift in and out thrusting his fists in the general direction of Bernie. He then went in for the kill, fully flailing his right and left arms, hoping to catch his big opponent with a determined connection that would end the confrontation once and for all.

Bernie, bided his time, stepping backward and then forward, and finally taking hold of Max's arm that had swung past, pulling his jumper and putting Max into a full headlock with his left arm, forced Max down to the ground while he kicked and thrashed his free arm in a frenzied defiance.

Bernie squeezed and threw in a couple of right hand punches to Max's head fixed under Bernie's forearm, and a gurgling, choking voice could be heard "let me go you fucking prick" Bernie tightened his grip and lay on top of Max, totally in control, with Max's head and neck buried under his considerable body mass, and then he said, "do ya give in".

Max wriggled some more, slapping out with his free left arm. His muffled cries were becoming more desperate as it was obvious that he was struggling to breath, with snorts of snot, and a desperate reddening of what face could be seen between Bernie's arm and shoulder.

Bernie leaned in and tightened the grip some more. Max was slapping out with his free left arm, forcing his cheeks open, gasping for air. He then tried in a stunted scream to say, "Let me go" Bernie repeated "do ya give up," and a grunted "yes" could be heard.

There was a long pause and a gasp from the crowd, who had thought Bernie, had killed Max. Bernie slowly released his grip and stood up, only glancing momentarily at Max.

He tidied his clothing, very quickly brushing down his arms and knees and then walked through the crowd in a defiant but triumphant manner, with Greg and Stephen following on.

Max lay still, trying to catch his breath, half hiding himself as he wiped the mucus from his face with slight blood smears from his nose, embarrassed by the attention. His friends stood close and tried to tend to him, but he hid his eyes and teary face. He pushed his way past them, in need of his own space to recover and gather his thoughts.

The crowd dispersed quickly with tales of how the fight had gone adding extra detail to the swinging of fists, blood, the final choking that nearly killed him. This was the stuff of schoolboy playground legend, that spelt out very clearly why and who you did not mess with for obvious reasons.

Stephen had very little physical threat from Max and his crew again and felt like he could in general go about his affairs in school in relative freedom. Even Dennis the punk, while with Stephen felt safer, but they still suffered the name-calling and verbal abuse.

Stephen liked to dress well and saved up his allowance with Christmas and birthday money after persuading his social worker, David Williams, to give him a little more for travel even though he walked to school. Money became more important to Stephen than ever, as he liked to be able to buy fashionable clothes and look the good mod, although he did let his hair grow as that was the popular guise in the 70's.

Astutely Stephen became aware that two of the 14-year-old girls, Margaret and Jasmine were always in the money, and it was common knowledge in 'Glenallan' that they were seeing older boys outside of the Children's home. Stephen had become friendly with one of the older girls called Sally, who had been at 'Glenallen' since she was 10 years old and knew everything about everyone.

Sally was 16 years old and due to move away to a lodging house when school finished in June. She was always saying, "I can't wait to get out of this fucking place", but the reality was that she was scared, unsure and totally unprepared about how she would get on in something so independent as lodgings.

Stephen felt that he got on better with girls than boys and was able to talk much more freely about things in life, also girls thought he was a good listener. Sally told Stephen, that Margaret and Jasmine were, a couple of tarts and that the older boys were pimps, and ex-residents, who had hung around 'Glenallen' for years.

Stephen was curious as to where they went and quickly realised that Sally was right and the girls were able to get away with staying out late when Stringer and McLennen were on duty.

Stephen had noticed that the 'pimp' boys would wait at the side of the building, by the bins to smoke, and that Stringer would meet up with them to smoke as well. They all seemed very friendly and one day, as Stephen left by the front door he looked back and down the side of the building where he was sure he saw a package, or something being handed to Stringer from the pimp boys. The girls were starting to walk from the garage that sat to the side of the building, and it was clear that Margaret was tidying herself as she was talking to McLennen.

He needed to avoid Stringer and McLennen getting on his case as Stephen had his own plans and he did not want to make it obvious that he knew what was going on.

Chapter 22

It was during the start of April 1977, and the day light hours were getting longer. Stephen was slowly approaching 15 years old. He was feeling that life was passing him by, that he had no friends or future around here. He decided to dress up and visit his mum and then spend some time in Edinburgh, however, he never got to see his mum. Instead, he made his way to the top of Leith Street.

This was a place that he remembered his mum talking about, where she used to live before moving to Craigshill. He arrived at Waverley station and walked around looking at the London signage and felt a yearning to go to London.

Leaving the station he walked along Princes Street passed Waverley Bridge, to the Scotts Monument and was amazed at the shear height of it. He then looked onwards to Edinburgh Castle where he paused to think about who had constructed such massive buildings and the ancient history of Scotland's great landmark.

It was a nice day and the park-looked spring like with blossom and a canopy of green leafy foliage as far as the eye could see. He then walked back along Hanover Street into George Street, which he remembered his mother talking about when she was a girl, and along to St. Andrew's and St. Georges Parish Church. He was not religious but once inside found the house of worship scattered with people who he assumed were praying as they sat facing the front, where a great multi-coloured stained-glass window shone light down through the centre of the church. Momentarily he felt a quiet peaceful reverence that he had not felt before. Stephen tried to imagine God who might dwell in this place, deciding to pray for his mum, thinking that he would like to believe that a prayer might make it good, but felt stupid and a little angry, then walked out.

Stephen made his way back to Princes Street Gardens and followed some steps descending to the main public toilets. Once inside the Victorian public convenience with large porcelain urinals, Stephen noticed a man looking at him, and he walked across to Stephen, stopping to wash his hands. Stephen did his pee and was aware that the man was going to talk to him as he walked to the washbasins. He spoke to Stephen by saying something about the weather changing. Stephen felt he was safe enough to talk to and agreed that he hoped that the last of the cold weather was over. The man smiled and asked his name; followed by do you want to come for a drink? Stephen paused for a short while and then thought why not and said "yes." The truth was that he felt a little excited to be receiving the attention from this older man and decided to go along with it.

He was not sure if this was right, but Stephen wanted something different in his life.

His name was Derek, and he looked well dressed, smart and spoke confidently about life, people and was funny. They both drank Coca Cola, and he kept looking at Stephen like he was so special and asked him where he lived, who his friends were. Stephen felt an excitement and an erection as Derek touched his wrist and gently affected a move to the back of his hand with a finger, slowly stroking and caressing it, which initially made Stephen feel a little awkward. He started to withdraw his hand for a moment and then realised that he liked it and did not care. He returned it slowly which made Derek even more curious and excited.

Derek asked how old he was. Stephen paused and then told him he was 16. Stephen also lied about where he lived and his friends but did tell him about Dennis and how being a Punk was too obvious and over the top like 'OTT'.

Derek stared at Stephen and said he thought he was older and laughed saying, "I like a nice piece of chicken for lunch". At that stage Stephen was not sure what he meant by this, but he did treat him to a chicken sandwich and Pepsi Cola in a nice café'.

They then walked through the Park and he stopped Stephen in a secluded space by a large oak tree and leaned his full body against Stephen. Derek started to try to kiss Stephen who was taken back and a little shocked. Derek realised that this was a new experience for Stephen who said, "I am not sure" Derek smiled and asked how old he really was? Stephen told him he was 15 years old and Derek relaxed his hold and gently stroked Stephen's upper arm, saying, "you, have a lot to learn" and kissed him on the cheek before asking, "when are you sixteen"?

Stephen liked this man and felt relaxed enough to respond to the kiss with a sexualized notion generated from his groin. He was then happy to allow Derek to touch his cock from the outside, which was fully erect. Stephen was excited and he really wanted him to bring him off. Then Derek took Stephen's arm and pushed it down the front of his trousers where Stephen felt the top of his hard erect penis, which made him draw his hand back a little. Stephen then became even more excited and took hold of Derek's erection.

Stephen's naivety and the excitement of doing this in the Park had caught up with him and before he knew it he was shooting his lot in his pants with Derek moving his hand over the outside of Stephen's trousers. He found himself clinging onto Derek as he grunted and smiled as the intensity subsided. Derek relaxed his hold on Stephen knowing that their reciprocal consummation had come to an end.

As they sat under the tree Derek looked embarrassed and talked about how he should not have done this, but gave Stephen £10.00 saying I hope that is OK? They walked back through the Park and Derek was very chatty but mainly kept saying that he would love to meet Stephen in 6 years' time and said he had to get back to work.

Stephen felt pleased with himself and liked the idea of having some real money in his pocket and thought about how easy it was.

He made his way back to 'Glenallen', feeling a new surge of confidence, but firstly needed to wash and a change of underwear.

That evening Stephen quietly thought about Derek and got another erection while looking at a 'Mirabelle ' magazine that had been left around. Also showing pictures of David Essex posing in a tight short sleeved three button t-shirt and jeans, with two sexy looking girls in shorts, draped across his shoulders.

Stephen started to think about naked boys and girls, getting several erections a day, particularly when he saw images of semi naked bodies in a magazine. He had kept his favourite magazine and newspaper cuttings and would find his way to a toilet to masturbate and fantasise about sex, while looking at the images.

The long warm summer holidays seemed to go on forever at 'Glenallen'. Sexual imaginings were a dominant feature, and he was curious as to what it was like. He knew that the girls were coming on to him, and were experienced, so he decided to get to know Margaret and Jasmine better. Feeling his best chance of exploring sex would be with one of these girls.

He found that they were a very tight couple, who, seemed to use secret glances and coded comments, whenever Stephen approached them. They would ask Stephen if he had a girlfriend and then they would giggle and turn to each other, laughing and whispering between themselves; "he's a poofter," "are you sure"?

There was a suggestion that Jasmine liked Stephen, but Margaret would always dominate the interactions by pulling Jasmine away and cupping her mouth to Jasmine's ear, talking in whispers and mutterings, to regain control.

Biding his time Stephen found Jasmine on her own after a meal, and he was able to ask her what kind of music she liked, she said anything you can dance to, stating 'Baccara ' "yes sir, I can boogie" is good. Stephen said he preferred real dance music like Disco, and Jasmine laughed, saying, "I mean modern music to dance to."

Stephen teased her by suggesting that Margaret was her 'girl friend', and Jasmine told him to 'fuck off man 'she likes boys. Stephen asked, "what about you" and she replied by saying, "of course I do", looking a little embarrassed at being questioned about something so basic. He then asked if she had a boyfriend, and she said, "that's for me to know and you to find out, do you have a girl friend?"

They could hear the others running about the building, and made their way outside, through the back door, smiling as they stepped around the corner to a hidden spot in the garden. Stephen felt confident enough to step in, readying himself for a kiss.

Jasmine was well aware of the signals, shifting forward allowing their lips to meet. Jasmine was a confident kisser and was open to the next phase when Stephen started to touch her breasts and moved down to her thighs and fanny over her clothing.

She confidently crouched in front of Stephen, unbuttoned and drew down the zip of his trousers, pulling them down along with his underpants. Stephen was clearly excited and found him-self enjoying the pleasures of oral sex for the first time. He touched her hair and head as she moved to create the limited friction that was needed. Jasmine looked up and said, "tell me when you are ready to come?" but it was too late, it was happening, and Jasmine laughed a little shocked, while directing the spurts to one side, still wanking him hard to properly finish him off. Stephen trembled and groaned as it happed then deteriorated into a purring satisfied male, like the cat who'd got the cream.

She knew what she was doing and even took out a tissue from her handbag to help Stephen and her-self wipe up. Soon he was frantically, trying to pull up his under pants and trousers, while saying, thanks that was great. She laughed, "No problems, that was a freebie, I don't normally give it away."

They walked back into the kitchen, where Bernie was making a cup of tea. Jasmine looked at Stephen coyly pretending that nothing had happened and walked to the kitchen sink to wash her hands. Bernie glanced in their direction, giving minimal acknowledgement to the two of them together, and then Margaret put her head around the door beckoning Jasmine to come. This she did with a sideway look and smile aimed at her suitor as she left the room. Which encouraged Stephen to grin in the knowledge that he had done something real and wanted more of it.

Growing in confidence he felt impelled to get out into the world. His action status went into overdrive. He was not going to be restricted by school, the controlling influences of Glenallen or the immaturity of the other kids in the home.

Chapter 23

Stephen three days ago, countdown. Sunday 23-01-1983.

It's 10.30am on a Sunday morning in January, and I had just left some old man I had met at the Dilly who called himself Ian. He was a nice enough person who I had been with before. I knew that he was basically a lonely man who bought his associations because that was all he really wanted, so he spent the night touching and stroking me, while trying to get a hard on.

He had paid me well, £30 to stay the night: we eat some nice food, creamy pasta with ham and tomato sauce and I drank as much as I could to dull my craving for something stronger. During the morning, in the bathroom cabinet, I came across a large bottle of codeine, which was a result, as I knew these prescription pills well, they were the strongest pain killers, better than paracetamol and a couple of them helped to numb out any bodily aches.

I tried to dip him for cash, before I left, but I think he was onto me, and kept an eye on my every move until I was out of his house which was somewhere in Islington North London.

Dougie wasn't around last night; I hardly saw him these days now that he had his new friends. I was lucky to be pulled by Ian just when I thought I would be sleeping rough.

I had £5.00 left from last night and another £30.00 from Ian. Without planning where I was going, I made my way to Highbury and Islington tube station and took the Victoria Line to Oxford Street, a familiar route. I intended to cut through to Charing Cross Road via Oxford Street and Berwick Street but on the way, by Berwick Street market I met Sam Blackburn who I knew had some gear.

He glanced at me, which gave me the incentive with money in my pocket to ask what he had. He told me he had some good Amps and could let me have 2 grams for £10.00, which was an ok price. They were good at keeping you focused and awake particularly with Scotch whisky. I ended up with 3 grams and paid £14.00.

Soho Square was nearby, but it was Sunday and no offie's were going to be open. I took a couple of the yellow and white capsules and codeine, while sitting in the park, and then made my way along Dean Street. I stopped at the Golden Lion again, and the Sunday lunch trade was in full swing, just right for a whisky chaser with extras.

I made my way to the same table I had sat at last night and was immediately aware of the attention I had received previously from the thin Scotsman with the metal rimmed glasses, dressed in a raincoat. I was feeling more upbeat and knew that the capsules were taking effect. The Scotsman was talking to some other men of a similar age, but kept turning and checking, waiting for a moment.

I got up to order a second drink and the man lit up a cigarette as he walked towards me. He asked how I was, while offering a Benson and Hedges open packet. I was not sure if we knew each other. Wondering whether he was an ex-punter or the old bill. I replied, "Yes I'm good." I realised that I was moving to the beat of 'Do you really want to hurt me', by 'Culture Club 'which was playing on the Jukebox, one of my favourite songs.

Moving forward I slightly lost my balance and was caught by his outstretched arm. I thought it was a pickup and made it obvious that I was open for business, and with a half-smile said, "Are you looking for trade?" The tall Scotsman leaned in and informed me that he might be, but that today was not a good time. I frowned playing the role of a naughty spurned lover, and glared a mischievous grin as if disappointed, which was a role that I had played so many times in my past.

I had found out that the man's name was Dennis, and that the Golden Lion Pub was his regular drinking hole and he was always there. There was no sense of attraction towards him. I left the pub feeling like there was an ominous, bad aura coming from this man, but I had learnt over the years, to always keep my options open, in case there was an angle and money to be earned. Anyway, I thought, "fuck um, who gives a shit, I don't care anyway".

I left the Golden Lion once again feeling lost, rejected, and reeling from the effects of the pills and alcohol. I wandered back along Dean Street to Soho Square where it had all started and collapsed on a bench. It was cold and the effects of the weather started to kick in. I knew that I had to find somewhere warm where I could sort myself out.

Instinctively I started to make my way toward the Dilly. I went back across Dean Street via Carlisle Street, across to Sheraton Street, Wardour Street, where I had partied hard in the past. I knew these streets too well and was able to make my way around as if on autopilot. I found myself in Berwick Street, where the daily market was in full swing, selling fruit and veg, general household goods, soft furnishings, fabrics, and a butchery stall. The smell of the bakery and fresh pastries drew my attention to one of the shops, just along from the café 'that smelt of fried bacon, eggs and tea.

Stopping for a brew in the Café I sat alone trying to work out what to do. I thought about 'Centrepoint' but was sure that they would not take me back. Being in Berwick Street reminded me of Lawrence, and I wondered if he would be worth a try. Lawrence was a guy who regularly came to the Dilly for rent. He worked for the government and described himself as someone who got things done for those in power. Hence a top-ranking civil servant who kept his sexuality secret from everyone he knew, closeted from the world, afraid of how this knowledge would harm his career. Lawrence lived in a smart flat in Brewer Street. He was someone who had taken a liking to me in the early years, and was a regular for some time, but was less welcoming now.

Leaving the Café I walked to the end of the market and through the alleyway. Continuing past the sex shops, flashing lights, cheap strip clubs that always seemed to be open, with the obligatory scowling male standing just inside the opening, menacingly looking out in anticipation for business or trouble.

Brewer Street was a busy road with a range of shops, flashing lights, girlie clubs, and bars. Big showy expensive cars were often driven, because of the easy access to Soho and the West End from the Brewer Street underground car park.

I wondered if Lawrence was home. Deciding to give it a try I called at the blue door, pressing the intercom, in the vague hope that Lawrence would be friendly and welcoming. A voice answered and Lawrence asked who it was. I tried to sound cheery and said "hi ya, how's it going? It's me Stephen" Lawrence paused but eventually said "yes, I am good, what do you want". I tried to sound upbeat and asked if I could come in, stating how cold it was outside, "I'm freezing my balls off." But Lawrence answered by informing me that he was just about to leave, "I'll come down." I sensed that Lawrence was not going to entertain me and I started to walk away.

As I backed off the door opened. Lawrence momentarily stopped while looking a little awkward. He had his black Crombie coat on and reminded me about the last time we had been together. I tried to explain that Dougie and I were only trying to have some fun and that we were well out of it and didn't mean any harm. Lawrence looked around uneasily and told me that he was not prepared to forgive anymore and that he was not someone who was going to continue to be an easy touch.

Little did I know that Lawrence had walked away feeling uncomfortable and guilty as he thought that I was fine on my own, without the influence of Dougie. He was also concerned about how disheveled I was looking but felt that he needed to make his point by being abrupt and deliberate in his actions, so that's why he did not look back.

I felt distraught and confused as I thought I could always depend on Lawrence.

I watched as Lawrence walked away then turned the corner. I half expected him to turn back. I started to follow him and before I knew it I was standing outside St Anne's Gardens. I walked in and found a quiet spot on a bench. It was cold. I felt lonely and hopeless.

I took several of my tabs and saw a broken bottle by the bench and picked up a shard. I thought about my mother, so called friends and punters, feeling that I had a worthless life and kept repeatedly saying "fuck her, fuck them, bitch, cunts".

I pulled my sleeves up to my elbows and turning my forearm to face me. Using the broken glass I started to scratch followed by a sawing action at my already scarred left forearm and then did the same to the other.

' Somehow I was, cleansing myself, it hurt, but it felt good, like I was ridding myself of bad things. As the blood flowed, I sensed that I was purged of my filthy wicked past, and the treachery that life had bestowed on me, and I watched as the blood seeped from the lacerations slowly dripping on the floor, and a feeling of numbness sent me into a stupor of quiet contemplation'.

Eventually I pulled my sleeves back over my forearms to cover the wounds, which took away the sight of the blood.

I started to shiver as the cold mixed with fear, blood loss and pain kicked in. I walked out of the gardens to Shaftsbury Avenue and looked up at the line of kids waiting at the 'Centrepoint 'gate, just before 8.00pm. I really needed to get in and feel safe. My forearms were throbbing, so I walked up the street and joined the queue. Chin on my chest and ready to shed a tear I waited my turn.

Chapter 24

Stephen was met and interviewed by Stewart who was one of the full-time workers. He could see that Stephen was different, shaking, and vulnerable, and asked Stephen how he was. There was little response, except, "I need a bed," which was not like Stephen, who was, usually much more talkative, even when he was pulling a story.

It was clear that he was particularly low. Stewart was also aware that Stephen had been told several times that he could not use the night shelter anymore, due to his extensive and casual use in the past.

Stewart told Stephen to wait, while he gave it some thought. He needed to discuss him with Gus the volunteer who attended the gate with him. They read the notes in the small, cramped office of the shelter and Stewart explained to Gus that the full-time staff team and team leader had had several long discussions about Stephen. The overriding decision was not to allow Stephen to use the facility again, because he was using it to sustain his existence in London, Piccadilly, and the rent scene. Centrepoint was a short-term emergency shelter not a hostel. However, they both felt that something was different. Stephen had not stayed at the night shelter for 15 months. There were some notes from 'The Soho Project' that updated what 'Centrepoint' had last recorded, that Stephen was about, he was using, and would drop in to see them, but was generally on the Dilly, renting, and that casual support and counselling was what Soho Project were offering. There was also the note from Linda last night, when Stephen was passing, stating that he looked a little grubby, which made Stewart think about why he had come to the gate two nights in a row.

Stewart and Gus arrived back at the gate and let the first group into the shelter and while Gus took them along the alleyway through to the back door, Stewart talked some more to Stephen. Stephen mumbled thoughts and indifferences, like; 'I feel like shit', 'I want to get out of the West End for good', 'I can't take it anymore'. Stewart decided, against all that he agreed to, with the team, that something was different and that Stephen needed the shelter even if it was to encourage him to go to 'The Soho Project' in the morning. It was Sunday, relatively quiet, and he felt Stephen must be desperate.

Fortunately, Stephen was surprised to be told that he could come in for the night, on the strict basis that he went to 'The Soho Project' in the morning.

Once inside he sat at a table where he was served some hot food by Gus, who was a little taken back to see Stephen walk into the Night Shelter with Stewart, but was privately pleased with the decision. Then as the evening progressed Stewart took the opportunity to sit with Stephen to talk. He struggled to get Stephen to open up at first, or even to take his coat off.

Stephen was relatively unresponsive but did eventually slip his coat back onto his chair before he took a swig from his mug of tea. It was then that Stewart noticed dried blood on his hands and asked Stephen what had happened. Without a word 'Stephen slowly drew the sleeves of his woollen jumper up his forearms, to expose two large lacerations on each arm'. The congealed blood was sticking to his jumper as he pulled the woollen weaves away from the sticky fresh forming scabs, that still oozed and seeped with thick coagulating red plasma.

It was clear to Stewart that Stephen would need to visit a hospital and talked to him about getting the gashes properly looked at and dressed. Stephen asked if it could be done here. Stewart explained that it was a serious injury and he needed to be seen by the hospital. Stewart asked Gus to accompany Stephen in the Ambulance to the nearest casualty.

Stephen and Gus waited to be seen in a relatively quiet casualty department. Gus talked to Stephen about his lifestyle, and how it could only go so far before his life would be in danger and that he needed to take some control back.

Stephen listened, stating that his life was shit, and promised that he would go to the Soho Project and take on whatever they suggested. He needed to change, stating; "I know, I'm not a kid anymore, I need to get myself sorted". The nurse attended to the wounds and the doctor said that they would keep him in overnight in case of infection and wanted to be sure that he was seen by their psychiatric services the following day. Gus reminded Stephen about his promise and said that Stewart would call the Soho project in the morning to explain all that they had talked about.

Centrepoint log: Stephen Addair. D.O.B. 10.06.1962. Date: 23.01.1983

Stephen came to the gate at 8.00pm and after some thought I decided to let him in as he was presenting in real need. This decision was justified as after a period of time trying to engage with him in the Night Shelter, it was found that he had freshly self-harmed and was in need of immediate hospitalisation.

I had to call for an ambulance and asked Gus if he would escort Stephen to casualty. He was to be kept in overnight, where they wanted him to see someone from the psychiatric services in the morning. He also promised that he would go to the Soho Project on Monday and try to get something sorted out.

I wish him well, let's hope that he is serious this time and makes a concerted effort to turn his life around.

Stewart

Chapter 25

Stephen slept in one of the recovery wards that night.

One of the older men in the ward, in a bed by the door, kept screeching and calling out to the nurse, followed by some other well-chosen expletives. Stephen's bed was the third on the left by the window.

When he awoke, he was given more painkillers, antibiotics, a breakfast and hot drink. His wounds were looked at again, cleaned and redressed. He could feel the warm rays of morning sun shining through the large thin-framed hospital windows. The dawn light was bright, for a change, on a London January morning. Life seemed a little better than yesterday. Dressed in a national health service, 'NHS 'bed gown, he looked down at his clothes, which were hanging out of a large green hospital plastic bag, on a chair, next to his bed.

Stephen felt uncomfortable and agitated when he thought about the previous evening at 'Centrepoint'. He was worried about what he had told them vaguely remembering the promises he had made. He wondered where his money and pills were and searched through his clothing bag and pockets, happy to find that they were all intact. He counted 16 capsules, two screwed up £5.00 and three £1.00 notes and a lot of loose change. He was unsure as to what he was going to do next, remembering the conversation he had had with Gus and the promise he had made to Stewart at Centrepoint.

His mind drifted to Dougie. He started to speculate as to where he might be and whom he would be with. Instinctively he knew that Dougie would be fine, as he always found an angle but wondered if he was trying to get in contact.

When the nurse appeared, Stephen told her that he was ready to leave. She informed him that the doctor was doing his rounds and would be in attendance soon. Stephen insisted that he wanted to get dressed, so she drew the curtain around the bed. He sat in his blue hospital armchair next to the bed and started to get anxious. The nurse glanced in, then efficiently pulled back the curtain, saying, "the doctor is in the ward, and will be here soon" She could see that Stephen was dressed and ready to leave and asked if he wanted a cup of tea.

When the doctor arrived, she explained in a no-nonsense way, that they were concerned because of the size and depth of the lacerations to his arms, informing Stephen that he was very close to the major veins and nerves that control the movement of his hand. The gashes were messy because the glass had shredded the superficial veins causing trauma to the forearm. She said that she had informed the on-duty psychologist who would be along soon for a chat and that the wounds would in time heal and repair, but in the meantime, he needed to have them properly dressed daily for a week or two.

Stephen had been thinking of Dougie and was feeling uncomfortable about the thought of having to stay around the hospital ward waiting to see a shrink. He became more flustered about the screaming nutter, whose voice reverberated through his head and the ward. Then some of the other characters who had wandered into the corridor were also beginning to rouse themselves, crying, calling for a nurse or moaning out loud. Stephen started to be affected by the loud murmurings, and told himself, that he did not belong here. He thought that maybe, he could go to the Soho Project, and on the way, pass through the Circus to see who was around. He waited for his chance, pretending to use the toilet and quietly walked out of the ward, through the main hospital and onto the street, quickly making his way along Tottenham Court Road then to Piccadilly Circus.

    He felt relieved to be out, back into the fresh air, and onto the familiarity of the West End. His arms were throbbing, reminding him of what he had done to himself last night followed by the sudden realisation that he had nowhere to go. Walking to the Soho Project he stood for several minutes outside the main entrance but felt embarrassed to enter. He did not feel like he could blag anything else out of them. Feeling in his pocket he came upon the bottle of codeine and took two, then another two before sauntering on.

UCLH, Casualty, Emergency Street Drop-in Unit. Stephen Addair. D.O.B. 10.06.1962. Date as recorded 24.01.1983. 9.00am

Stephen arrived by ambulance from Centrepoint youth homeless centre yesterday, Sunday evening at 10.30pm. He was immediately assessed as self-harming with 2 serious lacerations to both forearms and wrists. He had sliced across superficial veins narrowly missing the medium antebrachium and median nerve on the left forearm where the most damage was inflicted.

I have asked our psychiatric nurse to talk to him today, and he will need some housing advice and assistance as he does not appear to have a permanent address. His wounds should heal without sutures, as long as the scar tissue is kept intact using pads and dressings. I have prescribed a course of antibiotics in case of infection a codeine-based painkillers to help with any discomfort.

Dr. Shelby. Duty Team.

Chapter 26

Dougie had first met Stephen in Soho Square all those years ago, during a spring evening in May 1978. He had spotted him walking across Charing Cross Road and followed him to Soho Square. Dougie was well experienced in this kind of wee boy, young chicken, and pickup, feeling sure Stephen was there for the catching.

Knowing the patter well, he was usually able to befriend the vulnerable, who in general, were in need of direction and a friendly face. They were frequently relieved to have met a sympathetic peer, especially one who seemed to demonstrate acquaintance through accent.

Dougie was smart, confident, good looking and funny, everything that Stephen wanted to be. He took Stephen into a small café, bar in Wardour Street, called 'The coffee pot' where he seemed to know everyone. The customers were mostly male and were happy and welcoming. Dougie asked Stephen if he wanted a 'cappuccino'. Which was something Stephen was not familiar with, but politely said, "Yes, OK" when he got it, he saw that Dougie added two large spoonfuls of sugar to his, so Stephen did the same. He liked it and ran the name over in his head so he could order it again "Cappuccino, Cappuccino."

Dougie pointed to Lance and Keith and told Stephen that they were a good laugh and had good contacts. They were in deep conversation that kind of excluded Stephen, but Dougie gave reassuring glances that informed Stephen that Dougie was aware of him. Dougie had told Lance and Keith about something going on tonight; a good earner, and they both seemed up for it. He told Stephen, in a toned-down voice, that boys like us can make good money if you follow the rules,

"so remember; know what you are getting yourself into, get the cash up front, have some fun and leave them happy wanting more, then they will always come back." Stephen acted like he knew what they meant, understanding that he had met up with a group of guys who got money for doing sexual favours. Stephen did not have the confidence to question what was being said, pretending to understand.

Stephen felt privileged to be with this enigmatic young Scotsman who had chosen him. He was 15 years old, a little scared but excited to be walking through the streets of London, feeling like he had met a friend and someone who seemed like a winner.

Dougie told Stephen that he would do well, if he stuck with him, that he knew people, and then turning to the other two said, let's take him to 'Centrepoint' tonight, explaining to Stephen that it was just around the corner.

He quickly briefed Stephen, saying it's a safe place if you keep yourself to yourself. They will give you some food and a bed for the night, but have a story ready, as they will want to know all about you. "Don't tell them your real name, or that you are 15 because they will be on your back about all kinds of stuff. I will meet you here, at mid-day tomorrow, trust me you will be fine." With that Lance and Keith waded in with reassurances too.

Centrepoint log: Stephen Crombie. D.O.B. 10.06.1961 Date: 29-05-1978

Stephen stayed with us tonight. He presented as 16 years old seventeen next month. He told me that he had come to London from Edinburgh for work. Had very little to say other that his mum knew he was here and that he was meeting a friend tomorrow who would help him find work. That he was fine and only came to us because someone had told him that he could stay free, and that he did not want to use his savings.

I tried to get him to understand how dangerous London was for young people and that he really needed to get his visit, work and accommodation sorted out before he came. I explained that we were an emergency and advice accommodation service for young people aged between 16 to 21 years old, who might be at risk in the West End of London. He seemed to take all of that on, said he was fine, and would get himself sorted, but would attend the Soho Project tomorrow.

I was not convinced he was sixteen, and he seemed reluctant to discuss home, other than to say his mum knew he was *here, and that she had given him some money to be getting on with. Let's see if the Soho Project can get to the truth.*

Sally

The next morning, he was sent off to the Soho Project at 8.00am, instructed by Sally, carrying a printed basic hand drawn map and leaflet, spelling out what the agency could do for someone like Stephen and a luncheon voucher. He had been introduced to another boy, called Jack, who was 19 yrs. ' old, and had been staying at 'Centrepoint' over the weekend and knew where The Soho Project was from the week before. He reassured Stephen that The Soho Project was a good place and that the staff, were safe. Stephen did not feel he had anything to lose by not going. He had 4 hours to wait until he was due to meet Dougie again.

The poster in the waiting room said that The Soho Project was a West End Advice Agency, which was a grant-aided project, with charitable funds status, that it was a confidential counselling and advice service for young people.

Stephen was eventually seen by Barry, a fellow Scot, who was friendly and reassuring, he told Stephen that they could help him if he was serious about trying to get work in London, but that he had to be honest with them about his background details and age. They would help him sort out a National Insurance Number, as he could not get work without one. They wanted to know about home, his mum and exactly where he had come from.

Stephen felt that he was being cornered and started to say he would be fine, as his friend would sort him out with work. Barry asked him about this friend and then talked to Stephen about how dangerous the West End was for young people and how some people were very good at taking advantage and had stories of how to make money. They were really only after supporting their own ends. Stephen stuck to his story and when it was suggested that they call home, he became defensive, saying, "my mum does not have a phone."

Barry said that they worked closely with 'Centrepoint 'and that if they were able to move forward with clarifying something about him. They could guarantee him a bed tonight, and then could start helping Stephen with accommodation in the short term.

They asked Stephen about school and with that Stephen said, "I'm not going to school anymore" and asked if he could go to the toilet. Barry reminded Stephen that they could help, that he did not have to take their advice but could think about it today. He said, I will tell 'Centrepoint', that you were not able to move forward with the truth. 'Stephen realised that they were not believing him'. Barry knew that Stephen would need more time and said "I am sure they will take you tonight if you really need somewhere to stay".

Barry noticed that Stephen was becoming more agitated and started to nervously scratch at his wrists. He wanted to reassure him, that 'Centrepoint' would continue to support him. Moreover, that they would continue helping him, but would prefer it if he was honest with them. Stephen left to go to the toilet and then quickly went down the stairs and out onto the street.

The Soho Project Log: Stephen Crombie. DOB 10-06-1961. Date: 30-05-1978.

I met with Stephen this morning. I think he is still on the school roll and underage, but I could not clarify this. He was guarded in all his responses, but I feel that he has given a false name and is running away from something. I think he is probably in care. At first, he appeared relatively confident and told me that he had met people who were going to help him find work but would not tell me who they were. He mentioned his mum that she knew where he was, and that she was not on the telephone. He comes from Edinburgh, and I have made it clear that I thought Centrepoint would take him tonight if he needed a bed. I talked to him, reinforcing all the usual stuff about the West End dangers. I think and hope that we will probably see him again.

Barry

Stephen felt excited as if the streets seemed to welcome him. The buzz of the traffic, high-rise buildings and movement of the people made him feel alive and animated just as he had felt when he walked out of Kings Cross station yesterday. His thoughts were fixed on finding Dougie again. He traced his steps back to Shaftsbury Avenue, and as he walked, he somehow felt at home. He was in the centre of London and was walking past cinema's, theatres, a casino, fabulous clothes shops and tourist outlets; selling models of Big Ben, London double decker buses, Union Jack flags, T-shirts with 'Che Guevara 'and 'I love LONDON'.

He walked to the 'Centrepoint' gates in Shaftsbury Avenue, where he had been let in last night. The gates were closed, quiet and locked. It was still early 11.00am and he could retrace his steps back to 'the coffee pot' from there.

Sauntering onto Piccadilly Circus he was taken aback by the billboards that were lit up even during the day, with flickering multi lights glimmering and transferring images and nametags from one advertisement to another. He stood by the Eros statue and looked across at the lights, fascinated by the switch from one advertisement to the next. His attention was drawn to below the electronic billboard, to the Wimpy bar with railings sweeping around the pathway. There was a small group of teenage boys, who seemed to be just hanging out. He looked up once more, at the multi coloured lights flickering dramatically, and wanted to see them once it had become dark.

Strolling from Piccadilly, passing 'Playland' the gaming machine arcade, he noticed 'The Swiss Centre', where he then walked on toward Leicester Square to a green space with impressive buildings surrounding it. The Odeon Cinema took centre stage behind the large poplar trees standing majestic with their green leaves shading the sunlight around the square, casting shadows, but allowing long shafts of light onto the grass. The Poplar trees gently rustled in the cool morning air as if they were standing guard, or taking in the sights, in the same way that Stephen stood transfixed for a moment, before being shoved along, by the people pushing their way through the main thoroughfare, toward the small black metal railings surrounding the central part of the square.

He moved from the main thoroughfare through an entrance area into the grassy square and there was an instant peace. He sat on one of the many benches, to take it all in. Very soon there were pigeons everywhere, pecking their way around the bench that Stephen sat on. Some ferociously flapping their wings with the power of a small helicopter whooshing up the dried dirt from the ground. They came swooping down onto the grass next to Stephen, hoping to find any leftovers or remains of food from the previous night. One pigeon seemed to be waiting by his feet, hoping for a morsel or crumb and Stephen realised at that moment that they were survivors, like him, taking advantage of whatever was on offer, individuals, but part of a larger group, who took full benefit of their environment, taking whatever they were presented with to survive.

Stephen wandered over to the grand statue taking centre stage in the square. The figure was positioned in such a way as to look relaxed, confident and happy. He was leaning on two books with his right arm, his hand resting comfortable under his chin, while his left arm was lowered and his forefinger was pointing to a scroll that said, 'There is no darkness but ignorance'.

The figure was William Shakespeare. His immediate reference was to remember how his American teacher at school had tried to teach the class about, 'Romeo and Juliet'. How this man had written a love story, all those years ago. Star crossed lovers in Italy, with feuding families. Yet here was this grand statue in Leicester Square of the same man. He liked the phrase about 'there being no darkness but ignorance' not fully understanding it 's significant until later in his West End life.

Chapter 27

Stephen walked back to the Circus and stopped off in the slot machine arcade, where he was curious and amused to see some of the Pinball machines being played by a whole range of youths, some of whom he thought, should have been at school. There was a small group of boys gathered around a large blue and white box with space designs on it. They were looking down at a screen, totally immersed in whatever it was, continually tapping at the buttons and screeching with an intensity and excitement as they participated in the game.

Stephen played on a vacated pinball machine called 'Wizard'. The back box was brightly lit up, featuring a picture of a cool boy with a girl on his arm, who was wearing very little, with more girls around him posing semi naked. Putting in coin after coin Stephen tried to beat his last score. Weird enticing intense musical sounds screamed from the machine and lights flashed as he ferociously clicked the flapper's, in an attempt to send the ball bearing back around the random route, causing a frenetic clanking as it bounced between the brightly flashing sensors.

Stephen got the feeling that he was being watched, both by the other youths and a couple of men who were standing with some of the boys at the far end of 'Playland'.

After a short while a man called Andy in his early thirties, came and stood next to Stephen, suggesting how he could play the machine more effectively and informing him that 'you can get away with a nudge here and there', as long as you don't over do it, or the machine will cut out and your play will stop. Stephen hit the reverb station and the lights flashed with a volley of sound and energy, knocking up his score by hundreds at a time. He felt really good like he was beating the machine. Then as Andy suggested Stephen gave it a shove helping the pinball bounced from side to side, in an attempt to alter the direction towards the high scoring sensors. It worked, Stephen's score increased as he managed to change the direction of the pinball. Andy laughed and kept saying 'you are really good at this'. Stephen's confidence grew as he nudged again stopping the ball from rolling down the exit channel, gaining another few hundred points. Stephen had gone past his best score of 3800 and again tried to stop the ball from exiting and gave the machine a heavy bump, only to find the machine cut off and suddenly closed down to silence. Andy looked on, reminding him that he had nudged too hard. He offered Stephen the price of his next game. He played again but ended up getting his worst score of the session.

Andy said, 'let me have a go'. Stephen watched as this guy ran up a score twice as big as his, hitting the reverb button several times, almost making the machine sing and dance to his will as he played. The clackerty clack of the paddles smashed the large ball bearing back up into the machine sending it whirling and bouncing around between the flashing icons, pinging and scoring multiple totals. Andy kept talking as he played, asking Stephen if he was new to London, where was he from, where was he staying and did he know anyone? Stephen stood transfixed watching while answering Andy's questions. He then invited Stephen to meet some of the other boys who were beginning to watch as Andy played like a real pinball wizard.

Stephen was surprised at how easy it was to meet people. Andy seemed like someone who was friendly and fun to be with. The other boys in Playland looked happy enough, good-humored continually throwing out affectionate comments and lots of arms being placed around shoulders, that made it seem like, they knew each other very well. Andy would hand money to some who wanted to play another game.

Realising that it was nearly midday Stephen thought that he needed to be getting off, if he was to meet Dougie on time. Andy asked where he was going. Making it clear that he was usually in Playland and that if he needed anything, to come back and look him up. Adding casually, I can help you get somewhere to stay, work and make some money.

Stephen retraced his steps to the 'Centrepoint' gate and back along Wardour Street to the 'Coffee Pot'. Dougie was nowhere to be seen, so Stephen decided to have a Cappuccino while he was waiting. After some time, Stephen walked back to Soho Square thinking Dougie might be there, but he wasn't. Then out onto Oxford Street, which was heavy with buses and black taxis queuing to move along the main thoroughfare.

He started to feel a little lost as he walked up to Oxford Circus always keeping his bearings by thinking he had to turn left to make his way back to the dilly. He turned into Regent

Street suddenly realising that the shops looked bigger and very smart. The road was wider than the other streets, and seemed very long, curving around to a road sign, advertising Austin Reed, which seemed the grandest of them all. Stephen found himself back at Piccadilly Circus and standing outside of the Wimpy Bar, with various boys loitering about, laughing and playing together, promoting a lively atmosphere around the outside of 'Boots the Chemist 'and the burger place.

Stephen spotted some of the boys he had seen in 'Playland ' and they waved to him beckoning him into the fast-food restaurant.

Stephen had some food and bought another cappuccino in the Wimpy bar, for himself, Larry and Will, two teenagers who seemed to know their way around. He realised that his money was getting low as he only had less than £18 left. They asked him all kinds of questions and offered him a cigarette, which Stephen accepted. They were not surprised when Stephen told them that he had stayed at 'Centrepoint' last night. Both had stayed there in the past and also knew about 'The Soho Project 'saying that the staff were safe and would always help you if they could. When Stephen mentioned Dougie, Will said, he was around a couple of days ago, but nobody can ever keep track of him as he comes and goes.

They talked together about punters and told Stephen that he would do alright, as they liked them young on the 'meat rack'. Stephen acted like he knew what they were talking about and followed them outside to the railings. This was the showcase, a place where they presented themselves to potential buyers, like meat hanging in a butcher's shop waiting for a customer to point at their preferred cut. There was an obvious camaraderie between the boys, but when they were putting themselves out on display ready and psyched up, in preparation to work, the renters were not keen on Stephen joining them, and told him to, "get himself back to 'Centrepoint' tonight, when it opens at 8.00pm".

Stephen moved around to the underground station exit part of the railings at Piccadilly Circus, where he could feel warm air rising from the very depths of the underground system.

Standing under the arches he looked across Regent Street, then as he walked on, he was aware of the shove and push of the people crossing the road at rush hour. He looked to see an older male individual, who had moved towards him, giving a very subtle but obvious glance as he passed. He carried on walking to Piccadilly, only turning back to take a look across to where Will and Larry were standing by the railings.

The same man who had momentarily followed Stephen approached them and they stood chatting for a long while. Will was smiling and started to walk off with the older man. Larry was alone for several minutes looking about across the Dilly. A car pulled up pausing for a moment before moving onto Shaftsbury Avenue. Stephen could see Larry making his way towards the large white vehicle, and then getting in.

Later, at 7.40pm Stephen made his way to 'Centrepoint' and could see a small queue of young people waiting around the gate on Shaftsbury Avenue. He was beginning to feel tired and had come to the realisation that hanging out on the streets was, actually, an exhausting experience.

There was a complete mix of teenagers waiting by the gate, who were playful and a little intimidating for pedestrians as they walked along the street, sometimes deciding to cross over or to give them a wide berth.

Two girls about 17 or 18 years were running around screaming and chasing each other, almost like small children. They seemed incredibly happy and would stop and pause for moments, breathless, where one would fall to the pavement, laughing uncontrollably, continually smiling as the other sat half by her and half on her.

Some individual males looked nervous, anxious and worried as they queued, desperate to be let in and to have something to eat. In the middle of the line there was a lone teenage girl, and an older looking male who was talking to her and pulling at her arm as she tried to resist him. She violently drew her arm away curling backwards to free herself from his attention, making it clear that she was not going with him while desperately focusing on her place in the queue. The man became more insistent but realised that he was gaining the attention of the Centrepoint worker who had appeared at the entrance gate and quickly walked away.

Stephen spotted Jack and wandered over to stand next to him. Jack asked how he had got on today. He then explained that the Soho Project had sorted him out a bed and breakfast through his social services and said, "I'll be sorted after tonight, as they said I can move in tomorrow. It will be a shithole in Kings Cross, but at least it will give me time to get a job. They said that they could also help me with that". Stephen was impressed and when the queue eventually moved on and got to him, he was met by Stewart, one of the workers, who talked to him like he knew him. He was very welcoming, saying that the Soho Project had said he might come back tonight, 'but we can chat inside, after you have had something warm to eat and drink'.

Centrepoint log: Stephen Addair. DOB 10-06-1962 Date: 30-05-1978.

Stephen presented once again as Stephen Crombie, aged 16, but later in the evening told us that his real name was Stephen Addair and that he was actually 15, as we had suspected. He seemed a lot more relaxed tonight and told Kathy that he was still supposed to be in school and that he was in care at a place called Glenallen Children's Home in Edinburgh. He talked about not wanting to go back, that he liked London and had made loads of friends. I do not think he will go back in the short term. He is at risk in the West End, not sure how much help we can give him until he is ready to accept it? I think he is learning a lot fast and knows about the rent scene. I hope that The Soho Project can get that across when they see him tomorrow. He said he will go but insists that he is not going back home. Will speak to The Soho Project in the morning as we want to support him, but are in a difficult position if we offer him accommodation here on Wednesday knowing he is underage.

Stewart

Chapter 28

Stephen felt a lot more comfortable this time around and sensed that feeling of being safe with nice people, who welcomed him. The ground floor large Victorian room at the back of St Anne's Chapel had high ceilings, with four large windows to one side. It was set out with tables, chairs and a couple of large sofas. The room was heavy with the smells of cooking and steam that filled the space. The workers asked him if he was hungry, inviting him to sit down with a drink. He felt like they cared and were interested, curious to find out if he needed anything.

Music was playing over the loudspeakers, 'Baker Street', with that smooth saxophone rift that seemed to fill the room, making Stephen feel safe and supported. This was an infectious happy place and all the residents seemed content, chatting to the various staff. They served hot food and helped to sort out clothes for washing needs, plus other practical stuff.

One worker sat next to Stephen, introducing herself as Kathy. She asked him how he was. She explained that she worked as a volunteer and did he need anything. Jack sat with them, and they played cards together. Stephen was taught a new game. Stephen was taken by how friendly Kathy was and felt bad because he had lied about who he was. She asked him why he was in London and explained how difficult it was to get any help for him if they were unable to clarify his identity. Jack explained how The Soho Project had helped him get sorted and Kathy used that to clarify how they could help. Stephen explained that he wanted to stay in London and try to find a job but acknowledged that he needed help. She explained that if he was to stay in London, without support that would be an unsafe place to be. There were various people out there, on the lookout for males and females. They would pretend to be a friend, offer ways of making money, but were only interested in what they can make out of that person.

The evening progressed quickly to 10.00pm when the workers started to remind residents that it was time to sort out sleeping arrangements and getting to bed. The two girls were still loud and playful. Laughing, wrestling, and calling each other names, that at first seemed aggressive, angry and confrontational. Eventually their energy seemed to dissipate, and they settled down to cuddles on one of the sofas, situated along the back wall under the large windows that faced Dean Street, as Kate Bush sang 'Wuthering Heights'.

Stewart was busy talking to the single young girl for a lot of the evening, in-between answering the gate as the bell buzzed it's shrill sounding warning that another was seeking refuge from the streets of London. Eventually Stewart was able to catch up with Kathy who told him that she thought Stephen was probably underage as they had suspected. Stewart eventually made his way to Stephen and asked if he was OK. He asked him to stay back from going down to the dormitory so that they could have a chat. Stephen eventually told Stewart that his 16th birthday was on the 10th of June and that he was still at school and in care. Stephen said he was not going back to school and Stewart reassured Stephen that it was good that he had told them the truth, and that the Soho Project with us could now help him to plan and to get things sorted. Stephen went to bed feeling relieved that he did not have to carry on the lie and agreed to talk to the Soho Project in the morning.

The 'Centrepoint' male dormitories covered the lower basement 'crypt', while the girl's sleeping area was set-aside in a smaller side room beneath glass blocks from the pathway above on the Dean Street pavement. Passersby could be seen walking over the thick glass that reflected different types of light into the space, depending on the time of the day or night. The beds were old brown and slightly rusty metal sprung bunks with a mattress, that shook, creaked and rattled, with every movement of the person sharing above or below on their chosen resting place. Stephen was lucky on this night and had a bunk bed all to him-self and slept well, in the knowledge that he was not living a lie, and that apart from the noisy girls, all the boys settled pretty quickly, and went to sleep.

Chapter 29

The next day started well enough. Stephen was able to get some breakfast and was once again given luncheon vouchers and the information from Stewart about the Soho Project. He was able to get there with Jack again stopping off at a tobacconist booth that was happy to exchange the luncheon voucher for a pack of 10 cigarett's. He knew that they would be expecting him and met with Barry once again. Barry started by asking Stephen if he had been to Edinburgh, and he stated that this was his hometown. Stephen explained that he used to live there before he and his mum had moved to Craigshill, near Livingstone. Barry explained that he had talked to Stewart this morning and that as he had expected, was told that Stephen was underage. Barry explained that this was a problem as it would be difficult to help him get a National Insurance Number (NI), which would mean work and accommodation would not be possible until he reached 16.

Barry asked about his children's home and his mum. Stephen explained how he had wanted to come to London because Glenallen was boring and just a place to be. Barry said that it might be boring but at least you are safe and have your mum nearby. Stephen laughed when the word safety was mentioned, saying that "Glenallen was shit man, the staff don't care". Stephen did not want to talk about his mum only to say, "She's not well, and not very good at being a mum".

Stephen told Barry that Travis was OK. Brian asked Stephen if it would be all right if he called 'Glenallen' and tried to talk to Travis. Stephen said "yes, but I am not going back".

Barry found the number through directory enquiries and called the Children's home. McLennen picked up the phone and introduced himself in a very polite manner, saying, "he is in London, what's he doing there?" He informed Barry that Stephen had been missing for the last three days and two nights and that Travis was not due on duty until 6.00 pm. McLennen explained that he was the officer in charge, and that they had informed the police yesterday lunch time, that Stephen was a missing person. He asked how Stephen was and started to make enquires about getting him back. Barry explained that he had been staying at 'Centrepoint' and that with Stephen's agreement 'The Soho Project 'could arrange his return.

While holding the telephone to one side, covering the mouthpiece, Barry asked if Stephen wanted to talk to McLennen, but it was clear that he would not do that. McLennen asked for the details and address of 'The Soho Project'. Barry explained that they were, a confidential, drop-in advice service but that they could help get Stephen on a train. Barry informed McLennen that he needed to talk to Stephen, leaving his full name and telephone number and that he would get back to him soon. McLennen was aware of the legal implications for Stephen and explained to Barry 'we are in loco parentis' and that someone would come to London and collect him, adding that it was illegal for any agency to hold an under aged child without parental permission. He also made it clear that he would contact Stephen's social worker to make the arrangements. Barry asked for the name of the social worker and the contact details, but McLennen stated that he would call the social worker and get him to call Barry. Barry tried to explain that it was 'no bother 'that he could make the call, but McLennen refused to pass on the details, reiterating that it was Glenallen who would organise Stephen's return.

When Barry put the phone down, he gave a large out take of breath, quizzically looking at Stephen, with an expression of frustration, before passing on the gist of the conversation to Stephen. He explained that it was illegal for 'Centrepoint' to provide accommodation to an under aged person but instantly felt Stephen's growing resistance sensing that he might lose him again as Stephen had started to become agitated with the thought of being taken home. Barry quickly informed Stephen, that they could and would make provision for Stephen to go back to 'Centrepoint' tonight, as long as they were seen to be trying to look after his best interests.

Stephen wanted to leave, and Barry instinctively sensed it, saying that he did not need to hurry out, that he would try to make contact with his social worker David Williams, or that they could carry on talking some more tomorrow. Barry confirmed that they could help Stephen with his fare home, and that if Stephen was still adamant about his plans, to wait another month or so. "Once you are sixteen and have received your NI number, you will have a lot more choice in what you want to do." Barry tried to explain that he would be in a much better position to be able to help him, if he wanted to stay in London once he was 16 years, but it would be easier if he were to get the support of his home Social Service department.

Stephen was once again starting to feel a little trapped and began to make his way towards the door. He stated that he had to go now as he was meeting a friend. Barry reminded him to go to 'Centrepoint' tonight, and that he would inform them about the phone call to Glenallen and reminded Stephen to be careful and look after himself.

The Soho Project Log: Stephen Addair. DOB 10-06-1962.
31-05-1978.

Stephen stayed at Centrepoint last night and he informed them that he was still 15 years old. I tried to explain how difficult it would be for him to be able to work and find accommodation in London without a National Insurance Number but feel we need a little more time to get to know him before we push the hard line. I made a telephone call to his Children's home in Edinburgh called Glenallen and spoke to a Mr. Mclennen who said he was the head of the care home.

He was not interested in giving Stephen some time to think things through and wanted to make arrangements to come to London and collect him. It was interesting that Stephen did not want to talk to Mr McLennen on the telephone. I have traced down Stephen's social worker and will try to give him a call today. Stephen became a little agitated and was in no mood to co-operate and voted with his feet and left the building. I did get to remind him that I would be asking Centrepoint if they were able to take him back this evening, but he did not wait around to get conformation about that.

I spoke to David Williams this afternoon and he confirmed that Stephen was in care to Lothian Boarders Children's Services and was resident at Glennallen drive. He also confirmed that Stephen had been reported to the Police, as a missing child, and that he had been in their care since he was seven years old. He had explained that Stephen had very little contact with his mum and no father figure in his life. David understood that if Stephen was to return it would be better if he made the choice himself, but because he was legally a minor would have to inform the metropolitan police in London that he was a runaway from Edinburgh. I explained that we were a confidential advice and counseling service for under aged young people who worked very closely with Centrepoint homeless shelter, and that if Stephen turned up tonight, that they would refer Stephen back to us, where I would expect to see him tomorrow in the hope that we can encourage and facilitate a return to Scotland as soon as possible. I explained that as for now, Stephen had left and was out and about on the streets of London.

Barry

Stephen walked out onto the street and felt relieved and happy that he was free again, feeling that this new day would be good. Again, he wondered if he might see Dougie. It was late he had sat around most of the morning in the Soho Project waiting area.

He walked across Charing Cross Road and along Old Compton Street and across Dean Street, stopping at MacDonald's for a Big Mac, fries and a Coke. He was beginning to find his way around and eventually arrived back onto Shaftsbury Ave and Piccadilly Circus.

He went into 'Playland' and the 'Space Invader' machine was unoccupied, so Stephen played it. At first, he struggled to shoot down the alien shapes that came out from the side of the machine, building row upon row like attacking soldiers. He then felt like he had gotten the job done as he cleared the first sheet of beeping attackers. Then the second phase came, but this time a little faster. Once Stephen was better practiced, he shot them all down, only to be followed by the next page that built up too quickly and overwhelmed him as a player. Stephen was captivated by the high intensity of the machine and was desperate to get past the fourth page as he started to anticipate the speed and direction of the moving forces and nearly beat it, so had to try again, only to find out that he had used his last coin and had spent more than four pounds on the activity. 'Staying alive 'by the Bee Gee's was playing in the arcade and Stephen felt pumped at taking on the machine.

Stephen looked up and he then noticed Andy watching him from a couple of machines along, and smiling,

Andy asked Stephen, did he meet up with Dougie and then if he had stayed at 'Centrepoint 'last night? Stephen explained he had not found Dougie but that his day was good yesterday and then found him-self looking at Andy feeling a little awkward. Andy told Stephen that he could sort out somewhere for him to stay if he needed it, making a joke about poofs and young bodies being all the rage around here. Informing Stephen that money makes the world go around little boy. Stephen squirmed as he told Andy that he was not a poof, and Andy said, "you don't have to be, just play them along, they love it." "So, you see, I'm not after your body, bonny boy, but I know how it can make us both some cash, if you get my meaning".

Stephen paused to think then noticed three boys coming through the main entrance to Playland, emerging in earnest and walking straight towards them. One of them was Dougie and the other two were Lance and Keith.

Andy instantly changed his banter, threateningly pointing his finger in the direction of the oncoming pair. "Where were you two yesterday, you have cost me, I'll talk to you over there". He pointed to a corner of Playland. Dougie gave a cheeky smile aimed at Stephen, and quickly asked him how he was getting on, while giving a sideways nudge in the direction of Andy as he followed saying, "I see you have met the main man."

Andy talked over Dougie and tugged Lance on his sleeve, encouragingly moving him in the direction he wanted him to go. Dougie and Keith followed them to the corner of 'Playland' and very quickly they were encased in an intense angry debate that was being led and dominated by Andy.

Chapter 30

Two days earlier, in the coffee pot, Dougie had joined the boys where they had agreed to do a job that Andy had set up. Lance 17 years old and Keith 16 were to be his support act. Lance was small for his age and had a dark tone to his skin that he had inherited from his father who was born in Jamaica. He had soft Afro hair that he mostly kept short with a shaved parting line. Keith was very fair and would sometimes be referred to as a ginger blonde. He had pale skin and freckles down his arms and across his nose and cheeks. He looked the youngest being thin, slightly built, but was a couple of inches taller than Lance. They were friends and lovers, they had known each other for a few months, meeting on the Dilly, and had learnt how best to make use of their partnership. Dougie was the tallest with dark brown hair and a fluffy 'tash' that he had once shaved and probably needed to shave again. He had made his way to London from Glasgow over four years ago, when he was still 14. Dougie had seen and done it all.

A couple of days back, before Stephen came on the scene, Dougie had told Lance and Keith that Andy had organized a party for some rich politician pricks who wanted a group thing, saying the money was good. The address was in Pimlico and that the punters were Andy's special customers. "There might be more of us, so we will have to play it by ear and get the best out of it that we can". Dougie was invited because he knew what the gig would be about.

Chapter 31

Mondays were politician days, as they travelled into town, after the weekend at home, to get started for their week in the 'big house' Parliament. Dougie had a good idea about who would be there, as he had joined the party at various times over the last two years. He remembered the loud fat disgusting man with the northern accent, who liked to direct the boys, making demands that mostly involved a combination of voyeurism, pissing and touching.

When they arrived at the smart flats, they wondered where and how they were going to get in. Dougie who had been before, walked through the main gate entrance, leading Lance and Keith, from the busy road into a small car parking area set behind high railings. They rang the intercom doorbell. A doorman, or security guard opened it and beckoned them in. He went to sit behind a desk in the small lobby area then smiled begrudgingly, and asked, who had sent them? Pausing, as if expecting a code word in reply while waiting to hear the correct answer before allowing them in. Dougie said "Andy" and they were told to go on up to the first floor, to the end of the corridor to room 5.

Once inside the boys found that there were two men and one was the ugly fat man with the loud Northern accent who liked to be called Mr. C, and the other posh one was smaller, with an average build and light brown hair. Music was playing, and they both were smoking and had drinks in their hands. They started to smile welcoming the boys into a very smart lounge room with chairs and a sofa that backed onto two large Victorian windows. The long green velvet curtains were fully drawn closed. A compilation of music was playing; 'Cliff Richard 'was singing 'The Young Ones', followed by songs from Elvis, Matt Monroe and others of that period, late 50's early 60's. This flat had two bedrooms with a large bathroom and kitchen.

They were offered drinks and other forms of chemical highs from the men who continually made comments to each other about how beautiful they all were, saying what a good night this would be. The boys sat on the sofa and wondered how they could make more of what Andy had organised. Food was laid out on a table, mostly cold meats, bread and salad, so they ate and drank and snorted the white stuff set out on a mirror on a small table at the side. There were pills and a good supply of cigarettes.

Money was not mentioned as Andy had seen to all of that, but as usual a wrapper was left in an obvious place, in an envelope containing a substantial tip with two £50.00 and five £10.00 notes. It was left on the side table next to the amphetamines, with the inscription, for the boys.

Dougie opened it, looked inside giving a positive wink to Lance and Keith, and then glanced at the punters and executed a wavy hand salute like a jester getting ready to perform, which informed the Politian's that the boys were happy with the extra. Dougie knew that he would get the rest from Andy later.

The boys talked and laughed as the older men looked on pretending to have their own conversations. Dougie ate some food and started to consume a strip of cocaine from the mirror surface, flushed down by Bacardi and Coke in an effort to anaesthetise any sense of himself, knowing that he needed to get out of his head to get through. Then the boys followed suit using the pills to both numb and energise at the same time.

Both older men knew Dougie and were happy enough that he was there to help get things started. They had their sights set on the couple and asked pointed questions about their relationship. Dougie sensed their interest, knowing what they wanted to see, and suggested that the boys could perform, encouraging them by kissing each one and then directed the two of them together. This invoked an instant reaction from the big man, sucking on his cigar, who said "come on than lads show us what they can do" Dougie winked at Lance and started to stroke and pull at his cock over his trousers and Lance got the idea and did the same to Keith, unzipping his trousers and taking out his length while kissing his ears and neck. Dougie rolled away and took off his trousers, confidently exposing his tight briefs and the clear shape of his semi erect penis.

The punters were high and happy, that their party had started, with the fat one shouting instruction to Lance and Keith, "that's the stuff, suck it hard, take it all you dirty little poofs". The fair-haired politician unbuttoned his fly area and had taken out his piece. He was excited enough to wave Dougie over for some physical support to what he was doing, turning Dougie and slapping him across his bottom as he got close. He then started to remove his trousers and underpants and stood with his fully erect penis appearing between the front sections of his tailored white shirt. He expected Dougie to take hold of it suck and wank him as he watched the younger boy's sexual expression progress, feeling both stimulated and excited by the naturalness the boys demonstrated towards each other. Dougie helped him to satisfy his need, before taking some of his own clothes off, knowing that the Politician 'pig man' was also in need of some help as he struggled to get his cock out from under the layers of fat.

The night carried on to the point where the boys were invited and expected to stay the night. Lance and Keith ended up sharing with the posh fair-haired one who liked to be spanked with a riding crop hard across his rear buttock but also wanted flicks from the riding crop on his testis and penis. The boys duly obliged, taking pleasure inflicting pain, questioning what he was getting out of it. They kept the Monday Club man duly entertained until he decided that he needed to get some sleep.

Dougie drew the short straw with the disgusting one, who lumbered to the bathroom still wearing his blue pin stripe shirt, grey socks and heavily pleated oversized trousers held up with a pair of yellow braces to support the weight of the fabric. He drew down the braces and removed his shirt to reveal a white vest, where rolls of fat could be seen around his armpits and belly. It disgusted Dougie, he hated what he was doing but knew that he could get the job done, as he had so many times before, throughout his days when he stayed at Elm Guest House.

Mr. C asked Dougie to run a bath. Once filled, he maneuvered himself with great difficulty towards the bath and climbed inside, struggling to insert himself into the tub he barely fit into. He was oblivious to the great swell of bath water seeping out with every movement. Insisting that Dougie stood by him naked where he fondled Dougie's cock, balls and the cheeks of his bum. He wanted to be pissed on, holding his mouth open as Dougie aimed his urine at his mouth while intentionally aiming at his eyes, just because he hoped that would sting. It was expected that he followed this with an ejaculation over him, which Dougie had to work very hard at. Once dry and out of the bath the pig became tearful and asked Dougie to forgive him, then became aggressive and angry apologising for his grotesque form, mumbling that I know you hate me. He asked Dougie to come to bed and after some attempt at cupping and stroking, eventually, groaned and snored himself to sleep and left Dougie alone. There was still a bad odor emanating from the pig that smelt of sweat and stale cigar smoke that repulsed him. Dougie took his chance and slipped away from the snuffling slob, where he was able to settle down on the couch for the rest of the morning.

Both politicians were up the next day early and had gone paying little attention to the boys, telling them to eat and drink what they wanted, and to let themselves out. Dougie was wise enough to know that this was a gift and searched around for whatever he could make a few bob from. He gathered together as much of the pills, booze, cigarettes as he could find and came across a Rolex watch that had been left in the bathroom. He of course took it, knowing it belonged to the fat bastard. After all, what could he do, go to the police?

Chapter 32

When they left Dolphin House at mid-day the security man was nowhere to be seen. They made their way along Chichester Street and onto St. Georges Square where they bounced about for a while, having fun on the grass, running, grabbing, tumbling at each other and laughing at the silliest jokes. Doing anything to eradicate their experience of the previous night. They hated what they had been coerced into. Messing around helped to block it from their minds. But were quickly reminded of what had happened when Dougie took the two fifty-pound notes from the envelope and handed them to the boys, which they quickly and individually pushed into their trouser pockets. He kept the five £10.00 notes for himself.

Lance knew that Dougie had nowhere to stay that night, they both felt a little guilty as Dougie had taken on the fat man, so asked him if he wanted to doss down with them tonight. Dougie grimaced followed by a half smile, saying, "as long as that fat fuck won't be there, yes thanks", waving the packs of fags, plastic bag full of pink pills, and a half empty bottle of whisky, triumphantly pulled from his coat pockets.

They could have walked but instead made their way to Pimlico Underground Station which was one stop to Vauxhall on the Victoria line.

Lance and Keith shared a temporary one bedroom with two single beds, in a bed and breakfast hotel called 'The Heighten'. Which was found for them by 'Alone in London Service', (ALS) a youth advice agency that Centrepoint had referred them onto. They had set them up there a month ago and were on a waiting list for a full-time place in a Youth Hostel. ALS, was an Advice and Counselling Service similar to the Soho Project that was based in the Kings Cross area. They were good at helping boys like Lance and Keith get something more stable, recognising how difficult it was for two gay lads, who had to hide their relationship. Particularly if they wanted to find accommodation together.

Bertie was the manager and general do it all at The Heighten and spent his time mostly on the door. He was well aware of the problems encountered by gay men, as he himself had suffered the prejudices of his sexual orientation all his life, so was a sympathetic, soft touch.

Teens were considered difficult to manage and a liability, but this was one of the very few hotels that did allow younger males to share a room, turning a blind eye, since the law and restrictions had changed in 1967 for male homosexuals 21 years and over.

Youths were not considered to be able to make those judgments, while older consenting males together, in a private space were. Persons who were under twenty-one years of age or older men with younger males were viewed as criminals. If they were caught having consensual non-anal sex, they might have to face 2 - 5 years in prison, and anal sex could carry a life sentence.

It was one rule that was flagrantly dismissed by those who could pay or had the power to hide the so-called social misdemeanor. It was something that a rent boy rarely really considered, unless they were picked up by the police in the act, or busted at a private party, where those in power had the means and protection, to keep themselves a safe distance from any difficult questions posed by the law.

The next morning, they hung out in the hotel room, having to be careful not to give away that Dougie had also stayed the night, as it was a strict two-person occupancy and even Bertie would not allow that. The room was small and cramped and after a while Dougie was ready to leave.

Dougie, Lance and Keith decided to make their way to Piccadilly where Dougie was eager to cash in on some of the drugs he had taken from the night at Dolphin House and also wanted to find Andy to collect the second half of their hard-earned money.

Chapter 33

Stephen looked across the row of pinball machines at Playland. What he saw was Andy pointing hard at Dougies face looking angry and aggressive. He could hear Dougie saying, "give us what was agreed". Andy shouted in a threatening, low aggressive tone, "where's the fucking watch you thieving little cunt, this is going to cost me". Lance and Keith stepped away, leaving the face-off between Dougie and Andy, who were gaining the attention of the other gamers in Playland. The security guard started to walk in their direction, and Dougie chose that moment to push away from Andy, telling him to fuck off, leaving Andy looking like the aggressor, and vulnerable to the judgmental watching eyes of Playland and the security man.

Dougie made his way towards Stephen, saying, "let's go". Stephen followed and they made their way up Shaftesbury Avenue at a pace, only pausing to allow Dougie to light a cigarette, and to vent his anger at "that prick Andy, he is supposed to be on our side". Stephen knew this was not a good time to ask questions and looked on quizzically. They walked past the 'Centrepoint' gates and turned left into Dean Street and onto Chapel Street where they stopped at the music shop. Looking through the record sleeves, gave Dougie the time to slow down and regain his composure, while Bob

Marley's rhythmic beats could be heard singing 'Satisfy my Soul'. Dougie finally turned to Stephen and said, "Come on, let's see if Norman is in". Stephen followed dutifully feeling a growing sense of allegiance, confidence and excitement with this streetwise wide boy, only daring to ask, "is it far".

They arrive at Decca records office based on the 3rd floor in Great Marlborough Street and made their way into the very smart waiting area, where there were pictures of pop stars, The Rolling Stones, Lulu, The Moody Blues and Jonathan King.

Dougie had been there before and asked the very trendy female receptionist, if he could see Norman, remarking its quiet today. Beverly had met Dougie before and called through to Norman who immediately asked her to send them through. Stephen could not believe that he was in a record company office and was in awe of the various images of Platinum, Silver and Gold records displayed around the reception room.

Norman seemed predisposed as they walked in. He was looking down at his desk while challenging Dougie about why he had come to his office. Dougie seemed relaxed and familiar with the surroundings. He sat on the chair in front of his desk smiling confidently before introducing Stephen as a fellow Scot, new to London who needed showing around and have some fun. Norman acknowledged Stephen with a pleasant "ummm" sound, then looking at him and asked, how was he getting on. He inquired if he had seen the sights and pointing at Dougie said, "I hope this young reprobate is not leading you into bad ways". Dougie told Norman to fuck off, saying, "We are pals man, but I thought you might be interested", enquiring, "what's going on, any drinks on offer". Norman started to give Dougie a fiver, saying 'go get it for yourselves', then paused while handing it over and telling them that he had some tickets for Top Of The Pops (TOTP), recording tonight Wednesday at 'The Shepherd's Bush, Television Centre'. If they wanted to go, they had to get a move on. 'You need to be there by 5.30pm'. Stephen could not believe what he was hearing, looking at Dougies face for the reassurance that he was going to say yes. Dougie reached out for the cash first and the tickets second, showing off a very expensive looking Rolex watch on his left wrist. Norman noticed the adornment and told Dougie. "By the look of that, business is going well". Dougie waved it away by saying, "all in a day's work, a boys got to do what a boy can do". Norman smiled in acknowledgement. He then started to explain that all they needed to do was show their tickets at the main gates. Once you are there, they will direct you to the appropriate studio, where you will be told what to do, and which musicians were performing. "Boney M are number one, so should be a good show".

Norman was pleased to have been able to give them something, as he had a real soft spot for Dougie, which Dougie took full advantage of. He was also very attracted to boys like Stephen who had that impish young street boy look that he liked. Norman stood up and walked around the table, beckoning the boys towards the direction of the door out of his office, saying "have fun little chicks, see you soon, I know where to find you, and you know where I live Dougie". He gave Dougie a quick hug and half kiss on the cheek then did the same to Stephen who awkwardly responded in kind and hugged him back, grateful for the tickets to 'TOTP'.

On leaving the building, they walked back along Great Marlborough Street to Argyll Street, past the London Palladium, to Oxford Circus where they were able to take the Central Line to White City, which was a short walk to 'The BBC Television Centre 'in Wood Lane. They arrived a little early and had to wait on the road by the gates with other small groups of kids who were of a similar age to Stephen. Some of whom were accompanied by their mums who seemed similarly as excited, as the young people who were due to take part in this week's episode of TOTP.

Stephen could not believe he was here, he wanted to tell someone from home, instantly disregarding his mum, but thought about Wendy or Frank who he thought would have been very impressed. Dougie confidently chatted, while lighting up a cigarette with those waiting, including the mums, cracking jokes and quips about those who might be performing, and how they all mimed to their songs.

Several cars and vans pulled up and were checked and beckoned through by the security men. Eventually tickets were looked at, and they were herded toward the main foyer. Tickets were checked again before being led along a straight hallway, to the entrance of a large studio, which had three stages that were spaced around the room. They each had a podium but one had a long raised railed elevated special platform running along one side of the studio, leading from the main stage. There were large cameras on platforms being driven around and huge heavy cables trailing everywhere over the floor space, also lots of curtains draped against the walls. Various workers were busy moving stuff around and people were coming in and out of doors all around the studio. Lights were being turned on and off towards the main stage areas, and the central part of the studio were kept in a relatively normal light, so that the visiting kids could find their space to dance.

A loudly spoken man introduced himself as the floor manager and welcomed the audience by pointing out where the emergency exits were and that the cameras would be moving about a lot and not to get in the way. They were told to keep an eye on the two 'prompt 'people, who would show them when they needed to clap and cheer. They were then left to wait for a while, a space where background music was being sound checked, roadies were testing guitars, drums and microphones.

The anticipation was palpable and intense as the audience group looked around, sizing each other up, before a pause of sound that built up with the expectation that something fabulous was about to happen. Stephen felt relaxed and at one with where he was, he looked at Dougie who was in his element, conversing and jigging around next to those closest to him. There were beautiful looking girls and boys, their own age, all around. No mums were in sight; girls seemed to be appearing from doors around the room, dressed and made up, ready to dance their socks off, looking nervous as if they had something to prove.

Activity and anticipation were beginning to build as Stephen spotted Jimmy Savile, standing resplendently in his gold trousers, behind a roped off area, readying himself to one side, in front of a camera.

Dougie bumped Stephen on the arm and said take one of these, it will make you feel great, offering a small pink pill while taking one himself. Stephen followed suit and grabbed Dougie by the arm with a look of excitement like he had never felt before, saying, "look, it's Jimmy Savile".

The floor manager was counting the group in, as the introduction music started with the familiar saxophone hard beat, blending with the wailing lead guitar, and said, "OK its TOTP", and with that everyone shouted, clapped and cheered as the familiar credit music started to play. Which in turn was an indication to start dancing as wildly and as provocatively as one could.

The girls along the special platform, had unveiled their skimpily daring party dresses and looked great as they performed for the cameras that moved slowly along the row of lassies, zooming in and out on their most intimate parts, always searching for that clothing malfunction that they knew the producers required, but rarely happened. The girls on the special platform were the chosen ones, those that had some kind of golden ticket. The other girls on the main floor space, had their handbags at their feet, trying to emulate the platform girls, but got very little camera time, other than fleeting moments as the musicians looked down to the audience seeking out a connection, that the camera followed. The boys worked as hard as they could to get noticed. Dancing rhythmically on the spot. Moving to those tunes that allowed freedom of expression. Dougie was in his element gyrating to 'Night Fever' as Legs and Co performed on stage. Stephen was encouraged to show off his Tony Manero moves, strutting around Dougie throwing his arms out with a shake of the hips. The girls on the platform put everything into their moves, looking around at the competition. Trying to outdo each other. While others just went for that sexy pouting look, where dance was an expression of their ability to show as much leg as they could. They moved in unison with rhythmic hips, an exposed midriff and with most, a pulsating regular thrust of the chest and breasts that produced a native and free recurrent movement from head to foot.

Stephen felt great and was totally blown away to see 'Blondie', Debbie Harry, who was singing 'I'm always touched by your presence dear', followed by The Real Thing, playing 'Let's go Disco' one of Stephen's favourite songs. He was not sure what was making him feel so elated, thinking it could have been the pink pill, or that this was the best most exciting time that he had ever had in his life and he felt ecstatic.

This was disco at its best, and here Stephen was at TOTP watching Nile Rogers 'Chic 'playing 'Everybody Dance', followed by 'Tavares 'singing 'More than a Woman'. It was all too quick to take in. Each song followed by another great sound. This was what he had waited for and Stephen felt that it was his destiny, his place to be, where he could be himself. Stephen saw Jimmy Savile standing by the roped off area with a group of teenagers, waiting in front of the Camera, chatting to the crew and girls around him and he quickly walked up to him, to somehow try to show how excited and grateful he was to be there. Stephen thought a handshake would be the most correct way to greet him. Thrusting his hand forward, with a massive smile, he said "Hi Jimmy." Savile turned and looked at Stephen with an angry scowling face and told him to, "fuck off, I'm about to go on air". Stephen was taken back, and stood watching as the great man prepared himself, glowering into the camera, while steadying himself before turning into the Smiling, welcoming Jimmy, Stephen had seen on the television.

Dougie was sidling up to one of the girls who were part of a group watching him dance, as she moved, he took her by the hand, and they positioned themselves together. As the gentle flowing sounds of the song allowed them to express an instant intimacy that lasted halfway through the music, until Dougie let her go and took hold of another female of the group who was similarly watching and moving in unison. Stephen was in ecstasy as 'Heatwave 'sang, pointing to the audience displaying a peace and love symbol. They gently moved to the rhythms and swayed to 'Mind Blowing Decisions'. The room was enthused and in unity, although the girls on the platform had to slow it down a little. Then came 'Ian Dury and the Block Heads 'singing 'What a Waste 'that totally changed the whole mood of the studio. They all stopped to watch 'Dury' perform, strutting around holding half a microphone stand, making it clear that this was not live music. But when 'John Paul Young 'played 'Love is in the Air ' they could all get back to jiving rhythmically and showing off their best dance moves. Legs and Co joined with male dancers and performed to 'You're the One that I Want' followed by

Yvonne Ellerman on the stage miming to 'if I can't have you'. It sent the whole room into a delirious frenzied high, of posturing dance moves that made Stephen feel that life could not get any better.

There were some spaces between the songs, where the floor audience were flanked by cameras being pushed about, as the riggers manipulated the heavy cables to facilitate the cameras, to move around to get the best angles of the music acts. Eventually the climax of the event was reached. "And yes, the number one song this week is, Boney M, singing 'Rivers of Babylon', which allowed the audience to move rhythmically to the climax, that finished with the spectators steadying themselves, swaying from side to side in a rocking motion, as the rousing melody and chorus resonated around the room. Boney M swayed, smiling and pouting their way through the song, miming and mimicking in true TOTP tradition.

Chapter 34

Once it was over everyone seemed to slow down and take a breath. There was no more music, just the movement and a lighthearted chatter coming from the crew. Which then permeated into the audience before the floor manager shouted out his thanks, telling everyone to have a good journey home. Jimmy Savile was nowhere to be seen and the girls on the special platform walked down to the main floor area, only to then make their way out of the side door leading to dressing rooms and a hospitality space, for the chosen ones.

The audience floor group looked at each other and started to gather themselves together ready to leave. As this was happening Stephen and Dougie were approached by a well-dressed, suited man, who introduced himself as Chris Denning, stating that he was a Radio one Disc Jockey and handed them his business card with his name and a Decca Records logo across the top.

Once again Stephen could not believe that he was talking to a Radio One DJ. This famous person that he thought he had heard of. Denning told them that he had watched them dancing and thought they were good. Dougie stepped forward and took the card, hiding the fact that he knew Norman and Denning. Chris had told them that he was connected to Decca records. Informing them that, 'we are always on the lookout for young people who can review new music and bands, we give out free Albums for review, and he asked, are you interested'? Dougie took the lead and said that they were, and 'Denning 'pointed to his telephone number on the card, saying that they could call him whenever, before walking onto the next group of boys. Dougie handed the card to Stephen, with an air of dismissiveness saying, "I've met him before, he's a dick, and is only looking for the young ones, like you".

Stephen was buzzing and Dougie took Stephen back into the West End, saying "let's have some real fun". He led Stephen onto the railway arches, off Charing Cross Station. Dougie gave Stephen two more pink pills, saying they will keep you going and awake. When Stephen asked what they were, Dougie told him, Speed, but that meant very little to Stephen, all he knew was that he felt great and was ready to dance some more.

Chapter 35

They went to 'Glades' at The Global Village. It was the Wednesday night 'gay 'discotheque nightclub slot, advertised as over 21 and showed that Chris Lucus was the main DJ. Dougie warned Stephen to follow his lead as they were underage, informing him that they needed to check out what bouncers were on the door first. He said, "If Alfie is working, we should be fine". They were lucky and Alfie waved them through, no questions asked. Dougie knew that buying drinks would be difficult downstairs, so went straight upstairs, where it would be easier to mingle, buy and be bought drinks. They were able to blend into the dance crowd relatively unnoticed. Stephen was taken aback to find a room full of men, who were all together in a sexually charged atmosphere, happy and dancing to the clear rhythms of music that Stephen had never heard before.

Stephen was buzzing and grew in confidence when Dougie moved towards him, luring and inviting him to take action and dance. Stephen felt a heightened sense of chemistry with Dougie and started to move with him not giving any thought to the gender, concentrating and inspired by the constant beat, of the 'funkadelic 'sounds bouncing around him, he felt wide awake, and looked around at the other clubbers who were singing "One nation under a groove", some with their shirts off, with full moustaches, sweating and glowing like oiled Greek gladiators, as they swayed and clapped hands in unison.

Dougie moved off and was dancing with random clubbers leaving Stephen as he continued to dance, and felt the group bounce together, feeling at one with where he was, while also aware and flattered by the various looks and glances, that were clearly on him. Stephen was moving around the room, freely and uninhibited, lacking his usual restraint, he found himself in a tangible groin-thrusting tryst with one of the topless guys, grabbing onto his sweating torso with one hand while his other was holding the top of his leather belt. Stephen was aware that someone, who was intent on moving in on Stephen, was getting as close as he could. Stephen was intrigued and excited by the attention. He had a black tight T-Shirt with a heavy leather belt and large buckle hanging onto his black tight fitted denim jeans. Stephen let it happen and was moving in a synchronize motion with him, enjoying the closeness that made him feel horny. Stephen felt it was reciprocated and allowed the touching but drew away at a kiss, knowing that his partner was becoming more insistent. Eventually he beckoned and invited Stephen to the bar for a drink. Bacardi and Coke was all that Stephen could think of from the advertisement on TV. The suitor was not interested in anything other than the close intimacy that Stephen was resisting. It was starting to become difficult. Stephen spotted Dougie, who could see what the problem was and grabbed Stephen by the arm, taking him back to the dance floor. Dougie put his arms around Stephen and shouted in his ear, just loud enough to get heard, "don't take any shit from them, get what you can out of it, and if you want out, tell them to fuck off". Then danced and moved around, saying, "lets pretend to kiss, and he will think you are with me". With that Dougie put his hand over Stephen's mouth on the blind side, and gave him a massive snogging, which made Stephen smile, but he also thought that he wouldn't have minded if it had happened for real.

They carried on dancing through to the early hours and Stephen felt relaxed and at one with Dougie as he gently moved around his person, holding his arm and moving into a full embrace, where Stephen allowed a real kiss that felt soft and exciting as Dougie encouraged Stephen to reciprocate by guiding his hand around his waist and lower back. They moved between partners but always came back to each other as the pulsating fever of movement brought them closer together.

Chapter 36

When the club closed, they ended up spending the early hours of the morning in the 'all night café' on Northumberland Avenue and Craven Street. The boys were buoyed by their evening, still laughing and animated as they entered the smoky dower entrance of the cafe'. They came down quickly, as tiredness enveloped them, falling asleep with heads on arms, sitting at the table. The proprietor of the café', who was watching them, quickly moved in to wake them up, inviting them to buy something or to leave.

At the bottom of Northumberland Avenue, they turned left into Cardboard City under the bridge near Waterloo station and found themselves walking through bodies, stepping over and around a large grouping of homeless people who used this area as a safe unified space to sleep or just hang out in numbers.

It was a chilly late May morning in the capital and Stephen followed Dougie through the crowded village of boxes, blankets and sleeping bags to the Victoria Embankment Gardens. The sun was just starting to travel along the river. As they looked straight across, they could see, shards of bright light, glinting on the South bank, as the rising sun reflected off the surface of the gentle waters of the Thames. They could see Tower Bridge in the distance as the sun caught the tops of the towers and started to shine through the bridge onto the building across the river. Stephen felt happier than he had ever been in his life, thinking what a night, and for the first time he had felt a special bond, to this street vagabond who had made this all happen.

Once in the Gardens they found a seated shelter and sat shivering waiting for the day to warm up and the sun to hit them. They were too tired to think about the chilled spring morning and sat tight together. Dougie cuddled up to Stephen who reciprocated as best he could, hugging up against the green shed, sheltered by the wall, in an effort to keep warm, where they eventually fell asleep snuggled together.

They slept deeply but very uncomfortably until they could take it no more, then noticed people were arriving with paper bags and eating sandwiches, which reminded them of the time. The sun was shining fully onto the park grounds, and they carried themselves into the full glare to warm up.

While lying down on the grass Stephen looked up, and his attention was drawn to the gentle rippling motions of the trees above him. A light wind blew through the gardens causing a rippling action, which slowly calmed to allow him to feel the full warmth of the day's sun that was rising higher, distributing and sharing its midday Spring heat onto his face. At that moment he felt as happy as he had ever been in his short life.

They started to rouse at midday and Dougie recognised that he needed to pee. Dougie led the way once more, behind the seated shelter, allowing full flow and relief, after which, Dougie told Stephen that he had some business to attend to, and that they needed to split up. He told Stephen to go back to 'Centrepoint' tonight, and that he would be about tomorrow. Stephen asked, why didn't he go to 'Centrepoint' with him and Dougie said, that they would not let him in as they knew him too well. He told Stephen that he would be all right tonight. Stephen felt a little confused and sorry that they could not stay together, but Dougie was adamant and started to make his way up the embankment reminding Stephen of the quickest way back to the circus.

And that was it, he was gone. Stephen was left standing looking out across the river at the big OXO building and Dougie had disappeared in the blink of an eye.

He was alone again and questioned what he was going to do without him.

Feeling in his pocket, checking for money Stephen soon realised that he only had £6.00 in notes, plus some change left. He decided to make his way back to the Dilly and 'Playland', via Trafalgar Square.

On arrival at the south side of Trafalgar Square, Stephen was taken back by how awesome this place was. He gazed at the four fountains with the huge brass Lions seemingly standing on guard on massive stone plinths, around the central column, with Nelson on top.

There were lots of people milling around, children running, folk feeding the pigeons while posing for photographs.

He was feeling conscious of the fact that he had not washed and spotted the signage for the public toilets at the far end of the square, with the backdrop of an amazing building up high.

Once in the public convenience he felt very self-conscious, as he tried to wash under his clothing, in the large Victorian sink. People were coming and going quickly but he noticed someone taking a long time at the urinal. He kept looking around until he gave Stephen a short pert smile, followed by an acknowledgement nod, as he stood for what seemed a very long time facing the porcelain.

He waited until they were the only ones present and walked to the sink next to Stephen to wash his hands.

Stephen was confused by his formal manner, and by how straight talking he was in his effort to establish quickly if Stephen was working. The man was in his early twenties, smartly dressed, looking both anxious and worried with beads of sweat appearing across his forehead.

Stephen looked on, not sure what his next move should be, but the punter said, "You look the type". Stephen was taken aback by his abrupt manner and statement but knew what he meant and decided to respond by asking, "it depends on what you want". The punter nervously stated £"10 for a wank", while nodding towards the direction of a cubicle. Stephen was not sure how to respond, as he straightened his clothing deciding to go with it.

The money seemed good, and he thought it's just between him and me, nobody will know. He acknowledged the offer by tentatively walking in the direction of the cubicle. It seemed very public but added to the thrill. He found himself getting excited. Once inside the cubical it was locked by the man, who wanted to get the financial transaction out of the way, handing Stephen the ten-pound note.

He turned Stephen around so that he could stand as Stephen sat on the toilet seat facing him, while he unbuckled and dropped his trousers, exposing his erect penis.

Stephen felt that what was expected of him was pre-ordained, as this man had done this before. So, Stephen obliged by taking hold and did what he did to himself, rubbing the whole length, working it harder and harder as the punters excitement grew. Eventually the punter took hold of his own knob, wanking vigorously to finish himself off, cumming while aiming in the direction of Stephen then turning slightly as his ejaculated sperm hit the cubical wall.

There it was, splattered up the wall, with a little on Stephen's leg. He grabbed some toilet paper and handed it to the punter so that he could clean up, while Stephen dabbed his trousers with another piece in an attempt to wipe it off. The posh knob looked agitated and blurted out, "I hope you know that I am not queer, you fucking little fag." Stephen sat there looking at him wondering who this posh prick was, and told him "Fuck off to you, saying, neither am I." in his strongest Scottish accent. It all became a jostle and intransitive. The punter just wanted to get out of the cubical struggling to turn, then opened the door, peeped through the gap to check who was out there, and then left Stephen sitting, without so much as a thank you or goodbye. Stephen locked the door, then thinking, with a smile that he had earned a tenner. It was simple! He tossed himself off with the excitement of it all. This was the first time that he wondered if he might be a bit queer, as he had imagined being with Dougie when wanking, spurred on from the intimacy of the evening before?

Stephen left the public toilet and walked up to the big building looking over the square, finding it was the National Gallery and the view across Trafalgar Square was magnificent. He wanted to share this moment with someone and wondered where Dougie was. Walking on he followed his nose, passing the National Portrait Gallery that seemed so grand, then, looking back and across at St Martins-in-the-fields, walked along Charing Cross Road, turning left into Irving Street, and onto Leicester Square. Stephen was beginning to realise that it was easy to make money doing this stuff. He was learning and coming to the realisation that all these boys were here for a reason. You could make money and have a great time too. He kept thinking about last night. The best night he had ever had, believing that this was where he belonged.

Stephen wondered what his mum was doing and had some fantasy that he could earn enough money to bring her down to London so that he could look after her. Thinking that she would be different and it would be good for the two of them to be together.

Chapter 37

Soho Project log: Stephen Addair. DOB 10-06-1962. 01-06-1978.

Stephen did not stay at Centrepoint last night.
The word is that he has been seen hanging about the Dilly. We had our regular feedback with Centrepoint this morning and they confirm that he is vulnerable, as we all agree.
I talked to David Williams again today, and he said that he would try to organise someone from Glenallan to come to London to collect Stephen as and when he was picked up by the Police or was prepared to go back to Scotland. We can only wait to see and judge it then.

Barry Mountford.

Chapter 38

Stephen had left a bag at Centrepoint the night before last, which he wanted, with clean socks, pants and shirt, so he knew that he needed to return tonight. It was 5.30pm rush hour time. The West End traffic was busy, as he made his way across Shaftsbury Avenue. He walked to the Dilly railings and was met by Lance and Keith, who were messing around with each other, until they spotted Stephen and quickly became very insistent about asking, where Dougie was, and when did Stephen last see him. They said that Andy was well pissed off with him, as he should have turned up with the watch by midday today. Stephen remembered the really nice watch on Dougies wrist and realised they must be talking about that one. He eased away from them saying he had not seen him all day. They told Stephen to tell Dougie, that Andy was looking for him, if he did come across him, and that he needed to be careful and watch his back.

Stephen avoided 'Playland', worried that he might be spotted, wondering what would happen if Andy had caught him. He was also anxious about Dougie wondering where he could be. He decided to cut through Chinatown from Leicester Square where he was able to make his way around to the side of 'Centrepoint' to Dean Street, and walked back to Soho Square, where he sat for a while, in the hope that he might find his friend, but he was nowhere to be seen.

It was still light, and the hum drum of the West End was palpable, even from the relative tranquility of Soho Square. It was getting closer to 8.00 pm, so Stephen made his way back to 'Centrepoint' to wait in line for the gates to open. But, as he turned the corner from Dean Street into Shaftsbury Avenue, he virtually bumped into Andy who was chatting to another older man. They were waiting on the footpath looking down to where the back of the queue started. So, Stephen quickly stepped back to regain some composure, before deciding to face him. He was scared but kept thinking that he had not done anything to offend him, as it was Dougie he wanted to speak to. He decided to be bold and walked up to him as if he was unaware of any problems he might have, and was confronted by a very different Andy from yesterday.

Stephen thought he could say hello and then walk on past by looking innocent. But, Andy moved quickly to the side of Stephen and grabbed his left arm with his right and turned him around vigorously making him walk with him away from the queue and the gates, back into Dean Street. Stopping outside of the Golden Lion Pub, he held Stephen's arm tightly, while his eyes were in a fixed stare of intensity. He then asked very calmly but forcefully, how Stephen was, and when was the last time he had seen Dougie? Stephen decided to tell a half-truth, which was that they had gone to the Top of The Pops show last night together, but that they had split up after, and he hadn't seen him since then. Andy wanted to know where they had got the tickets and Stephen said, "not sure where it was, but they were from some bloke in a record office". Andy told Stephen that Dougie had something that he had to return, or it would end up costing him a lot of money.

Stephen bluffed it out by saying that he did not know what he was talking about and had not seen Dougie all day. Andy released his grip and asked Stephen if he was going to 'Centrepoint' tonight, saying, you will be OK in there, but if you see Dougie, come down to Playland tomorrow and I will make it worth your while.

Stephen joined the Centrepoint queue and followed the group as they moved together towards the Iron gates. The line had already got smaller as the majority were probably returning from the previous night and had just walked straight in. Worried and more scared than he had ever been and sensing the need to constantly look back towards where Andy had been, he walked on. Stephen started to feel safer once closer to the gates.

He stepped forward anxiously as the night shelter worker looked up from his clipboard with all the names. He could see that Stewart had been watching what had been going on, and asked in a quizzical manner, if everything was all right? Stephen was questioned about where he had stayed the previous night as they walked along the tunnel from the gates, towards the rear entrance to the night shelter. Stephen told his exciting story about being at the recording of TOTP last night. Unfortunately, to his great disappointment, 'Centrepoint' did not have a television, so Stephen was unable to watch the show, which would have been aired now. But he was able to wash, change his clothing and also have his dirty stuff cleaned ready for tomorrow.

Stewart had to inform Stephen, that this could be his last night at 'Centrepoint', as they were not allowed to provide accommodation for under aged children, meaning under sixteen-year-olds, unless it was an emergency. The childcare law in the United Kingdom stated that any child under the age of sixteen, including those in care with a care order, who had absconded from home, had acted illegally. He explained that Stephen could be arrested on sight by a police officer without a warrant, and returned to the care provision, authority they had run away from. He also informed Stephen that anyone, within an organisation, found to be harboring an under aged child could be charged and arrested. The night shelter or refuge facility could also be closed down. Stephen was not very alarmed by this information as had seen similar messages about being underage in London while waiting at the Soho Project.

Stewart tried to talk to Stephen about using what the care system had to offer, and that once he was 16 that he could start to plan his life, job training, and in time, an independent place to stay. He explained that the Soho Project would be able to get in touch with his social worker to sort out a return to Scotland and 'Glenallen' tomorrow. That his social worker would organised for someone to meet Stephen in London to take him back. Stephen asked who that would be, but Stewart stated that he did not know and asked who he would be prepared to meet with.

Stephen had been giving the threat from Andy some thought and told Stewart that he would like it if Travis could collect him. Stewart asked Stephen if there was anything he wanted to tell him in regard to 'Glenallen' and also asked him about what he had been doing while he was in London, making a very direct reference to the man who he had seen harassing Stephen in the street. Stewart tried to reassure

Stephen with all the skills and experience that he had developed as a youth worker over the years that they could help him get it sorted. Stewart told Stephen that this would be a good place to start. Again, Stephen gave it some thought as he knew he could do what he wanted once back to Edinburgh. He told Stewart that most of the staff at 'Glenallen', were fine. That he really liked Travis and that he would be 16 years old in 9 days' time and he could go visit his mum when back in Scotland. Stewart was not convinced but carried on with the pretext that all of this might happen tomorrow.

Centrepoint log: Stephen Addair. DOB 10-06-1962 Date: 01-06-1978

Stephen arrived at the gate around 8.05pm after disappearing for a night. It seems that he has made friends and knows all about the Dilly. I think he is very adept at hiding what is going on, but I picked up that he was feeling a little threatened, as I saw him with an older male, who was holding him back, as Stephen was trying to walk away. I tried to get him to talk about it, but he avoided my questions by telling me about how he had attended a TOTP recording session on Wednesday evening and was very illuminated. It sounds like he saw some top bands.
I have told him that we will not be able to offer him a continued stay at Centrepoint, and the reasons why. However, he is extremely vulnerable, and we need to keep a look out for him. Soho Project has been in touch with his

social worker in Edinburgh and is ready to assist in his return. He told me that he gets on well with Travis, his key worker, at Glenallen, so will pass this onto the soho project in the morning, but he was reluctant to discuss how he found the place, only saying that it was somewhere to stay. I am not sure if he will return just yet, but we need to keep up the persuasion, and it is essential that we get the clear message about what the night shelters position was with under aged runaways. He was very tired and went to bed early and struggled to get himself up and ready this morning.

Stewart.

Chapter 39

In the morning, when Stephen left 'Centrepoint' he was worried and cautious, looking out for Andy. He wondered what might have happened to Dougie, and kept flipping between, he'll be fine, to questioning and doubting his confidence. The weather had turned and it was raining. London seemed a different place, with people rushing around trying to grab shelter, with raised umbrellas bumping against each other, as they passed by. Stephen walked to the Soho project with two of the new girls, who were 16 and 17 years old, feeling safer in numbers. They had spent two nights at the shelter and were making their way back to the Soho Project. They told Stephen that they had talked to Vikki who had helped them apply for money to get a bed and breakfast in the short term. Stephen felt a little safer with them, as he was worried that Andy might be about and waiting for him.

When they arrived at the 'Soho Project' along with another group who had also made their way from 'Centrepoint', Stephen was seen first by Barry once again. Barry had to be very clear and frank with Stephen about what was best for him. He questioned his friendships and talked about the dangers of renting. Stephen became very defensive and said that he knew what he was doing, and when his sexuality was mentioned Stephen clearly informed Barry that he was not queer! Barry told Stephen that whatever he was into was up to him, "I am not here to judge anyone, but there is danger out there, and we have supported lots of young men, who thought that they could handle what they were doing, and for some, it all went wrong for various reasons." He explained that kids from Scotland, 'in care', were in a difficult position, because a child, was required by a supervision order, to reside in a residential establishment. If they abscond can be arrested without a warrant in any part of the UK. Stephen knew that he was being pushed very hard and would normally have made an exit by now, but something deep inside was telling him to go and see his mum, even though he was also a little worried about being out and about on the streets of London. He agreed to return. Barry made the call to David Williams, who talked to Stephen over the telephone, and explained that he would arrange for someone from 'Glenallen' to come and collect him. They would look up train times and get back to them. Barry asked who would be coming, mentioning Travis as Stephen's preferred person, David replied that he could not promise, but would make enquiries. He'd get back to them, with all the arrangements.

The Soho Project log: Stephen Addair, DOB. 10-06-1962.
02-06-1978.

I met with Stephen today and he has agreed to go back to Edinburgh. Stewart from Centrepoint seemed to think that someone on the streets has spooked him but I did not get to the bottom of what it was all about, but he got tickets to TOTP on Wednesday evening and said he went with a friend called Dougie! I did not talk to him about our involvement with Dougie Banner but told him that we knew him well. It seems that Dougie has shown him around and then disappeared.

I received a call from John Stringer from Glenallen, who told me that he had booked the 08.45am from Waverley Station and should be at Kings Cross by 4.30pm.and had booked a straight turnaround for 5.30pm. I agreed to escort Stephen to Kings Cross Station, and to meet John in time for the return. Unfortunately, when I informed Stephen he became a bit agitated and said "not him" but it was too late to change, as he had left Glenallen for the train journey this morning.

Barry

Stephen reluctantly agreed to meet with John Stringer, fearing what a six-hour train journey with him would be like. They met as agreed, under the big clock, and Stringer presented as normal and friendly as anyone could be. He told Stephen that they had all been worried about him and told Barry that it would be fine and that he could take it from there.

Stephen was left with Stringer who asked Stephen if he had eaten, saying that they just about had time to grab a sandwich to take on the train with them, which they did. During the train journey home to Scotland, Stringer tried to be friendly, and asked Stephen what he had been doing, did he make any friends? But Stephen was reluctant to discuss any of it with him, and only said, "It was good, I would like to live there someday soon". Then Stringer, in a more stoic voice, started to inform Stephen about how he was in care, and that he could not go anywhere until he was discharged. "That this escapade would cost him a loss of pocket money, and a week's evening curfews". Stephen mentally cut off from what he was saying, choosing to turn away and huddle down into a sloppy scrunch, thinking that he had failed, which left him feeling an overwhelming tiredness, as he fell asleep for a good five hours of the journey, waking as the train proceeded through Dunbar, moving ever closer to Edinburgh.

When they got back to 'Glenallen' it was raining during the very early hours of the morning, and Stringer sent Stephen to his bed saying, 'we will talk in the morning'.

Chapter 40

Stephen was grounded right through to his birthday, but refused to go back to school, saying that there was no point. So 'Glenallen 'took away his pocket money for longer, informing him that, 'the moment you go back to school, you can get your allowance back'.

Stephen had a new confidence, and he became a bit of a celebrity in 'Glenallen'. The girls wanted to know all about London. Asking: where did he sleep, who did he meet, was it as big as they say? When he told them about his attendance to TOTP, they all had doubts, thinking he was lying, but when they asked him questions; where had he got the tickets from, and who he had seen? They were so excited and nearly dropped to the ground and screamed with a total disbelief, when they recalled the show from Thursday. They remembered who had played and in what order they had performed. Margaret took the most convincing, saying that he could have seen it on the Television and was just good at remembering the order. But when he described Jimmy Savile and the studio, they were all convinced.

He told them about the shops, cafes, Trafalgar Square, the pigeons, Piccadilly Circus, the River Thames and how easy money could be made. He also told them that he had stayed at a place called 'Centrepoint 'for free, and how easy it was to make friends down there but remembered to tell them that there was no point going until you were sixteen as the police will just bring you back. 'Centrepoint' will not be able to take you if your underage. Jasmine was all over him and asked about the girls. He exaggerated and told them about London girls as though they were models, the lights, the West End, and those city ladies who were all up for it. Stephen told them that he was going back once he was 16 and that no one could stop him.

Stephen's confidence and self-assurance sent his coolness ratings through the roof among the residents. He was able to put his arms around Margaret and Jasmine as he hung out around 'Glenallen', and even crept into their room, where they questioned him, some more, about London and TOTP.

Sitting then lying on Jasmine's bed, he made sure to always talk quietly aware that the staff was always about. Jasmine was eager to get close which meant that Margaret sat on the next bed on the other side of the pair. Jasmine snogged Stephen who lay alongside her. She allowed him to touch and stroke her legs with his right-hand finding access under her night dress and between her thighs to her moist fanny. He attempted a fingering action that seemed to arouse Jasmine to an intensity that would have allowed more to happen. He wanted more and was prepared to let it happen, but Margaret liked to keep control and put a stop to it, stating that they were making too much noise, fearing the snooping ears of the staff and that it might get back to Doc and Jackson. So, after a while he climbed out through the window, and back to his own room where Greg was waiting, and wanted to know all the detail, about how far did she let him go, what was she like, did you do it? Bernie listened into the conversation and smiled when Stephen told Greg a little bit too much about Jasmine. Greg had always fancied the girls, Jasmine in particular, but knew he did not stand a chance as Doc and Jackson were always about. They were two older boys who used to be residents at Glenallen, when Greg had his first stay at 11 years old. He hated them, and as big as he was now, he was still scared of them, as they were bullies, who had hurt and abused him in the past, and had a special relationship with Stringer and McLennen.

Chapter 41

It was Stephen's 16th birthday, the 10th of June 1978. Stephen felt a calmness that allowed him to take risks, he was not worried about what the staff would say or do, as he knew they had no real hold on him, now that he had somewhere to go. He knew that Jasmine was up for it but was also aware of being watched by the staff, mainly McLennen who seemed to have some claim on the girls.

The girls knew what to do, and Jasmine took Stephen to the place where she would do favours for McLennen, at the side of the house under the carport, in a hidden spot. They kissed, fondled, touched and got closer to penetration when Jasmine stopped and told Stephen, "it's your birthday, you can fuck me for free this time, but it will cost you next time", and from her bag, she produced a rubber Johnny, then she efficiently tore the wrapper open with her teeth and rolled the Durex over Stephen's erect penis with the self-reliance, confidence and experience of someone who was well practiced at this task. She then turned around, flipping her skirt up, to allow Stephen to enter from behind. Clumsily and within what seemed like seconds it was over and Stephen could say, on his birthday, that he was no longer a fuck virgin.

His new self-confidence allowed him to go back to those parts of Edinburgh where he thought money could be made. His plan was to get out of Edinburgh and back to London to find Dougie as soon as he had enough money. He felt emboldened now that he was a legal sixteen-year-old, encouraged and reassured, with a better idea of what London could be.

Chapter 42

Dougie was aware that Andy was looking for him, as they had history from way back when Doughy first arrived in the West End as an underage runaway.

Dougie Banner grew up in Glasgow with his mother and father and five older siblings. He was the baby, the youngest, the accident, and had four older sisters and one brother. His brother Frankie was the firstborn, who Dougie looked up to. Dougie always viewed Frankie as the man of the family, as he was 21 years his senior, and was in and about the home when he was a small child.

His sisters were the most prominent and important people in his life, and he would share and play with them as much as he could. When he was a baby, he was their living dolly, a plaything. They would take total control of the feeding, nappy changing, and dressing him up. Their mother, Molly Banner, was in her early forties when Stephen was born, and was working most of the time, to supplement the family income at Dunn and Moore's, which was the local bottle-washing storehouse. She worked as a general supervisor of the female workers. His dad, Michael Banner, was a tough workingman, 12 years older than his wife. He was a ship builder, welder, at the 'Fairfield Shipyards 'on the Upper Clyde, but poor health, followed by difficult times and closures in Glasgow ship building industry during the mid-sixties, impacted on him hard.

He had worked right through the war and the bombings, at the boatyards and docks. The hard manual work of a welder had come at a cost. He had respiratory problems from metal inhalation, and the constant smoking of tobacco as he was rarely seen without a roll up hanging from his lips. He persistently coughed, blaming it on the damp Glasgow Clyde air. As time passed, he had an endless wheeze during the day and night, which prevented him, along with everyone else in the house, from sleeping. He therefore struggled with the rigors of the job as an older man in his early sixties and through ill health he slowly, and painfully, passed away when Dougie was 7 years old.

After the death of his father, Dougies mother found money was difficult to come by. Frankie, who worked on the dock yard helped out with money, then in later years, the older girls Margaret and Gillian were able to work with their mother in the bottle-washing storehouse. They were also able to contribute to the family funds to pay the bills. This allowed Dougies mother Molly to stay dignified in poverty and to be able to keep food on the table.

Dougie had loved his dad, even though he only had a few memories of him. He remembered his father's open coffin being placed in the front room, and all the funeral activity as family and work friends from the docks, came to pay their respects. The procession of mourners who followed the hearse from his house to the church, and the long service the next day followed by the burial at a graveyard just outside of the city. He saw his mother crying for the first time at the grave, along with his sisters and wondered why he did not cry. His mother, brother and sisters grieved for some time. There was a great sadness in his home, with a reliance on the church to help them through. His mother was a devout Catholic and ran the house in accordance with her rules of obedience and daily prayer. Dougie's nearest in age sisters, Jessica and Sylvia were his go to people, if he needed some reassurance or a cuddle, but he rarely went to his mum who seemed to constantly rebuff him.

Chapter 43

Some years later the Banner family life became more deprived and impoverished with the looming closures of the Upper Clyde Shipyards (UCS) in 1971. Dougies brother Frankie was a strong Trade Unionist who found himself involved in the battle to stop the termination of the yards, which were threatened with being shut down due to the short sightedness of Edward Heath's, 'Tory party'.

The various dockyards had been amalgamated in 1966, but by the early 1970's were seen to be losing money, even though they had a full order book and were forecast profit in 1972. Jimmy Reid was the union representative voice that was shown on the TV, who spoke about not going on strike but, instead they would go on a work-in. Jimmy wanted to show the shipyard Scottish workers in a different light to the common public perception of strikers. He demanded that they showed discipline in their struggle, and instructed them that there would be no hooliganism, vandalism and no bevvying. This call struck a chord with the British working class and the people of Glasgow in the 1970's where 80,000 strong came out onto the streets to support the rallying cry of the ship builders of Clydeside.

The Banners felt the hardships of irregular pay packets, for some time, as they depended on Frankie's wage to keep food on the table. Molly prayed for the ship workers struggle, but she was ever resilient, and made sure that

Margaret, followed by Gillian, got their jobs in the bottle washing plant, which in turn helped with the family's income.

Dougie was made to attend Sunday school along with his younger sisters, and during 'Autumn 1970' he was chosen to sing in the church choir when he was 11 years old. This was an important passage in his life as he enjoyed that feeling of having a special talent and being in the company of the other boys who in general came from better off parents and were on the whole fun to be with. They were not fixated with sports and girls, like most of the boys at his school.

As Dougie grew up, he sensed that he was unlike the other boys in his school, as he felt safer in the company of girls, but as he got older, he realised that he was attracted to boys, even if they were not concerned about him. His mum was aware that he was different, particularly when he was playing with her younger daughters, Jessica and Sylvia. She would tell him to go out, and find some boys to play with, encouraging him to make some friends of his own age and gender. Dougie would get angry at his mum's attempts to direct and push him into doing things that he didn't want to do. He would reject this by ignoring her, which in turn would infuriate his mother, who would leave him to the girls to sort out.

He found little solace in his mum's prayers and would get quietly angry when she used God and sins as a way to discipline and control him.

Dougie was a bright boy always full of fun with rebellious laughter around his sisters. He liked dressing up with the girls. He had a charm and sense of humour that would get him out of trouble in most situations, and he had learnt how to manipulate them all.

They would constantly dance to the music on the radio, and the sisters would say that they were Rolling Stone fans, rather than the Beatles, but in reality, they liked all kinds of popular music, particularly Motown, because it had rhythm, and was the best music to dance to. Stevie Wonder singing 'Up Tight' was a favourite, and The Supremes, 'Baby Love'. When Dougie danced, they would laugh and tell him how special he was, that he had a real talent for movement, and they would work out moves with him. Eventually he could do better than his sisters. He loved to dress up, entertain and dance, pretending to be a pop star, with his favourite singer being Diana Ross.

Dougie loathed school and could never understand why people sent their kids to a place where, you were bullied, threatened, and indoctrinated with religion and forced to comply. If the teacher, Nun or priest so desired they could hit you with a fist, open hand, cane, slipper and even the wooden blackboard rubbers that they used to wipe clean the chalked up black board.

He attended St Saviour Catholic School, and during his early teens, moved along the road to a senior Catholic school for boys, and his sister Jessie was in the school next door, a Catholic school for girls. The schools were divided by a long black metal railing at playtime that stretched between the two playgrounds from the building wall to the exterior fence. The only time they came into contact during the school day was at breaks, lunch times and after classes as groups congregated outside of the school before moving onto their chosen locations or home. Dougie would always make his way to the far railings, with a friend called William, as that was where they felt the safest. He could talk to his group of girls through the metal stays. He would pick up on the flirting and female chatter about which boy, each of them liked, and the endless comparisons of who fancied whom. Dougie found himself making the same judgments about the boys too.

St Savior's had a mixture of priests, nuns and others, called teachers, who worked at the school. Some were retired Army people, who liked the sound of their own voices and the sense of power over children. When they ran out of things to talk about, and were struggling with the lesson material, the trusted subject textbook that had been around forever was shuffled through, in an attempt to find some content that might stimulate a discussion. Or a copying and fact-finding task, that would be thought up during the teacher led dialogue with the class.

Dougie was a choirboy and had to attend mass on Sundays, in the big church across the road from the school. At school they had morning worship assemblies every day that seemed to last forever. Dougie liked to sing and had a good voice. Dougie would do anything to get out of boring morning assembly, and felt himself lucky because every Tuesday and Thursday, he and William would have to attend practice for the church choir. A choral group, which was an elite set of ten choirboys from two-year groups. They were taught to sing a range of sacred choral works that would be performed on special occasions like, Easter, Christmas, Baptisms, Weddings and Confirmations. Each boy would receive a small weekly pocket money payment, and a bonus when performing for those special ritual events, marriages, births and mass, but marriages were the best earners. Dougie did feel obliged to hand some of his earnings to the family, but would also save and keep some back, so that he had the freedom and flexibility to be able to spend his money, as he chose to.

Chapter 44

When he was 12 years old in 1972, the youngest, Jessie 15 years old and Sylvie 19 years still lived at home, while the other two sisters had married and had lives of their own. They used to attend mass together joining most of the services with their mother, who with her two daughters was becoming more and more devout. Where Margaret, Gillian and Frankie had moved on from the family commitments and to their mother's disapproval, had become part time lapsed Catholics and hardly ever attended, apart from special events. His mother volunteered as much as she could and took charge of flower arrangements and decorations in the church, along with her daughters. Sylvie became one of the only female 'Usher's 'in their church and even got involved with preparation of the holy sacrament for Father Ball and Father Deacon Stanley Murphy.

The Reverend Father Paul Ball was Priest to the main Catholic Church as well as teaching some religious instruction in the boy's school. He took a particular interest when auditioning members to the choir and his choirboy group. Deacon Stanley Murphy was the principal choirmaster, who organised and ran all of the practice sessions. He had specific musical skills, being able to play the piano and the church organ. Stanley was funny and tried to make singing and learning the choral works more interesting. He liked being with the boys and got to know them really well over the months and years he worked with them. The boys would call him 'Stan the man 'behind his back and refer to him as Stan when they talked, which was not a problem for him. The boys enjoyed the familiarity with him, particularly during down time, but he made it very clear, that they could only call him Stan when there were no other adults present.

The Reverend Ball would visit the choir once or twice a fortnight and share some of his wisdom and knowledge. He would always sit with the boys, and join in with the singing, which he would say, brought back memories of when he was a choirboy. He had a particular interest in Dougie, who had matured into a dark haired, good-looking, 13-year-old boy.

Dougie was aware, and somehow flattered, that Father Paul would intentionally pick him out to talk and sit next to. He would speak about how the choirboy was one of the closest spiritual vessels to God, in church, as they carried our songs of Worship to the Heavens, which pleased and allowed God to celebrate man's place on earth. He would sidle up to Dougie, putting an arm across his shoulder, continually rubbing his shoulder and upper arm, as if it was a friendly gesture. When they were sitting, he would hold his thigh, squeezing and moving his hand around.

He asked Dougie how he felt when he sang his favourite Choral works, which were; 'O Sacrum Convivium' and 'Jesu Salvator Mundi'. Dougie would play along with him by stating, 'what an honour it was to be able to sing to God'. He would be looking around for William, while expressing some embarrassment at what he was saying, but also had to smile at the twaddle that Father Paul was coming out with about the glorification of God through the choirboys.

Father Paul seemed oblivious to the uncomfortable secret gestures between the boys. Thinking that he was liked and accepted as part of their group. He even thought that the boys were a consenting collection of cherubs who accepted his touching, as part of his place in the group, as a friendly father might be.

William was `Dougie's only real male friend. Dougie's soon realised that William was attracted to him, as he followed him about wherever he went. Sometimes Dougie would intentionally be cruel to him by grabbing his belly and wobbling it. He referred to him as 'Tub's 'and 'fat arse', slapping his bum to gain a reaction, but William just took it all, as he did not want to fall out with the only friend he had. They spent more time together over and beyond their time in the church and school. Dougie was aware of his fledgling feelings of sexual arousal, and embraced those emotions with his sensual thoughts about, good-looking actors, male models, and pop stars. They both liked David Bowie, this new and exciting androgynous person who was not afraid to dress up and be different.

To try and impress Dougie, William would talk about how Ziggy was "so good looking and exciting". Dougie was frustrated with not being able to have fun with people he felt were like him. William was the nice friendly tubby kid, who tried to please everyone, but there was no excitement. If anyone was to take the lead it was going to have to be him. Dougie had always felt that he was special, that life was waiting for him and that he needed to find somewhere else, where he could express himself.

Chapter 45

'Stan the man' had organised a weeklong visit, to a Catholic retreat, for the choirboys to practice their Choral songs. Paid for by the church as a thank you for their work in the choir. This was a youth work exercise for city kids to provide and enable them to have some fun and reflection in the countryside They were picked up on Monday morning, outside of St Saviours, in school uniform, and taken by Minibus to St Vincents Seminary, in Renfrewshire. The building was set on a hill and was a magnificent grand house. The focal entrance was through a large, gated access, along a straight path leading to the main door of the big house. The boys were taken around the side of the estate to a second entrance that led to the annexed buildings where the priests in training at the Seminary and guests stayed. The main building could be seen from the annex across two beautiful grassy quadrants. The chapel was set to the left facing the manicured areas, with pathways running around each green space, and a main path joining the annex to the big house. There were grounds all around the buildings, with a magnificent view of the Firth of Clyde from the side of the grand house, where visiting clergy, and senior priests would have their accommodation. The large bay windows spoke of an affluent time when the Catholic Church supported the Scottish Church and people, as a gesture to the rest of Britain during the 18th century that the Church was a grand and an independent authority serving the people of Scotland. The seminary was run by a team of, 'servants of God', that included, the senior priest, the young seminaries, nuns, a cook, cleaners, and a gardener.

The boys were welcomed by Father Keith O'Brian, who explained, that he would be looking after them while they were at the seminary, and took them to where they would be staying. Dougie, William and the other boys were directed to a stark, dormitory, with six bunk beds, three to each wall, which was linked to a large social area where they ate, and also carried out the indoor, organised activities. Stan the man, told the boys to sort out their own sleeping arrangements, as there were 12 beds but only 10 boys. They were very excited to be given the freedom to choose their beds and bed pals, so Dougie and William chose the bed in the corner close to the window, and the first thing they had to do was make the beds as the linen and woollen blankets were folded neatly at the bottom of the beds, with a single pillow on top. This was the first time he had ever slept anywhere other than at his own house. The boys were a mix of 12- and 13-year-olds and Dougie felt confident within the groups, as one of the oldest at 13 nearly 14, in September.

To the back of the annex were two sports fields with rugby goals and then a clear view across the rolling hills and woodlands in the distance. It was June so the weather, on the whole was good, with some hot spells. They had four days to enjoy their freedom since leaving home. After changing from their school uniform into more leisurely clothes and throwing a few pillows at each other, they wandered out into the communal room and onto the playing fields where they ran about shoving each other and rolling about on the grass laughing out loud in gay abandonment. The freedom and excitement of being away from home and transported them to a shear consciousness of liberation.

They were starving by now and wondered when they would be fed, and Dougie was thinking that he might have to break into the lump of cake his sister had given him in case of emergency. Just as they were all thinking food, two nuns arrived with a basket of bread, cheese and apples and a tray with beakers and a large jug of water, which they all shared and ate sitting by two large trees on the other side of the two Rugby pitches. The Nuns blessed the food, and the boys were pleasantly surprised by how friendly they were, introducing themselves as sister Diane and sister Marie. They asked lots of questions about Glasgow and home. As they were finishing their food Father O'Brian and Stan turned up smiling, to inform them that they would be playing tag on the rugby field. They needed to get their runners, shorts and rugby shirts on, and pointed to a door in a wooden building, which led to the changing rooms. Also, after evening tea, they would all go to the chapel where they would show Father O'Brian some of the Choral pieces that they had learnt.

The games were fun, even though Dougie was not a great fan of running around and sports, but because he was one of the eldest, and the others were not particularly sporty, he felt confident and in control of his performance for once. It was different to his experience in school, where the sporty kids always dominated.

After the games they were ushered back to the changing rooms, where they were expected to shower. Something he always tried to avoid at school but now felt particularly pressured and conscious of this expectation with his choirboy friends. He had started to grow hairs around his penis and felt embarrassed and different. Previously the closest that they ever got to undressing together, was when removing a jacket or shirt to put on their cassocks. When the group undressed in preparation to enter the communal shower together Dougie was afraid that he would lose face, and cause a fuss, he pretended to be distracted by talking to William, who was quite bold and confident in his undressed state, and had not yet reached puberty. Confidently walking around naked like there was nothing to it.

Dougie waited until nearly all had left the communal shower and were in the process of drying, when he moved quickly into the full spray, holding his towel to cover up until the last minute, hurriedly getting wet then vacating quickly with his towel tightly wrapped around his torso so he could leave with William.

Dougie felt even more uncomfortable as he became aware that Father O'Brian was standing in the changing room throughout, and had felt him looking, particularly when Dougie held back with William, who still audaciously strutted around unassumingly drying and dressing, like a big happy, cuddly teddy bear. Dougie was the last to dress and William sat and waited until he was ready to leave. Father O'Brian had moved around the dressing room trying to look busy wiping around the Shower and toilet area. He asked the boys what their names were, and when Dougie put forward his name, Father O'Brian said, 'oh yes, I have heard about you', and Dougie looked on curiously wondering why. Just as he was going to inquire how, the Father asked if they liked sweets, informing them that he had chocolate hidden in the changing rooms. They could have some later if they wanted to meet him after Choral practice here. The boys innocently looked at each other, not knowing what was happening. Father O'Brian asked if they could keep a secret, as he did not have enough for everyone. Dougie confidently spoke up by proclaiming that he did like chocolate and we are good at keeping secrets, saying, "see ya later," and walked off with William to meet the others.

The Choir practice went on for 2 hours, and the boys kept thinking about the nice Father who was going to give them chocolate. Stan the man dismissed the boys and told them that they should go back to the dormitory where they could have 50 minutes of free time before needing to get ready for bed.

Dougie knew that this was their time to get the chocolate and was excited by the secretive liaison with the good Father. He went to the changing room with William and when they arrived, they could hear the shower running and then heard him shout out, 'hi boys, sit yourselves down I am just coming'. Father O'Brian appeared naked from the shower, and walked towards the boy's semi erect, talking all the time about how he needed to wash away all the sins of the day. The boys looked astonished, as he appeared from the concrete shower block, and quickly the Father said, "no need to feel uncomfortable, this is how God made us". Dougie was focused on his wet, lean, muscular body and pubic area which half dilated seemed enormous in length and girth. The dark moist hairs all over his torso and legs exaggerated his pale skin complexion. The Father reminded them of how the boys were naked and showering earlier and that it was normal for us men to wash together, as cleanliness was close to Godliness. He then asked if they wanted some chocolate as he held his phallus, casually rubbing it as he talked. He enquired whether they did this? While with the other hand he reached into a small bag, where he produced two Cadbury's milk Chocolate bars and handed them, one at a time, to the boys. William looked at Dougie as he held his bar of chocolate. They both awkwardly stood up together, as William said, 'thank you, we need to leave now and get back to the dorm'. Father O'Brian reached out for his towel and reminded them that this was their secret and that he had lots more sweets for another time.

The boys left the changing rooms staring at each other, before waving the chocolate bar triumphantly, as if they had gained the trophy, they had set out to obtain. They did not discuss what they had seen, as they felt it was what it was, but both of them were independently thinking about naked bodies, hair, and big penis's and that this is what being a man was.

The next day started with a prayer before breakfast led by Father O'Brian. All Dougie could visualise was the Father's naked body.

After they had eaten, the morning activity was arts and craft work in the dorm room. Father O'Brian along with the two nuns from the previous day led the class. Inviting the boys to make a poster advertising their church and the choir using coloured crayons, coloured paper and pieces cut from a stock of old magazines. It had been raining for most of the morning, and the afternoon activity was the hike down to the water's edge of the Clyde. The trek back up the hill was wet, mucky and hard to navigate through fields and narrow overgrown paths. They were instructed to get their muddy clothes off once into the changing room, and to shower and place their wet stuff into a large laundry bag, where it would be taken away, to be washed and dried.

All that Dougie and William could visualise when undressing was the father standing on the spot naked openly rubbing him-self.

The image had awakened a sexualised curious notion that played on their minds. When he appeared urging the boys to get showered and back into warm clothing, Dougie was aware that this man of the cloth was scrutinising them all very carefully. Dougie and William made sure that they stayed with the other boys throughout, and ran back to the dorm as a group, just as another shower of rain was building up again.

When they arrived back at the dormitories the nuns had once again prepared their evening meal, which they had to eat quickly as they were expected to attend the chapel at 6.00pm for choir practice. Father O'Brian joined them for food and encouraged them to gee up when it was getting closer to going across to the chapel. When they arrived at the chapel they were surprised to see that Stan was in full conversation with the Reverend Father Ball, and when the choral group had gathered, he introduced the Father by informing the boys that he was visiting for two nights and that they needed to show him the new choral piece that they had been practicing and learnt.

They proudly sang; 'Holy God, We Praise Thy Name', and Father Ball clapped, while shouting 'splendid' and once again talked to the boys about, music to the heavens and beautiful cherubs. Father Ball watched the whole two-hour practice, rolling his head around, in a complete adoration of the music, until it was finished. As the boys filed out of the choirstalls he stood and embraced each boy in turn, smiling with arms outstretched, as if performing a special act of appeasement, consciously taking each boy and pulling him close, before moving on to squeeze the next. When he got to Dougie, he became even more vociferous in his attempts to show his full appreciation of what the choir had achieved. Stan looked a little embarrassed but did not question the Father's enthusiasm. He viewed him as his greatest allied fan who, always promoted, found funds for the development and progress of the choral mission at St. Saviours.

When the choir practice was finished, Dougie began to view Father Ball in a very different light, as he was aware that when he got his cuddle, it was not like when his sisters put their arms around him, as his hands moved intentionally down his back from the nap of his neck to the small of his back, just resting on the top of his buttocks, forcefully pulling him into his groin area. The curious nature of these encounters with the Father left Dougie feeling that this must be some kind of a normal way of interacting, if you are a member of the church.

On the third day Father O'Brian came into the dormitory and individually woke the choir boys, by standing or bending at the beds, stroking hair or a cheek, and pulling the covers down, while encouraging them to wake up to a new day.

Another glorious chance to follow Gods will, by getting out into the golden rays of the sun, which was predicted for today. It was all happiness and fun, and the activity in the morning was a treasure hunt, followed by some trust building in the afternoon.

After morning blessings and breakfast, the boys were instructed to pair up and use a fact sheet to try to uncover the 10 clues, to where the treasure was hidden. William was very excited and dragged Dougie around the grounds seeking out where each clue might be. By the time they had worked out the fourth clue Dougie was becoming a little bored with the game, but William steadily pushed Dougie on, systematically telling him it was fun. We can win this he declared. They wandered around the grounds of the big house and found Father Ball sitting on a bench, looking reflectively at the stunning coastal vistas, across and down to the Firth of the Clyde River valley.

Father Ball acknowledged Dougie and asked if he was having a good time, patting the bench space next to him inviting Dougie to sit and take in the wonderful views that God has given us. William was more interested in getting on with the treasure hunt, not feeling that he was being invited to sit anyway. He started to run down the hill, telling Dougie to catch up. Father Ball asked Dougie about home, as he knew his mother and sisters well, avoiding any mention of his late Dad. When he was alone with Dougie, he told him to remember that he was special, and that God knew this, and that we are looking for young people to train as seminaries here, for our church, and placed his right hand on his bare legs continually moving it up and down whilst smiling and patting, saying, 'what do you think about that'. The physical hand movements once again made Dougie question what the Father was doing, but he was beginning to take it for granted, that this was what he did, like it was normal, but the doubt lingered.

William was calling to Dougie, from a bush at the bottom of the path, informing him that he had found the 5th clue and they needed to run around to the big tree now. Dougie used this cue to pull away, informing Father Ball that he had to go and get on with the game. Father Ball, with a final squeeze, disappointedly let go of Dougies leg and waved him on, encouraging him to catch up with his friend.

Father Ball grew in strength and determination, as his perverted urges were forming in his head, taking him closer to wanting a more intimate relationship with Dougie. He then found Father O'Brian patrolling the game and encouraged him to join him in his private room in the big house. The two of them had a history, where Father Ball had tutored and dominated Father O'Brian as a young seminary student.

Once in the room, along with himself, Ball would demand that they knelt in prayer. Ball would take his clothes off and physically help to remove O'Brian's and ask that they pray for forgiveness together. While praying, Ball would chastise himself with a short leather whip across his back, shoulders and genitalia, and then turn his efforts onto O'Brian who passively engaged in pleasing the good Father, whilst being whipped until orgasm had been reached. Father Ball would then insist that they individually took a cold shower for forgiveness and as a punishment and penance for the sins of man.

Dougie and William had lunch and some free time to explore then they went straight onto the field where Father O'Brian and Stan-the- man were running the next game. They were told that psychologically we have automatic physical responses to danger and feeling safe, and that to trust the group to protect us we need to truly let go of any auto physical responses that prevent our human psyche from dominating how we go about our lives. He produced two blindfolds and asked the boys to split up into two groups of five, where one boy in each group would take turns to be blindfolded. A number of chairs benches and assorted objects were used to produce an obstacle course, and the trust games started.

The instructions were to get around the course blindfolded while being encouraged and directed verbally by the team, where each had a go. They then had to stand on a chair blindfolded and fall backwards, where the remaining four in the group would encourage a fallback into safe supporting arms.

After the full trust games had finished Father O'Brian then asked them to sit down in front of him, and they evaluated what had happened, and he questioned them about how that had felt. He asked; 'how was it having to trust each other, did you have faith in your friends, and why did you give your trust?' There was some discussion about being in it together, supporting each other and a belief that they would not allow anyone in the group to get hurt. Father O'Brian spoke about how faith was important, and that sharing experience and belief was a fundamental part of being human. But that being a Catholic and believing in God's love and forgiveness was the most important message.

He looked around at the group and straight at Dougie and William, who were sitting at the front of the gathering, and asked, "Do you trust in God, do you believe me". "I entrust you all to carry Gods work to the people, and persuade them that hope, forgiveness and love are the real messages that God wants us to share everyday".

He spoke about how their singing in the choir was bringing hope and love to our church and community, and that we all have to serve and fully repent our sins, saying; "forgive me for my sins" twice, with the second phrase silently dropping lower, as his voice softened and wavered on the second sins. Dougie could see tears welling up in the Father's eyes, and the boys could sense a restrained quiet moment. They paused awkwardly, waiting for Father O'Brian to move, as he stood head facing the ground. Then he walked away, gesticulating to Stan to carry on with the feedback. Stan stood still for a moment as he looked at the confused group of choristers, and then said, 'right, who wants hot chocolate and a short bread biscuit 'pointing to the nuns who had just appeared from the dormitory room. With a wave of his hand, he gesticulated in the direction of the reward, and with minimal encouragement the boys ran as fast as they could to get there first.

On the third evening they were expected to perform their three practiced pieces and some of their usual ensembles, which was once again led by Stan, with Father Ball watching on from the pews. The rest of the team at St. Vincent's College, which included several seminaries, nuns, cook and the gardener joined them. Father Ball arrived just as they were starting their first piece and sat on his own at the back of the small church. When the choirboys had finished, they all felt elated by the performance, and filed out of the church back to the dormitory in one group.

Stan followed with Father Ball and Father O'Brian, eulogising about how well the boys had performed. They all had supper together before going off to their beds, where father Ball followed the group into the dormitory, as they were dressing for bed, to do a reading. He informed the boys that he was leaving in the morning and would see them on Sunday at St. Saviours, and to have a lovely last day tomorrow.

The boys were all tired even though it was the last night. Dougie and William were the last to settle, talking about getting home and missing their mum's cooking. They decided to creep out of the Dorm and run across to the changing room to see if Father O'Brian would come through with his promise of sweets. When they arrived, they could see that the lights were on, and carefully opened the changing room door before peeking in. They could hear the shower running and they were aware of Father O'Brian and Father Ball's voice. They were talking to another younger man and encouraging him to get into the cold shower and wash away his sins. Father Ball was the most verbal, demanding trust and devotions as the sound of a, swoosh and slap could be heard, followed by low whimpering's of 'yes Father'. The boy's fell back with astonishment at what they could hear, looking at each other transfixed as if they had fallen upon a secret tryst amongst priests.

They decide to leave, and William was the first to clumsily exit, followed by Dougie, who briefly looked back from the opened door. He was spotted by Father O'Brian who had looked around from the shower area standing fully naked catching the movement of Dougies body and face as he withdrew from the access. The boys quickly ran back to the dormitory fearing that they would be followed. Once in the social area William spoke to Dougie about feeling scared about what they had heard. Dougie reassured him by saying he would look after him, that they needed to stick together, and he put an arm around his shoulder, followed by the other arm, to give a reassuring hug. William grabbed onto Dougie around the waist, enjoying the closeness of their bodies, not really understanding why it felt so good. Dougie urged William to get into bed and sleep, but Dougie was left with the image of Father Ball's nakedness and questions about who the younger seminaries voice in the shower was, and if Father O'Brian had seen him. Dougie eventually got to sleep but wished that he was back home and looked forward to seeing his sisters again.

The next day started with Stan and Father O'Brian waking the group and informing them that for their last day they would be going on a nature hunt, and hike into the woodlands, followed by lunch. All before they would be leaving in the Minibus to return to Glasgow and their families. They were told to pack as best they could, strip down the bedding and leave it in the large laundry container. The nuns joined them, where Grace and breakfast was had.

As a group they hiked up the hill to the woodlands, where using a worksheet, they had to find and identify specific leaves, trees, plants and evidence of wildlife. Once back to the Dormitory they ate lunch, changed into their school uniform, and said their goodbyes to the nuns, some of the young seminaries and Father O Brian. As they went to collect their bags from the main sleeping area Father O'Brian pulled Dougie to one side and surreptitiously handed him a tube of sweets, saying, remember don't tell the others, it's a secret. Dougie took the sugared jellies and hid them in his pocket silently acknowledging the instruction, while thinking, that was a good result feeling reassured that there was no reprimand from their foray the previous night. That the events had provided him with a transaction to his favour and

Dougie was left to surmise that these secret occasions could be a profitable venture.

Chapter 46

Dougie was pleased to be home and told his sisters about the great house, gardens, dormitory, the games and the choral performances. His sisters smiled and acknowledged that Dougie had experienced his first bit of independence from home. Dougie felt a new grown confidence, reinforcing his feeling that something special was out there waiting for him and that change was possible.

When his mother quoted the Bible and how Jesus loved us all and forgave us for our sins, Dougie was able to silently comment to himself, 'particularly if you are a priest, a seminary or a choir boy '.

Chapter 47

During that year Dougie's voice started to break and he knew that his choirboy days would soon be over. Puberty had helped to develop his muscular shape, vocal tone and pubic hair. He could see when sharing the communal shower at school, with the other boys that he was not the only one with hairs under his arms, on his chest and around his Willy. He was getting aroused at any thought of naked bodies, particularly males.

Father Ball would constantly turn up at choir practice and go through his usual routine of eulogising, followed by direct contact with the choristers. Dougie was starting to feel neglected, as Father Ball had moved onto another younger boy and avoided any contact with him.

William was still his little follower, who did everything he could to please Dougie, including buying him some sweets each week. He knew that Dougie liked sweets and would do anything to please him. William also turned up with a half packet of cigarettes and asked Dougie if he wanted to try it. Dougie was familiar with smoking as his dad used to smoke all the time along with his big brother Frankie, also Gillian who kept it a secret from her mum. William's whole family smoked so it was easy to access cigarettes, and he had tried it and liked it. He felt quite grown up as he lit up in front of Dougie, coughing slightly while trying to disguise the effect. Dougie felt that he also needed to keep face and gently sucked on the end as William lit him up. He was surprised and slightly turned off by the taste but liked the thought of standing holding a cigarette and eventually enjoyed the relaxed feeling it gave him deep inside.

Chapter 48

It was just before Christmas, December 1974 and Dougie was 14 years and four months old. He knew that this would be his last festive celebration as a choirboy and tried to hide the fact that his voice was unreliable and had started to change. He was also concerned about, how a lack of income would affect him, as he had become used to having some money always readily available. He liked the level of independence, though minimal, that it afforded him. Allowing Dougie to save and buy, within a reasonable teenage price range, goods that included magazines, single records, the odd item of clothing. He had bought some flared trousers, much to his mother's disapproval.

On Saturday the 21st of December as he was going to choir practice, as usual. Walking through the nave of the Church to change into his cassock, he noticed Father Ball, and to his surprise, that he was talking to Father O'Brian intently. Dougie was taken back and thrown off guard, as the father had become one of his sexual fantasies from that evening in the locker room. There was a nod of recognition from Father O'Brian and Dougie walked on through to the small room, where the other boys were. William had become the lead boy in some of the choral pieces and was nervously running through his phrasings. Dougie went straight up to him, excitedly informing William, that Father O'Brian was in the vestry with Father Ball. William acknowledged the information by confirming that he had also seen him.

After some time Stan-the-man stepped into the room to do his pep up speech, informing the choir that they had some familiar, but special visitors, so they needed their finest voices today.

The boys performed to the best of their ability, wanting to impress the Father from St. Vincent's College, singing the Christmas choral pieces, they had been learning. They sang with gusto, strong and clear. Father's O'Brian and Ball clapped with their usual level of appreciation and spent time talking to the boys. Stan told them to get dressed back into their home clothes.

Stan and Father Ball left together in the direction of the vestibule, leading out through the main entrance. The boys filed out of the small back room, dressed for home, chatting and happy.

As the boys were leaving, Dougie was aware that Father O'Brian was directing much of his conversation in his direction. As the boys filed out, Dougie boldly held back hoping to talk to him. William stayed with Dougie even though Dougie kept stressing that he would meet him outside, emphasising the 'outside 'until finally the penny dropped, and William realised that he was being directed, and was not wanted at that moment in time.

Once alone Father O'Brian informed Dougie that he had grown since the summer and now looked like a youth rather than a boy. Dougie stated that he was 14 now and politely asked how Sister Diane and Sister Marie were. The Father said that they were fine and that they had asked him to pass on God's love to you all. He then asked if he had given any thought about joining the seminary when he was older and did, he still like the sweets. Dougie smiled and passed this off awkwardly by saying 'not really and yes'. The father invited Dougie back into the vestry, saying that he had more sweets in his bag in the office.

Once in the vestry he reminded Dougie about the secret that he had promised to keep. Dougie recognised the hanging robes that father Ball wore for the various ceremonies and the vestment objects used in the Liturgy. He felt in the presence of explicit church grandeur.

Father O'Brian asked if Dougie had ever carried the Chalice and invited him to hold the Sacred Goblet, whilst informing him that the Chalice worked miracles. He stated that, "the liquid from this trophy could transform how one views the world". He drew a small flask from his pocket and poured some fluid into the Chalice, pretending to drink some of it. Then he invited Dougie to take a mouthful. Dougie was both nervous and excited and swallowed the strange, sweet fluid that resembles the taste of a fiery fruit juice. He felt an animated thrill, as though he was doing something naughty and daring. He drank out of the church Chalice a second time before placing the Goblet onto the nearby table, wondering what this was all about. He looked directly into Father O'Brian's eyes and could see an anxious, watery-eyed man who was reaching out to Dougie. Pulling him closely religiously kissing his forehead and holding him tightly to his chest. Then chanting God is good, forgive me my Father, before leaning down to kiss Dougie's ears and neck. Manipulating his hands so that they could reach around and down Dougies back to his waist and trousers. He slowly reached to his buttocks, caressing and squeezing each cheek, pulling him towards his own groin. Dougie could feel the Fathers erect phallus pushing against him. Dougie was transfixed by his eager suitor, but felt strangely heady, aroused and emotional, as the good Father pulled his trousers down and turned him. Maneuvering his-own body and clothing to a place that allowed full penis to skin contact. He thrust at Dougie whilst reaching around and holding Dougies boyhood tightly in his right hand. Then with the briefest hand contact, quickly turned Dougies erection into a spitting torrent of warm fluid. As Dougie, uncontrollably climaxed, he could feel Father O'Brian's penis pushing hard between his rectum cheeks and upper thighs, with the occasional pause as he rubbed Dougies ejaculation around to promote a level of lubrication. Dougie was frightened but felt unable to resist, feeling his mind was shutting down, as the thrusting intensified and then stopped. Dougie fell to the floor in an unreal state of dreaminess and pensive exhaustion, not really understanding what had happened. Father O'Brian knelt next to him, hands clasped together, as if to pray, asking God for forgiveness.

  It was some time before Dougie felt steady on his feet and conscious of what had happened. He was aware that the Father was upset and suddenly became angry, hitting his fists hard on the floor. Dougie was struggling to fully comprehend what had taken place. He gradually pulled his clothing back on while observing Father O'Brian slap himself with his own leather belt several times across his back and legs. Dougie stepped away still groggy from the effects of what he had drunk, not fully understanding what had transpired. He was growing more fearful of the good Father, who was not the person he had previously fantasised about. Dougie moved to the side of the room, away from Father O'Brian's gesticulations, and watched as he began to dress. Father O'Brian then looked at Dougie, giving half a smile as he gathered his thoughts in preparation to address Dougie. Needing to seek out Dougie's response to the preceding events. He quickly reminded Dougie that it was their secret and pulled over his bag to take out a 'Cadbury's Mars Bar and a large tube of Smarties', offering them to Dougie saying, "I know you like a sweet payment, and now I see how much".

He started to walk towards Dougie and handed over the reward. Dougie groggily took the sweets, but as he started to regain a greater degree of consciousness, he felt uncomfortable and reacted by shuffling away from the virtuous Father, who asked Dougie to stop and take a breath. He held out his arms and open palms, pausing whilst reassuring Dougie that everything was fine, it was their secret, as long as his mother did not find out about what they had done.

Dougie had not thought about his mother until then, and an overwhelming fear and sense of guilt welled up inside of him. He began to dread what would happen if she found out, and what would his sisters say. He then became conscious of an uncomfortable anal wet stickiness and the overpowering feeling that he needed the toilet. He became aware of soreness, that he thought going to the toilet would put right.

Dougie's instinct was to get home, so he left via the door, back into the church, and walked to the front where he found William still waiting in the vestibule. William was curious as to what had happened with Father O'Brian and followed Dougie, asking as many questions as he could think of, before Dougie stopped, and in a controlled but forceful manner told William to 'shut up and go home'. William was taken aback by Dougie's aggressive response, but took it, because he always did.

Chapter 49

The next day Dougie was due to return to the church for the final rehearsals for the Christmas Eve choral event. He had arranged to meet William in the park.

Once up and in the bathroom, to his horror he looked into the mirror and found a large white spot between his left outer nostril and cheek, and another just starting on his chin. Should he squeeze it or bath it with hot water until it popped? This was not his first experience of these vulgar protruding swellings that jutted out from his facial skin. So, he went with the gentle dabbing with hot water and a flannel. In general, it left less of a mess on the skin than the more satisfying, 'squeeze and bleed' method that always appeared worse afterward and took longer to heal.

He wanted to look good, and dressed in his flared trousers, shirt and turtleneck jumper. At the breakfast table he gazed at his mother, fearfully wondering if she could tell that something had happened, that his life had changed forever. He had felt that she seemed to always know about everything and chose her moments carefully to inform and control her family. What if she knew about Father O Brian and what had happened between them? In a panic Dougie tried to second guess how she would react, if he told her what had happened, but every possible confession led to his mother getting very angry and blaming him for what he had done. He then imagined that she would call out for his sisters and tell them what a dirty little sod he was, to be doing unnatural things with the good Father.

Chapter 50

Breakfast porridge oats were the first meal of the day, and his mother always expected the day to start with a blessing and 'praise be to God, for delivering us all from evil', particularly on the Sabbath. There was no formal early mass this morning, due to the pending Christmas events. Dougie sat uncomfortably at the kitchen table, with his sisters Jessie and Sylvie, still feeling heady from the events of his time with Father O'Brian. He started to think about how it might be, having to come face to face with him again today. His sisters were aware that Dougie was starting puberty, and that his voice had dropped a tone, also he had spots.

While his mum was out of the kitchen, Jessie teased him, asking if his change was affecting his ability to sing. Jessie tormented him about pubes, stating that a hairy fellow would mean big changes in his life. Sylvie shrieked at the thought of her little brother having pubic hairs anywhere. She reminded Jessie to be civil at the breakfast table, warning that mum might hear. Dougie got angry with Jessie and told her that it was 'natural', asking what she thought of her 'hairy fanny', is that why you can't get a boyfriend. He looked to Sylvie for some support, but Sylvie scowled at the two of them, forming an awkward silence as their mother came back into the kitchen. She had heard everything, but still asked what had happened, stating that God was ever watchful, that sins would be punished. Dougie reacted indignantly, by saying 'some might, but it depends on who you are'. His mother recoiled and reminded him that, it was not for them to pass judgment, as that was between God and the Holy Fathers to decide.

Jessie looked embarrassed as she knew that this had started because of her goading and throw away comment, but feeling self-justifying, she said to Dougie, "yes, it is natural, but remember girls have it earlier, and worse than boys". She looked at Sylvie and her mother for some support. Their mother spoke in an angry and direct tone, aimed at Jessie, but she turned to Dougie and said, "I will not have these words spoken during breakfast, and in my home, that's it, stop". She pushed back her chair forcefully from the table, informing them all to clear up, do their chores and be grateful for God's forgiveness. Moving to the front door, she put on her coat and hat before leaving without saying another word. They looked sheepishly at each other, and then Sylvie quietly got on with clearing up the breakfast things, while Dougie still incensed, dressed and got ready to leave the house, slamming the front door behind him.

Chapter 51

It was a cold, but bright, Glasgow mid-morning as Dougie walked along Drumoyne Drive and across Langland Road, in the direction of Elder Park where he knew he would find some peace and a quiet place to think. William eventually arrived in the Park and met up with Dougie, who was sitting on one of the swings. He asked him how he was, while offering him a cigarette. Dougie was still fuming quietly, making it difficult for William who was struggling to say the right thing. He talked about Christmas Eve rehearsals, what they could do with the pocket money. Making reference to him being a 'Day dreamer' like David Cassidy, when finally,

Dougie replied with a Bowie song, 'Is there life on Mars 'Come to that is there life anywhere? William could see that Dougie was still upset and mentioned Father O'Brian as someone who was fun to be with, asking what had happened in the Vestry.

Dougie nearly told William about it, but then looked into his eyes, aware that he could ask anything of him at that moment and he would do it. He leaned in, taking his arm and pulled him close and kissed him lightly on the lips, stopping to check that William was happy to continue. There was an awkward silence, and they tried again, but this time they held their lips together for a longer period and a natural longing took over as they tried to open mouths to gain a lengthier intensity. Dougie pulled away inwardly smiling that it had happened, his first kiss, even though it had been with dumpy William. William was embarrassed and felt awkward, not really feeling confident enough to do anything other than to say, "that was different, a real Bowie moment".

They walked on through the park to St Saviour's Church to continue rehearsals, and as expected Stan was waiting to greet the boys along with Father O'Brian, who sat quietly in the front pew. William was still reeling with the effects of the kiss and kept looking at Dougie in awe and adoration. Dougie could feel the intensity of the previous evening in the Vestry with Father O'Brian and was aware that he was fixated with the man of the cloth. He felt an arousal and awakening for this man, that had truly sexualised the boy to man in him.

Dougie sat with the other choirboys waiting and watching as Stan started the count for the first Christmas song, which was 'Silent Night 'in two-part harmony with the lead sung by William. The mood was happy, and Father O'Brian sat looking at the choir in quiet contemplation. William was aware that he was the focus during his solo and looked at Dougie for approval, but Dougie was more interested in catching eye contact with the Father. As the rehearsals finished, there was applause from the back of the church where various people were sitting, one of which was Father Ball, and Stan gave them the last instruction about Christmas Eve and what time to arrive, Father Ball made his way down the central aisle clapping and sat next to Father O'Brian.

As the boys stood up to leave, Dougie was surprised that Father O'Brian totally disregarded him, turning to his fellow men of the cloth, seemingly in deep conversation. William made his way to Dougies side and tried to talk about how the rehearsals had gone, expecting some kind of recognition for his solo but Dougie indignantly strode on totally disregarding William's call for companionship.

Dougie sauntered away from the Church feeling confused and rejected, making his way along Langland Road back to Elder Park. It was late afternoon and Christmas lights were beginning to flicker from some of the houses and flats. The winter gloom was slowly starting to rear its mournful self. Sundays were the days when the house was empty as his mother and sisters were preoccupied with their duties at the church.

He could go home but decided to walk around the park. During this time Dougie's thoughts were solely about Father O'Brian. He was aware that he had started to get physically excited and was struggling to contain a hard on and wanted to relieve himself. Dougie found his teenage self, having to readjust his clothing to account for the direction and force of his phallus. Approaching the park toilets, he decided that he needed to relieve himself but had learnt that peeing down was the most difficult thing to do, with an erection. He found himself spraying upwards beyond the urinal and onto the wall in an uncontrollable action, but as his stiffness subsided, he was able to hit the porcelain, and eventually the drain hole.

While facing the urinal he was aware of a low moaning and grunting sound coming from the direction of the cubicles. He stood still silently trying to make out what was going on. He could hear quiet whispering followed by some commotion and decided to get out of the building before he was noticed. Then he sat on the park bench just along from the entrance to satisfy his curiosity.

Eventually an older man left the convenience looking slightly agitated, examining the terrain right and left as he departed. Within minutes a younger boy exited, while zipping up his parker coat. He was calm and at ease as he lit up a cigarette then ran his hand through his thick red hair, cut in a bobbed style, parted through the middle. The boy spotted Dougie and glanced to one side and then the other, before coolly making his way to where Dougie was sitting. Dougie was captivated by him but got a little nervous. He started to wrap his duffle coat tightly around himself, pretending to be doing his own thing, not really sure whether to stay put, or start to walk away. Before he had time to make that decision it was obvious that he was coming in his direction. He stopped in front of Dougie and asked him if he was all right.

"It's a wee bit cold to be sitting there" and offered him a cigarette. Dougie was unsure of what to say and do but decided to take a ciggy and placed it in his lips. Graeme then held out his lighter, allowing the flame to hover just in front of the tobacco tube. Dougie drew in the first lit vapor and struggled to resist coughing. Graeme informed Dougie that this was no place to sit as it was getting dark and the park wardens would be around soon to close the gates. Dougie thanked Graeme for the cigarette and started to stand up ready to leave. They walked on together and Graeme joked about the strange bogeymen who lurked in this park, informing him that 'they wait for unassuming teenage boys. They approach bearing gifts of money and sweeter incentives, but what they really want is your innocence'. Dougie laughed and started to feel a real connection with Graeme, picking up that they were similar. Graeme told Dougie that he was 17 years old and that he had just come back from London where the real action was. "You can earn some good money there, as long as you stay clean and look after yourself". He asked Dougie how old he was, assuming that he was a similar age, and Dougie replied by declaring that he was 15, deciding to add a year, thinking it was better to be a similar age. Graeme invited Dougie back to his place, stating that he had just bought a new Roxy Music album, declaring, "I'm their biggest fan".

When they arrived at Graeme's house, which was in a posh part of town, with smart Victorian houses, Graeme warned Dougie, that he lived with his mum, she was a hippy, so don't be shocked if she's a bit strange, she likes her wacky-backy.

His mother answered the door dressed in a full-length smock dress, with a long woollen jumper draped around her shoulders and welcomed the two of them enthusiastically. Then she made her way back into the front room where Dougie was aware that there was a strange poignant smoky smell mixed with a distinct aroma that Dougie later found was called incense sticks. They looked like long reeds standing in porcelain holders, burning and smoldering their way down to the receptacle's that held and caught the dying embers, as they dribbled into a grey ashen stem that eventually extinguished itself.

Once in the bedroom Graeme lit up a spliff and offered Dougie a share, and after several drags of this new experience, Dougie felt contented and satisfied. He watched as Graeme explained and discussed, with great enthusiasm, his record collection. Graeme was keen to show Dougie his singles and long players, which he kept in his bedroom on a low shelf, and instantly brought out Roxy Music 'Stranded' Brian Ferry's third album. He played the first track 'Street life' which was an upbeat song that had bounce and tempo, allowing Graeme to dance on the spot. When it had finished, he eagerly put on 'Virginia Plain', which had the best rhythm and Graeme's favourite song. He encouraged Dougie to stand up and dance, which at first, he tentatively did, Graeme moved in close, turning and smiling as he grabbed his hands encouraging some movement in unison. Dougie felt free, like he was doing what he loved, with someone who was like him, and danced with the gay abandon that he had felt when dancing with his sisters. Feeling proud that he had some moves, as a wave of joy filled his soul, through the rhythm that took hold of him. He had not really known much about Roxy Music but was a fan now. Graeme showed him pictures of Brian Ferry that were on his wall and in magazines, in his glam rock outfit. This great looking man, wearing makeup that looked a little like David Bowie. When Dougie mentioned Bowie, Graeme went crazy saying how he loved him and put on 'Ziggy Stardust and the Spiders from Mars' singing out loud, "let me put my arms around your head, gee its late let's go to bed"..... The rest of the evening was one of the happiest times that Dougie could remember, they kissed, and touched, and Graeme exposed Dougie to the kind of natural love, that he previously, could not have imagined was possible, showing Dougie what to do and how to do it.

Chapter 52

Leaving Graeme's that evening and walking home, he felt elated as though his life had started. He kept thinking that this is what it feels like to be young, alive free to be who I am, do what I like. He felt fresh, awake and kept running the events of the evening through his mind, reliving the sensuality of first love.

He found himself comparing what had happened with Father O'Brian, the intensity, physicality and roughness of the older man, knowing it was a sin, but still finding him-self-starting to become excited with the thought of another liaison. Even though it scared him and he knew that it was very wrong, now that he had experienced the innocence of this real love with Graeme.

Chapter 53

The next morning came quickly, and Dougie felt different, more confident, and relaxed, with a distinct feeling of self-worth. He knew who he was, and why all this time he had struggled with the other boy's innuendos, his mother's self-riotousness, and his sister's comments about girlfriends.

Later that day Christmas Eve choir had gone fine. Dougie had mimed most of the choral pieces and thought he had got away with it. At the start of choir practice, Stan had asked Dougie to sing individually, then sat him down to explain that singing days of a choir boy was short lived. That is why God gave boys this gift but took it away from men. We all have to finally grow up as our bodies change. Dougie smiled at the notion of being 'grow up 'and acknowledged that he had been struggling for some time to hit the high notes. Stan accepted Dougies explanation and reminded him, that he could still continue coming to Church. That once his voice had fully broken he might consider joining the senior male and female singers. Dougie defiantly told Stan not to worry as he never much trusted or believed in God. Stan reminded him about the community, his mother, sisters, choir-friendships, but Dougie brazenly told him that he did not plan to hang around much longer and wanted to get on with his life, 'on Mars'! Stan looked quizzically and sympathetically at Dougie, feeling the pressure of the other choristers who were impatiently waiting for the practice to start and finish, so that they could get home. Before leaving, Dougie told Stan with a grin on his face that, "at least I don't have to come to choir practice anymore." Dougie was pleased to get away from an experience that had bored, confused, sexualised, and sometimes enthralled him. He was sure that there was much more on offer now that he had met Graeme.

Dougie and Graeme spent most of their days together throughout the Christmas holidays. The thought of going back to school in January became an irrelevance to what Dougie wanted. The excitement of being with Graeme, having real sex with slow full-filled kisses, while exploring an eroticism that just felt good as they tried deeper reciprocated oral contact that stretched their throats to the point of a gag reflex, that they both tried to overcome, with ropes of spit that felt like the climax to ejaculation. They would explore each other's tender spots, learning that hygiene was a prerequisite to great sex.

Chapter 54

His sisters could not understand what had happened to Dougie as he was dismissive of them and was hardly ever at home. Graeme had talked to Dougie about London and had planned a return visit. His mother started to demand a greater degree of attendance and duty around home, which set up more conflict between the two of them.

He would stay at Graeme's overnight, in the clear knowledge that he wanted to make it obvious that he was not going to be controlled by her, which in turn set up disagreement, resentment and argument as she demanded that Dougie should be home before 6.00pm with little attempt or willingness to question where he had been.

His reaction was to push it further by arguing or ignoring her demands. His sisters tried to question his change in attitude, struggling to understand why he was so hostile with them and blamed it on puberty.

Graemes mother was the complete opposite to his mother. She was welcoming and totally supported Graemes freedom and the choices he made. He was able to do what he wanted, checking, as they came through the door, asking if they were hungry or did, they want a drink. The smell of incense and weed were the prevailing aromas as you entered the house. The feeling of calmness and peace was the overriding ethos of Graeme's mum and their home. She had enjoyed the sixties, where she travelled the Silk Road, as a single mum, with a small child, and had lived for more than a year on an Israeli kibbutz in a collective community. She was fortunate to have been able to return to Glasgow at the end of the sixties to live in relative comfort. She had inherited her grandparent's property, and a small but substantial amount of money from their will.

Chapter 55

Frankie the hard man, had moved out of the family home years ago and was making his own life, but was called to arms by his mother to force Dougie to go back to school, and follow her orders, in and around the home. Frankie waited for Dougie to return and was sitting in his father's old armchair. Dougie knew it was serious when he spotted Frankie, and with the briefest nod of acknowledgement he went straight past him, to his room.

Frankie followed Dougie up to his old small box room and forcefully pushed open the bedroom door, where clearing his throat, he awkwardly spoke about how Dougie was hurting mum, that she was not getting any younger. That if he was to live in her home Dougie had to live by her rules. Wearily reinforcing his argument by saying, "that is the way it is, you are only 14, and anyway you are also upsetting your sisters".

Dougie was not used to arguing with his older brother, who had rarely spent any time with him over the years. He felt somewhat intimidated by his overbearing and demanding tone. On the other hand, thought, how privileged he was that Frankie would even take time out of his day to talk to him. There was no attempt to ask what Dougie was doing, why he was not attending school, so Dougie obstinately, told him that he was leaving and going to London. Frankie derided this declaration by saying, "there's nothing for you there", calling Dougie a fucking fantasist. "There's nothing but trouble in that place, you won't have anywhere to stay". Dougie angrily told Frankie that he was going with a friend, who had been there before, and knew how to get hold of money. Frankie told Dougie "You stupid fool, you will end up in trouble with the Police, stop being a selfish little prick". Dougie told Frankie "It's my life, and I will do what I want". Frankie left the room locking the door from the outside and shouted to Dougie "you'll do what you are told, I am going to talk to Mum".

Dougie had never been locked in before and banged on the door, shouting, "let me out, mum". Dougie felt desperate and blamed his family for his unhappiness. He eventually decided to pack a bag with essential clothes, climbed out of the bedroom window, grabbing onto a gutter downpipe so that he could get to the ground floor and promptly set off to Graeme's house to inform him that he was going to London with him tomorrow.

Chapter 56

It was a drab February evening when they arrived in London, it was dark and late, and on the way, Dougie felt that he should tell Graeme that he was really 14 years old, and not 15 until September. Graeme had explained the things that he needed to look out for, the Police, Skin heads, Nasty old queers who did not think that they should pay, Pimp handlers pushing drugs and that if they got split up, that they should always meet back at the 'Dilly'. Graeme was astute enough to know that 14 years old was risky. That it would make it more problematic if picked up by the law. Graeme was clearly in charge and took control and managed the whole journey to London.

Graeme knew some people in the West End, and had hoped for an overnight stay with Darren, who was an older ex-punter, that Graeme had lived with for a short while when he was in London last year, in May. He described Darren as a nice guy, but needy. He will try to control you if you let him. When they arrived, Darren was wearing a colourful floral silk dressing gown and little else.

He continually stroked his hair, checking that it was flat at the sides, seemingly demonstrating a lack of confidence and embarrassment. He led them into his home, with an exaggerated, swish and swoon beckoning gesture, that Dougie soon found characterised Darren's very nature and style. Once seated and settled with a cup of tea, conversations ensued, questions were asked and Darren explained that he worked as a make-up artist in the West End theatre. He described how he was working on 'Jesus Christ Superstar 'at the moment, a brilliant new show, with a hunk of a young actor called 'Paul Nicholas', who is playing 'Jesus', written by two new fabulously talented musicians and writers, called Andrew Lloyd Webber and Tim Rice at 'The Palace Theatre', adding "you must come and see it, I can get you tickets".

Darren had a meager one-bedroom flat in Soho and lived with his cat called 'Fluffy' and two goldfish, 'Wai Wai' and 'Mai Mai', and seemed to know which was which. He was welcoming when they both arrived, introducing Fluffy to the boys, asking her to be friendly and 'keep your claws to yourself baby', adding, 'she can be a little minx at times'. Graeme made it clear that they only needed to stay one night and would be out of Darren's hair by morning.

Darren was a kind, happy, camp, queer parody of a gay man, who demonstrated extreme effeminate behaviors that Dougie had not seen before. He was pleasantly surprised by the ostentatious nature of this person and his home, which was beautifully presented, with colourful throws and cushions draped over furniture and around the room. The radio was playing quietly in the background as the DJ introduced the number one record of the week, by Steve Harley and The Cockney Rebels ' Make me Smile ', which suited the mood and the moment as the three of them got to know each other. Darren spoke in a concerned manner when he asked about the boy's intentions while in London and reminded them about how tough it was for someone as young as Dougie.

Chapter 57

It was Saturday 22nd February, and the sun was shining for once. The previous evening Darren had told the boys, that as much as he had enjoyed their company, they had to be out by 9.00 in the morning, as he had a matinee and needed to be at work by 10.00am.

Graeme was excited at the thought of showing Dougie around London but first walked past the 'Centrepoint' gates on Shaftsbury Avenue, informing him that if he ever needed to stay somewhere in an emergency, he would be well looked after in there and that it was a safe place. They then walked to Piccadilly Circus and Graeme explained that this was where he made his money and they could both do well together. Dougie was so excited to be among the Capitals buildings and wanted to go to 'Nelson's Column', where they fed the pigeons, and then walked onto the 'River Thames' and 'Big Ben'. He was surprised to find how close together all the significant places were, and how easy it was to walk to each famous landmark. Next, he wanted to visit the big shops. Graeme took Dougie to Oxford Street, but by then they were hungry and stopped for a burger. This seemed like a happy town with music and buskers all around. Graeme knew that they needed to make money soon as spending for two was expensive. What little cash he had would run out fast.

They found a cheap bed and breakfast in Euston on Saturday night and Sunday, but money was running out. Dougie liked the time that they had together in the shabby dwellings and even the smelly beds. They were able to make love at will and in a private space, exploring every aspect of each other's bodies. Dougie enjoyed Greame moving his mouth and hands slowly down his shaft feeling his knob stiffen and swell to bursting as he made him cum again and again. They sucked each other's dick in turn, rolling foreskin back feeling the soft flesh on tongue and at the back of the mouth. Ropes of spit embarrassingly fell out of Dougie's mouth as he drew away which he pulled to one side as he sucked harder bringing Greame to a full climax. They finally went to sleep but were disturbed by the constant hum of traffic and the sound of car horns that intercepted the silence of the night.

On Monday morning Graeme told Dougie that they, he needed to earn as money was getting low. He took Dougie to the Dilly telling him to sit by the Eros statue to watch and learn, as Graeme hung out along the meat rack waiting for his first pick up. Dougie was not sure about sharing Graeme with others but was curious and interested in who might be interested in him.

During this time, Dougie lost concentration and started to look around at the neon signs moving and changing shape from Coca Cola to Skol Lager. He looked up at the outstretched under foot of Eros then the various groups of people who were hanging out with each other around statue. Time seemed to be running on and when he looked across the road to the railings near to 'Boots the Chemist 'he realised that Graeme had gone. He walked across the road to the railing not really fully understanding what had happened.

He remembered that he should always meet back here and waited until it was getting dark at 4.30pm. He only had £2.26 in his pocket and was getting hungry and walked across the road to the 'Wimpy Bar'. He bought a Wimpy, chips and coke for 35p. After that he waited outside, leaning on the railings, looking about for Graeme. While he was waiting, he was aware of a man who moved slowly along the barrier until he was standing next to Dougie and introduced himself as Andy. He asked Dougie if he knew anyone. Dougie quickly explained that he was waiting for a friend. Andy said, "you and all the other lads along this path", Dougie was not sure whether to laugh at this but thought that Andy had some experience of these things and was sounding him out. Andy told Dougie about the Playland arcade over the road and invited him to come and play a few games with him while he was waiting. "Don't worry, it's on me, I will pay, come on it will be fun". While walking Andy asked Dougie how old he was and smiled as he put his arm on his shoulder. When Dougie told him he was 16, he laughed, and said "come on, I am not the Police, what's your real age"? So, Dougie, with a wry smile, said he was 15.

Andy played the machines with Dougie, and they started to develop a banter that charmed and seduced Dougie. Andy's intimacy was subtle and professional. He touched

Dougies arm and hands, offering suggestions to help with the maneuvers and tactics on the pinball machine. Eventually Andy intimated that he could help Dougie make some money. He reminded him that he could catch up with his friend tomorrow. Dougie was excited at the thought of spending time with Andy who was good looking, charming, and old enough to excite him in the way that Father O'Brian had. However, he was reluctant to leave the Dilly, as he felt sure Graeme would return.

Winter darkness had fallen, and Andy explained that Centrepoint would be a good place to stay overnight, but that it would not be open until 8.00pm. The streets in the West End were teeming with people and predators, so Andy took Dougie for a hot chocolate at The Wimpy Bar to get to know him better. Dougie told Andy that he was happy to go to the 'Centrepoint' place tonight as Graeme had recommended it. Andy told him that he would be safe there, knowing that he would see him again tomorrow. They walked along Shaftsbury Avenue to the gates, but Andy stood back once they arrived, informing Dougie to tell them that he was 16 and wanted to live in London, or they would 'dob 'him into the police as a young runaway.

Chapter 58

Dougie rang the bell and waited outside of the large metal gates on Shaftsbury Avenue, wondering what was on the other side, but trusting what Graeme and Andy had said about the place. A welcoming, friendly lady came to the gate with a clipboard and asked Dougie some basic questions, name, age, where was he from, why was he in London? As they walked through the alleyway around the building to the back door, she explained what they could offer once inside. She reassured Dougie that they could help with some hot food, a shower, a bed and some advice about where he could seek out future accommodation if needed. The Night Shelter felt scary at first, but safe. There were various people, male and female who all seemed to be getting along, eating food and playing cards and board games.

Dougie was shown into the large social room area, and was offered some hot food, which arrived in a matter of minutes. Music was playing and the excited friendly sound of the other young people in the room helped him to feel safe. Then very soon after finishing his food another woman sat next to him and asked about home, and why he had decided to come to London. She was curious about his age, not really believing that he was sixteen, but explained that they may be able to help with some emergency short-term accommodation. That he would be sent to an Advice Centre in the morning where they would be able to talk to him about options.

Centrepoint log: Dougie Spencer. DOB 05-09-1957. 24-02-1974.

Dougie arrive at 8.45pm, with a basic change of clothes in a bag. He told me that he was 16 and 17 in September, but I suspect he is younger. He struggled to talk about home, saying that he lived in Glasgow and that his mother knew he had come to London. When I asked him how he had found out about Centrepoint he said a friend had told him but could not remember the friend's name. He seems very young but has seen some of the sights in London as he talked about Trafalgar square and Big Ben. I will refer him to The Soho Project in the morning, to see if they can get a little bit further with the truth.

Anna

The basement dormitories smelt of old socks and the washing and drying machines seemed to rattle and run all night. Dougie was knackered and slept relatively well. In the morning, he had the Centrepoint breakfast that was a hot drink and juice, cereal, toast, bread, spreads and porridge. In the morning Anna talked to him about how important it was to go to 'The Soho Project 'and tried to pair him up with others that were also going to the advice and counselling agency.

Once out on the streets he decided to skip Soho Project and made his way back to the Dilly in the hope he might find Graeme. It was early, cold but bright enough for the winter. Once on the streets at 8.30am he observed how fast and assertive people moved, the stations were crowded with people, streaming out, to their respective destinations. Dougie waited for an hour but there was no sign of Graeme. So, Dougie made his way to Leicester Square, wandered around, and came back and walked across to the Dilly, but still there was no sign of him. He thought about going back to Darren's, but was not exactly sure where he lived, and just when he was beginning to worry Andy turned up and asked Dougie how he had got on at Centrepoint. He spoke reassuringly about things being cool, and that he would look after him, until he met up with his friend again. They walked to 'Playland' where Andy introduced Dougie to some of the other boys, who were hanging out, while waiting for the afternoon trade to start on the Dilly.

Chapter 59

Andy was an experienced pimp, who had been part of the Dilly scene for many years. He had found that setting up connections was more profitable and less humiliating, than providing the service him-self, even though he was good at it. He knew how to take advantage of a young queer, by sharing his experience to gain trust, through dependency, desire, and affection. He asked Dougie if he spotted his friend, knowing that he hadn't. Supplied him with cigarettes and took Dougie for a Burger and 'Knickerbocker glory' at the Wimpy Bar always questioning, praising and flirting throughout the liaison. Once Andy was confident that he had Dougies trust, he invited him to his top floor two-bedroom council property in Vauxhall, on the 'Coronation Buildings Estate', which he sub-let from a mate called Colin Jordan. The flat was well laid out with modern furnishings, a big television, records filled the shelves, and he had an eye level electric cooker, which looked very American and totally new to Dougie.

Andy was in total control of the situation and placed a record on the turntable, 'Bridge Over Troubled Waters 'Simon and Garfunkel, and showed Dougie around the apartment ending in the spare bedroom, which was equally as well furnished as the first bedroom. Dougie was drawn to the pictures on the wall that depicted two semi naked men posing provocatively in boxer briefs and the second was of a young

Marlon Brando, wearing a leather jacket and jeans. Andy confidently lay on the bed and asked Dougie if he liked Marlon? Dougie felt excited by this older male who was unzipping his fly and drawing down his trousers to expose his penis. He asked Dougie if he knew what to do, and Dougie felt obliged to demonstrate his sexual knowledge and newly found experience. He performed an oral mouthful on his semi while his hand pulled and rolled in a reciprocating fashion on Andy's expanding swollen piece. He detected a pungent urine smell as he placed his lips around his foreskin, which he slowly drew back, allowing him to lick and insert the tip of his tongue around Andy's pee-hole.

Andy's arousal prompted him to push himself as deeply as possible into Dougies throat, pulling his head as he exposed Dougies willingness to take it to a gagging deeper throat state. Dougies eyes watered at the intensity of the oral thrusts, prompting the wiping clear of ropes of glandular spit and a running nose, while pushing Andy away as he was left gasping for air.

Andy's intense sexual aggression reminded him of Father O'Brian, which scared and aroused him at the same time. Andy wanted to fully test his young apprentice to the full, and removed Dougies trousers exposing Dougies erection, which Andy ignored. Then turning him face down onto the edge of the bed, began lubing himself with his spit and, penetrated slowly at first, but when he was sure that Dougie had done this before, fucked the boy to his own climax, coming as he withdrew.

Andy had judged his apprentice well and continued to dominate him with, charm, offers of money, cigarettes, pills, sweets, and a promise of excitement and fun. Andy pushed, persuaded and enforced his expectations throughout so that Dougie was completely caught up in Andy's stories of meeting celebrities and other important people. It transfixed the boy taking him to a state of full subjugation. Dougie spent the night with Andy who praised Dougies sexual knowledge, informing him how he could earn good money doing that stuff.

Chapter 60

The following day Andy was clear that this was a one off and that he had business to attend to, but that he knew a house where Dougie could stay, that would provide Dougie with work to help him pay his way, as long as he was able to do the stuff he had done the night before. He gave Dougie five pounds warning him to work hard and listen to Carole. That he would keep in touch and would take him out once he had settled in.

Dougie thought about Graeme and felt guilty but had been clearly informed by Graeme that they would both need to earn in London and that he had probably been doing the same thing with someone else. Dougie kept in the back of his mind that he could always make his way back to the Circus where he might meet up with Graeme or go to the 'Centrepoint 'place he had stayed two nights earlier.

Andy used his car to take Dougie to Elm Guest House in Rocks Lane, near Bares Common, Southwest London. The building was a three-story hotel run by Carole and Haroon Kasir. They had two top floor rooms that housed three boys but could accommodate six. Carole and Haroon lived in the one-bedroom basement, and ground floor apartment, with an integrated kitchen and living room space. The entrance and first floor contained a large reception, entertainment space, with a separate dining room and kitchen area, with a through door. There were three guest rooms, one of which was called an executive suite with a separate entrance through a back door.

Carole took charge of the boys and made sure they were fed, washed, and medical needs taken care of. Carole, who had been forewarned, that Andy was heading over with a new chicken, welcomed Dougie. She had alerted the other boys and had prepared a bed and some food for Dougie, who was nervous but trusting that Andy was looking after him.

Andy told Dougie to do as he was told and make him proud. He said that the other boys would explain what this place was about, that Carole would look after him and also give him pocket money. He told Dougie that he had a special job coming up with influential punters and wanted him to demonstrate to Carole that he would be able to help her out with some of her clients.

Dougie was disoriented and struggled to fully comprehend where he was or what he was expected to do but played along by chatting with the two other boys who were a similar age to him. Carole and the boys showed Dougie around the main entertainment rooms and accompanied him to a back door entrance to her basement flat, where he would get meals and just hang out if they wanted to. Carole was welcoming and friendly and offered Dougie the choice of a mixed bowl of chocolate bars presented on the table placed next to a square Tupperware box full of different sweets. She told Dougie that he could help himself whenever he wanted, as she bought them for her boys.

Haroon who had been upstairs organising the rooms, introduced himself to Dougie by stating out loud "So you are the new boy, has Andy already gone" Before Dougie could say yes, Carole intervened by saying "Dougie this is Haroon, my husband and we both work together in the entertainment business, he will be around all of the time, particularly when we have guests". Dougie nodded with the acceptance of a good choirboy and reached out for a Toffee crisp.

Chapter 61

Brian was 16, the oldest, and had been part of Elm Guest House for the last nine months. When Brian was 13 years old, he had been picked up outside of Charing Cross station by Roger Gleaves, who proceeded to groom, manipulate and frighten him into being part of the Paedophilia network he ran, which procured and supplied a catalogue of younger children to paying customers.

Gleaves connections with a Bromley children's home were integral to his syndicate and he used two henchmen to carry out his affairs. Brian had been traded to Elm House when he was 15 as he was older than the age range that Gleaves preferred.

Aiden and Connor from Wicklow, Ireland, were 14 years old like Dougie. They had sneaked upon the Dublin to Holyhead Ferry and then made their way on a Victoria line coach to London. Aiden and Connor were gay and had been bullied relentlessly in their small hometown. In the summer, decided to run away to Dublin together with a small bag of clothes and very little money. They did most things to survive, including stealing beer bottles from behind Off License's and getting the return price on the bottles. They would clean around warehouse, and the warehouse manager would drop them some coins if they did a good job. While in and around the docks they found better reward when they noticed boys hanging nearby the concourse who were making money from passing trade. Aiden was the most confident and after checking it out with a regular, made himself available, making five Irish pounds. Their arrival in London was difficult as they did not know anyone, had little money and had no idea how big this city was, as it just seemed to go on and on.

Victoria station was their first place to hang out but they were aware of the Police and did not want to have their collar felt and sent back to Ireland.

Andy had met the boys at 'Playland 'earlier in the year and had brought them to Elm House after taking care of them for a couple of days.

They were nearly 15 now and knew the score, telling Dougie to play along but only do what you want. They explained that they had some regulars who wanted twos, but most were singles who were looking for a connection with a boy, just do it and take what you can. Carole and Haroon do well out of it, a lot better than they let on, but they will expect you to perform. Brian listened in and told Dougie, "Get what you can from it darling, at least you are protected here if they turn aggressive". Brian was camp and proud of it; he was wearing a poly/cotton dressing gown and smoking by the window with it slightly ajar to keep most of the cold air out.

The next day, Carole took Dougie shopping for clothes and underwear. She bought serviceable clothes that looked right, making sure that he kept the youthfulness that she knew her customers preferred. That first evening all four of them were to be clean and dressed smartly. They were beckoned to join Carole and Haroon in the reception room and given a drink each to help them settle their nerves, similar to the drink she would give them each morning.

Carole prepared the drinks, asking what each boy preferred. In the mornings most wanted hot chocolate but, in the evenings, it was Cola or Fanta. She mostly added a cocktail of Codeine, Mogadon in a diluted sedative as a supplement to the drinks, to nullify their energy, transporting them to an accepting state. She had found that the drugs helped the boys perform better in their transactional activities with her clients.

Before the first customer arrived, she would brief the boys about who they were expecting, always using a pseudonym to hide their real identities. Adding, "he was a very important person, or a public figure". "Once they arrive you will have to be on your best behaviour". "Remember I will be listening out for all of you and will be close by if anyone needs me".

Most of the clients would arrive through the front door and have a drink as they chatted to Carole or Haroon who would normally be running the bar. Once the niceties had happened, they would indicate a choice of boy to Carole who would escort him into a room with his drink. She would then brief the child who in a nullified state entered the room where Carole would introduce him to his perpetrator.

Chapter 62

Month's on, Dougie struggled to understand what had happened to him. Constantly feeling tired and speculating where Graeme was. Wondering how William and his sisters were and worried about what his mum would do if she ever found out what he was doing. He often had confusing recollections, flash backs of what had transpired with Father O'Brian, which became mistaken puzzling feelings, about what he had been doing with the visitors in Elm House.

Andy had come back to the lodgings at various times to collect his payments from Carole and to ensure that his property was being looked after and available for his needs. He had talked to Dougie about how he was getting on, bringing him some gifts of magazines, chocolate and a modern blue chiffon shirt with a high rolling collar. He explained that he might have some separate work for him next week and that he would bring him another present. He had taken the Irish boys a couple of times and they had stayed out for the night, returning tired and had slept most of the next day.

Chapter 63

It was late August; Dougie was approaching his fifteenth birthday and Andy picked Dougie up in his car. Dougie was wearing his new shirt and Andy commented on what a good fit it was, which made him feel special. He informed him that they were going to a party in Surrey where they would be seeing a radio one DJ and some other pop celebrities. Dougie felt apprehensive but also excited by the thought of something away from Elm Guest House and the old perverts who used the place. He was pleased to be finally going somewhere, even though his morning hot chocolate had left him feeling tired.

He was taken to a large, detached country house where two huge metal gates barred their way to the grounds leading up to the front door. Andy rang the intercom bell and spoke into the speaker. Dougie could hear him talking to a man who eventually appeared at the front door and could be easily viewed through the wrought iron structure. As he approached, the gates opened, and Andy drove onto the ample driveway. Andy smiled, as Chris Denning told him that Norman was inside and that Jonathan was on his way. Dougie was taken into the front hall where there was an impressive stairwell leading up to the first floor. Dougie could see two children silently hovering around the landing stairs looking down at the new arrivals. Denning took them through to the very large kitchen living room where they were offered drinks. Denning talked about how busy everything was. He kept dropping names and telling stories about male and female pop stars connected to Decca records, getting out of their heads, cavorting naked, when they visited this house and the parties.

Norman, then joined them as they walked back into the lobby area, and invited them into the kitchen, for something to eat. Dougie could see that Andy knew this place well, and that he had a long-standing relationship with them, particularly when Jonathan turned up.

As the day progressed King spoke about going to 'The Walton Hop" tonight, which was a local discotheque for young people. He asked Dougie if he could dance, and snuggled up to him, insinuating that he would like to see that young tush move a bit, adding you will have to dress up and pretend you are 18.

King like Denning spoke about celebrities he knew and also showed Dougie some pictures of naked women and men. One of the photo's included a full frontal of himself posing in a top hat and cane, where he said, "how did that get in there", acting slightly embarrassed he put his hands in front of the image, to seemingly hide the picture, with a title that read 'let it all hang out'.

The other children were too young to attend and were looked after by Terence who was the house cook, cleaner and general do it all. He commented on Dougie's trendy shirt and said lets find something to go with it, helping Dougie find trousers, and a smart jacket from the general wardrobe that he looked after, saying, "there you are baby, you look a treat, very modern, do yourself proud, they will love you", and planted a huge kiss on his right cheek, saying, "you could pass for 18 maybe a young 19", Dougie smiled, and told Terrence that it was his birthday next week.

When they arrived at 'The Hop 'there was a small group of girls and boys hanging out at the entrance and the two bouncers ushered them it. The main dance area was sunken and centrally placed with the Disk Jockey looking over the floor, playing 'When will I see you again 'by The Three Degrees. The bar encircled the far end, with tables and chairs placed all around the dance floor with rails running throughout, with entry points on and off the discotheque level.

They arrived after nine and the disco was in full swing. The far end was reserved for King and his group. Most regulars had seen him before, but a buzz went around as he arrived, with the usual pointing and acknowledgement that a celebrity usually gets. Dougie was in total awe of what this place was, young people like him, hanging out, having fun, dancing and free to be with whom they wanted. King and Denning sat and watched as Dougie danced with Andy and Norman moving to 'Rock Your Baby' by George McCrae.

Dougie knew that the men could not touch or get too close together in public, particularly the older men who were in fear that it would be frowned upon by most of the others in the disco.

Dougie did find himself getting intimate with one of the girls who seemed to move near to him. They got into the rhythm, he locked his right thigh hard into her groin and a natural gyration occurred and he felt a sexy connection, thinking of Graeme as an ideal partner. Then Kung Fu Fighting was introduced by D.J. Mike Smith, and the whole floor began to jump and bump to the 'ha 'as the karate moves were mimed, dancing freely with Andy and Norman, all united in the mutual hip thrust associated with the song, aimed at each other. Dougie found himself moving freely about the floor as the music progressed to an oldie but rousing, 'Spirit in the Sky 'that captivated the mood of the evening and even made Denning and King get onto the dance floor. Dougie enjoyed the feeling of being in a club disco with everyone, along with the oneness of the music that brought people together.

Once King had had enough and wanted to go, they were taxied back to the house in Burwood Park, Walton on Thames. Dougie was expected to join King and Norman, after a few more drinks, while Denning preferred the younger variety.

Dougie played his part with them both, as he had learnt how to get through these events from his work at Elm House.

He had been given some pocket money of sort from Carole, but nothing of any real value and Norman had slipped him a £10 note in the morning, just as some of the others had done. After the events of last evening, he had decided that he needed to get out of that place now and make a life for himself. He made his mind up that once he was fifteen, he would get away from Elm House. He knew that 'Centrepoint' was an option and still hoped that Graeme might be around the Dilly.

In the morning Andy told Dougie that he would be taking him home after breakfast. Dougie became angry and told Andy, "That's not my home", but Andy ignored him and went about cordially chatting to Norman and Denning, who screwed up their faces looking at Andy sarcastically in response to Dougie's hissy fit.

Andy helped himself to some of the small packets of cocaine contained in the drugs drawer. Dougie realised that they had value and similarly secretly helped him-self to a few packs. Followed by a handful of purple pills, which he stashed quickly in his pocket. When they left Dougie knew that Andy was not going to let him go easily and that his best bet was to wait until he was gone and make his escape via Elm House the next day.

Chapter 64

The next day he avoided unnecessary contact with Carole and the boys. He had breakfast but avoided the hot chocolate, as he knew it always made him feel tired. Instead, he dipped a wet finger into one of the packs of white powder, sucking in the substance, which livened him up and made him feel stronger. He still had the clothes that he had worn to The Walton Hop and was able to take his original bag when he first arrived. He hid the packets and pills he had taken from the Surrey house in a separate section in the bag, and without informing anyone left the property through a back gate and made his way to a bus stop that listed Kensington and Chelsea as a destination. On arrival he got onto an underground train to Piccadilly Circus.

Chapter 65

It was summer and the atmosphere was lively, full of tourists, and warm. He remembered the chicken run and Playland but was frightened that Andy might catch him. He positioned himself by the Eros Statue, looking out for Graeme, and watched for a while. Then stood under the arches outside of Swan and Edgar's before walking past the railings and then up through Shaftsbury Avenue. He decided to check that Centrepoint was still in the same place. It was. He read the signage that said open at 8.00pm. He wandered around and made his way along Berwick Street, back down to Brewer Street, aware that this was the place for girlie shows and sex action. He had wanted to try to remember what route he had taken with Graeme, hoping he might be able to make his way back to Darren's, but struggled and got lost.

He then found his way to Soho Square, which was a green peaceable haven. It was a hot sunny summer afternoon in Central London, a place to eat his crisps, drink his cola and try out one of those purple pills he had taken from the drugs drawer in Surrey.

While sitting he watched a sandal wearing, group of strange looking men singing and dancing in procession, all dressed in orange robes, with bells and bangles on their arms and legs, and had orange marks dashed in places on their heads. They rhythmically sang 'Hare Krishna 'while hitting drums and playing bells, hung between their fore finger and thumb, that sounded tranquil. Quietly it drew Dougie into a steady movement. He sat questioning and admiring their dedication to who they were. One of the singers was carrying a box to collect any donations but stopped at where Dougie was sitting and smiled in a kindly manner. Dougie uncomfortably looked away. He said, "may the Lord Krishna look after you, if you are hungry and need to eat, come with me to our kitchen, we are close by, look". Pointing to a street leading from the square. Dougie declined, saying he was fine. They walked on and away, until they eventually had moved beyond the square, where he could hear them slowly make their way along Soho Street where the sound stopped. Dougie followed them and it was clear that they did offer food, only asking for payment as an affordable donation. He did not recognise anything on the menu apart from rice but thought he would give it a go thinking 'you never know, it depends how hungry you are'.

Dougie felt more energised after eating and took another pill, then went back to the square and started thinking about home and wondered what his mum and sisters were doing. He thought about William, Graeme and even Father O Brian, realising now that the older man had taken something from him that was not his to take. He became angry at what the priest had done to him, along with all those other perverts who used and abused him. Turning him into what he had become, a loser with nothing. He was determined to turn his life around and vowed to himself that he would not go back to Elm House, that he needed to find his own way and take control of his own being and destiny.

Chapter 66

As the sun was starting to get lower in the sky Dougie made his way back to the gates at 'Centrepoint'. He was still frightened that Andy might show up, and maybe it was the pills, but he had gained strength from his escape and grew even more confident. He was welcomed back into a place that cared and treated him like he mattered.

He decided to tell a degree of truth as could not admit to what he had been doing these last 6 to 7 months and found himself gabbling on about going back to Scotland and then coming to London again. That he had a friend that he had stayed with, but they had let him down. He told them he was 15 years old and 16 in a few days' time, 2nd of September. That he was not hungry, but once presented with food, kept eating. He wanted to keep moving about. He chatted with lots of the other users, who viewed him as a kid who was speeding or in some state of hyperactivity that prevented him from relaxing. He danced to the Glitter Band music coming through the speakers in the main social area, 'Just for You' feeling safe, buoyant and stronger.

Centrepoint Log: Dougie Banner DOB 02-09-1958 Date: 29-08-1974

Dougie says that he stayed with us in February this year and made a name up, Dougie Spencer. I could not find his card in the index, so not sure why. He said he came to London with a friend and that they had run out of money so went back to Glasgow a couple of days later. He arrived with a small bag, mostly of clothes and seemed a little high and hyperactive. I am still not sure if he is sixteen in four days' time. Dougie was very confident around the other residents, and we found it difficult settling him down, but he eventually crashed and slept after coming up stairs a couple of times asking for a drink. I felt it was not appropriate to push him too hard for the truth this evening. Will try to get him to 'The Soho Project' tomorrow and hopefully it will all become clear.

Dougie was a little more settled and quieter this morning. I asked Bonnie and Craig to encourage him to walk up to The Soho Project with them.

30-08-1974 a.m. I spoke to Mick this morning, who said, they had just arrived and that Dougie was with the bunch of them and would be seen soon.

Janice

Dougie felt protected with the others at The Soho Project. He was playful and again had it in his head that he might find Graeme today. It was Friday and the weather was still hot.

He talked to Mick, a straight speaking Scottish advice worker, who Dougie liked and trusted. After some questions about home, Glasgow, and the streets in London Dougie talked about his dad. Saying that he had died when he was young from his work, he was a strong family man who had strict views on life. Mick explained that it would be difficult to stay in London without proper identification and Soho Project would struggle to help him without the full truth.

Dougie finally admitted that he was still 14 and nearly 15, and when Mick pushed him about home, it was then that he got worried, and started closing up, saying, "I can't go back, my mum and sisters will not understand". Mick then gently asked, "what won't they understand". Dougie said, "I can't say". Dougie becoming visibly restless with each subsequent question where Mick eventually found that Dougie had been in and around London since February, and that he had been staying with people, but refused to say with who and where.

Mick sensed that he was stirring up deep anxieties in Dougie and backed off with the questions, suggesting to Dougie that 'he should stay at Centrepoint tonight and come back again on Monday once he had time to think'. Mick's assessment was that he needed more time with him. That he would ask 'Centrepoint 'if he could stay with them over the weekend, because Dougie was vulnerable and it was better to continue the working relationship, in the short term, until he can persuade him to look at options.

The Soho Project log: Dougie Banner. DOB 02-09-1959. Centrepoint feedback: Friday 30-08-1974

I spent some time with Dougie this morning and believe he is a very vulnerable boy. He is 14 years old but will be 15 in three days' time. He became upset and withdrawn whenever I approached the subject of his mother and family, saying his dad had died when he was young. I do believe that he lived at home and not in care but will check later. I tried to talk to him about being looked after by Social Services, but he was not interested in that. I will continue to see what is available. P.M. Feedback to 'Centrepoint'.

I have made some phone calls, and he was reported missing in Glasgow back in February this year, so who knows where he has been in the meantime. He has a mother and sisters, and they live near the Clydeside Glasgow. The Police are duty bound to log and report that we have been in contact with him here in London, and they will have to report him found to his Mother, who is Molly Banner. Centrepoint have agreed to hold him over the weekend and try to get his confidence. I will talk to him again on Monday. I also called Social Services who, knew he had been missing and said that his mum had contacts through the church, and that they had a good volunteer care service who might be able to support Dougie when he returns.

Mick

Dougie spent some of the day with Bonnie and Craig who were waiting for 'Centrepoint 'and The Soho Project to find them some temporary accommodation, with the view to something more permanent with, 'Brent People's Housing Association'. Who throughout the 1970's along with other housing groups, campaigned for affordable homes, and were part of the pressure group who helped secure the July 1974 Housing Act. The housing project was allocated a small percentage of their housing stock specifically for homeless young people, who were identified and supported by the West End Agencies.

Dougie sensed that Bonnie and Craig wanted to be on their own, and decided to go back to the Dilly, still hoping to find Graeme. He was careful and kept an eye out for Andy, but found that punters approached him, as his incognito style of watching and waiting was viewed as interesting.

He was unsure about what he might get himself into and also didn't like the look of them all. He also caught the eye of other renters, some of whom were on the lookout for Dougie, and had been briefed by Andy.

Sheriff was one of them. He had been about and on the scene for some time and had attended some of the parties where Andy had recruited boys. He knew that Dougie was important to Andy and decided to approach and befriend him.

Sheriff was a smart gay who wore Ravel platform shoes, tight flared trousers, a smart wide lapel jacket, large shirt collar and seemed to Dougie to be coolness itself. Dougie liked the way he looked, and found that he was easy to talk to, and very quickly spoke about his friend Graeme, and asked if he had seen him. Sheriff explained that lots of boys pass through here and that some you get to know, while others keep themselves to themselves. Sheriff was aware that Dougie had been kept at Elm House, and knew the place well, and that younger boys lived there. Andy had introduced him to Haroon and Carole last year and he had worked for them a couple of times but had quickly realised that renting independently was a better financial option, than what was on offer from Andy at that place.

Dougie told Sheriff that he was staying at 'Centrepoint', that it was his birthday on Monday, and that he was going back to Glasgow to find Graeme. Sheriff knew that he had time to pass this information onto Andy, as it was Friday, and Dougie would be at 'Centrepoint 'for the weekend.

Sheriff invited Dougie for a cola in the 'Wimpy Bar', where he was able to get a good idea about what Dougie had been doing for the last six months, realising why he was of value and of interest to Andy. Dougie asked Sheriff questions about what music he liked best, and established that Sheriff was into funk and soul and asked where he came from as he had dark skin and a different accent to anyone else, he had ever met. Sheriff told him he came from Bradford, and talked about some of the clubs in London, adding that Dougie would need to be a bit older to stand any chance of getting in. Dougie showed Sheriff the two packets of coke, and the pills, he had found at Denning's place, and Sheriff's eyes widened as he looked at the white powder, knowing that they had street value. He told Dougie he could get a cash return for them. Dougie offered Sheriff a pill and took one himself saying they make you feel free as if you can do anything. Sheriff knew they were amphetamines and questioned Dougie some more about Denning, asking if King was there too. Sheriff said he could get anything between one and two pounds for both packs and Dougie naively handed them over saying he would be happy with £2. Sheriff handed Dougie two £1.00 pound notes, and pocketed the cocaine, knowing the street value would be quadrupled for each. Sheriff kept looking around for Andy then invited Dougie to go to Playland with him, but Dougie made an excuse, about wanting to hang out here still hoping to find Graeme. Sheriff made his exit and went straight to Playland, but Andy was not around.

Chapter 67

Dougie made his way back to 'Centrepoint' at 7.40pm, not knowing where else to go, and hung around with the others who were waiting for the gates to open. The way that Centrepoint worked was that one full time paid worker would be responsible for that evening, night and morning shift, and would manage the case load, along with 5-6 volunteer staff, who worked a regular one night a week at the shelter.

One of them was the team leader, and usually the person with the most experience, or just had the right aptitude to train, galvanise and organise the volunteers. Volunteers were charged with physical, hygienic and caring roles to support the practical and emotional needs and demands of the residents.

Young people could legally be supported by Centrepoint between 16 and 21, with an up to age of 25 years old, if they could be of some help, but staff were reviewing the upper age range due to the increasing need to offer a service geared more specifically to 16- to 21-year-olds.

It was illegal to accommodate under sixteens, but Centrepoint knew that there was a moral argument, and took the risk with the law, in the knowledge that they were providing specific short-term emergency help. Not aiding and abetting underage young people from running away from home. They were always aware of the consequences if something went wrong.

The volunteers would arrive at 7pm and started to organise the food for the evening. Preparing the beds ready for sleeping and arrange the social area. The paid worker would have been fully briefed by the full-time day worker, who had received all of the feedback from the advice, housing, drug and other assorted agencies, when coming on shift at 5.30pm. The full-time worker would gather the volunteers together, before the gates were opened to fully brief them on who and what they would be expecting that evening.

Eventually dead on eight o'clock the gates were opened, and a small melee of young people pushed their way to the front knowing that they had their place booked, leaving the others to step back and wait for their turn, knowing that they would be called forward soon. The main full-time worker had a clipboard and called out the names in order, briefly chatting to the residents who were happy and relieved to be safe, fed, comforted and back for another night.

Chapter 68

Dougie was bouncing around the group, annoying some of them still high from the pill he had taken with Sheriff earlier. Sarah, who was the full-time worker that night, had her notes from the Soho Project and was expecting Dougie knowing his vulnerability, but was also concerned about his erratic behaviour. She took Dougie away from the waiting residents to the far end of the passageway entrance. Knowing by experience that he had taken something. She asked him about his excited and loud behaviour, and informed him clearly, that, people who are taking unhealthy substances cannot use this place. She added, we want you to stay, but first you need to tell me what you have been taking. Dougie quickly realised that they were seriously challenging him and decided to show Sarah the few remaining pills he had, saying, "Here you can have them all". Sarah asked if that was all of them, questioning, "do you know what they are"? Dougie explained that someone had given them to him, and that they made you feel good, and awake. His feeling of familiarity to this place was changing. He stepped back thinking that he was not going to be allowed to stay. Sarah quickly reassured him that he could stay but needed to eat something, drink lots of fluids to help flush whatever he had taken through his system, and to sleep if he could. She informed Dougie that she would dispose of the remaining pills and that he needed to turn up in a better state tomorrow before his return to the Soho Project on Monday. They walked Dougie into the main social area where she introduced Dougie to Kathy who was the volunteer team leader. She helped Dougie sort out a hot drink and some food. Sarah then went back to the gate to process the rest of the night's residents.

Centrepoint log: Dougie Banner DOB 02-09-1959
Date: 30-08-1974

Dougie was waiting at the gate and seemed very lively. I had to take him aside from the other residents and inform him about our drug rules. I decided to still let him in, as it is clear that he is vulnerable, young and needs lots of support, but I needed to make clear about our expectations.
He seemed to understand and responded well after my warning. Kathy spent the most time with him this evening and thinks he has been involved in the rent scene. Need to try to get a bit more from him tomorrow evening.

Sarah.

Dougie spent Saturday walking around the West End but kept coming back to Piccadilly and Leicester Square. He would be drawn to the railings where the other boys congregated, like a moth to a flame. Something pulled him in, his thoughts transfixed by the mysterious prospect of meeting someone new, finding Graeme, and playing cat and mouse with Andy.

Sheriff spotted Dougie as he approached and quickly walked across Shaftsbury Avenue to Playland to report into Andy.

It was a warm, yet balmy evening in the centre of London and the tumbling rolls of thunder could be heard echoing in the distance, followed by the flashes of lightning that sparked across the sky.

Andy made his way to Dougie largely unseen, before making himself known by standing tightly up against him, arms locked onto the railing, smiling and asking, "where have you been mate". Dougie scared and shocked, turned around and tried to duck under the tightly locked arms, of the older man, who stood over him. Andy pushed in closer to consolidate his hold.

Dougie looked straight at him and shouted, "let me go, I'm not going back there". Andy calmly reassured Dougie that everything was fine and loosened his grip slightly, saying, "I can't make you stay with them, it's your choice". Then let go completely, as he noticed that he had a few people glaring at him. He continued to remind Dougie that it was his choice, and he had heard that he had been staying at 'Centrepoint', and that was good, asking, "What are you going to do for money, I can still help you with business". Dougie looked about and could see that some people were watching, and spotted Sheriff, and at that moment realised that it was he who had grassed him up to Andy. Sheriff stayed well back and waited to find out how this would play out, but Andy stepped away, recognising that Dougie would be around for some time, and could be a useful little money earner at some point in the future. He handed Dougie a couple of pounds and reminded Dougie that he was always around if he ever needed work, before striding away from the rails towards Shaftsbury Avenue.

Sheriff approached and asked what was going on, but Dougie less naïve now, was wise enough not to trust Sheriff again, but kept his options open, informing Sheriff that he must know Andy if he worked around here. Sheriff looked away awkward and clumsily reached into his pocket and offered Dougie a cigarette, which Dougie took knowing that he had one over on Sheriff, and had learnt that this world of rent boys was ruled by survival of the fittest

Chapter 69

Dougie was welcomed back into 'Centrepoint 'on Saturday evening and the atmosphere was friendly and full of optimism, as residents spoke about turning things around, sorting themselves out, finding work and a place to live. It made Dougie think more about home, his sisters and Graeme. Music from Radio one was being played in the social area, with 'Sugar Baby Love', followed by 'Waterloo 'by ABBA that seemed to raise the spirits of the room as the sound filled the space in between the laughter and continual murmurings of the group in the packed room. It was a hot thundery summer evening, and the rain had only briefly appeared earlier at 6.00pm, lasting minutes, but freshened up the dusty streets enough to feel and smell like the air was momentarily clean.

Dougie played cards with Bonnie and Stuart and two other boys, one of which was a volunteer at the night shelter. Then at 10.00pm as the other players moved away, Dougie found himself chatting to Mark about what he wanted to do next. He told Mark that he realised that he had missed home, particularly his friend Graeme, who he had originally come to London with. Mark had let Dougie know that he was Gay, so was able to explain how hard it had been for him when he was under 21. That the 'coming out 'to his parents was the most difficult thing he had ever done. Dougie spoke about being

Gay too, but did not mention his mum other than to say, 'even if I told her she would just dismiss it or call me a nasty name'.

He talked to Mark about Graeme, while also making it clear that he had also been with older men. He tried to explain that some but not all of the older men he had been with were nice people. But if his family knew about them how difficult it would be to live at home. His mum and sisters who were all Catholics and would plainly not accept what he had done or that he was gay.

Dougie was happy and confident and found him-self flirting with Mark and becoming aroused with the thought of a liaison.

Mark informed Dougie that he was worried about him as nobody can survive London without money, support and a place to stay and told him that he needed to at least reach 16 years to be able to live within the law, work, and get somewhere to stay.

Dougie thought he had it all worked out and told Mark, when I go back, I can stay with Graeme. Mark told him that sometimes what you want and what you get are two completely different things, particularly if you are under sixteen and gay. He explained that his mother had specific legal duties of care and that under the law he should be at home, or if the authorities so decide could be placed in another supervised environment like a Children's Home. Dougie listened, realising that his options were limited.

They were all called to get to bed and move to the basement area where bunks were made and ready for each resident. The final song rang out on the radio, 'Band on the

Run' by Wings, which played like a tribute to the bedraggled mix of young people, all looking for their own personal way to find some security, peace, harmony and a way to move forward with their lives.

Centrepoint log: Dougie Banner. DOB 02-09-1959. Date: 31-08-1974

Dougie was happy and in control when he arrived with no sign of substance abuse. Bonnie and Stuart have befriended him and seem like a positive influence. Dougie once again came across as confident, playing cards most of the evening with Mark who seemed to gain in confidence. Mark said that he clearly described himself as gay, and that he was knowledgeable and open about his sexual experiences, which have included an older boyfriend, and some older men that he did not want to discuss and closed up when I tried to query some of what he was talking about. His mum and family do not know he is gay and he is pretty adamant that he will not go home, as life was impossible for him in that house. Mark added that he was worried about him as he is going through a lot. We need to feed this all onto Soho Project on Monday morning.

Janice

It was a long weekend full of anticipation for the occupants who streamed out of the side door, at eight o'clock, onto Dean Street, on a Sunday morning. The residents moved wearily along the streets, separating and making their own way in differing directions. The long day until 8.00pm was a journey to be taken by all, as time slowly slipped on.

Dougie started by walking with Bonnie and Stuart again, but left them by noon. He sat around Trafalgar Square and then onto Leicester Square and while sitting watching the flashing light surrounding the Odeon Cinema was approached by two very tall Policemen. They had trailed Dougie from Trafalgar Square and decided to stop and question him. Dougie felt threatened, but decided to play it cool, and answer their questions pretty honestly. With a few slight deviations from the truth, he gave his real name, but changed his year of birth, to September 1958 and that he was sixteen tomorrow. That his mother knew he was in London as it was his birthday. He tried to explain that he had stayed at 'Centrepoint' over the weekend, that they were sorting him out with a place to work and live. However, he was shocked to find that the Police were going to take him to the Police Station, as he was underage and listed as a missing person.

Dougie tried to explain that the Soho Project were dealing with it, but it made no difference, and they escorted him to West End Central Police Station where the desk Sergeant called for a Westminster Emergency Social Services worker to attend an interview to act as an independent responsible adult, as they explained police procedure. Which was that Dougie would be detained until officers from the Clydeside Police could arrange for Dougie to be picked up.

Dougie waited for what felt like a day. By late afternoon he was informed that he would be collected sometime in the next 12 hours and returned to Scotland.

Centrepoint log: Dougie Banner. DOB 02-09-1959. Date: 01-09-1974

Dougie did not show up tonight, which is worrying. Bonnie and Stuart said that they had been with him up to about 12.30 and that they had not seen him since?
I will report to the Soho Project in the morning.

Linda

Chapter 70

Stephen two days ago, countdown - Monday 24-01-1983.

I walked away from the Soho Project and my over riding feeling of failing friends, Centrepoint and myself, washed over me like a dark cloud that enveloped my heart and soul. I felt useless and after taking the codeine I searched in my pockets for the Amps that I had bought from Sam Blackburn, and swallowed a handful, struggling to consume them without a drink, but eventually got them down. My forearms were throbbing, and it was a cold late January morning. I felt useless and wondered where my friends had gone.

Instinctively I seemed to walk to Soho Square, and aimlessly made my way along Oxford Street, then into the underground at Oxford Circus to find some warmth. I sat on the longest line, coloured light blue on the tube map. The Victoria Line tube train allowed at least 50 minutes dazed half sleep until you reached Walthamstow Central. There the train stopped, as it was the end of the line. Once at a standstill I was encouraged to disembark the train, by the attendant station staff and had to wearily cross the platform before taking the next waiting train south towards Victoria Station and Brixton.

I would find myself, sleeping and waking as the regular jerking motion brought about a broken half sleep, my mind full of drifting thoughts, and memories. Only to be jerked back to reality with the stops and momentary pauses.

The doors opened and closed, bringing that mixture of cold and warm air venting through the carriage with repetitious draughts of dusty toxic currents that flowed along the tunneled chasms, washing through the carriage at every door opening, forming a thick vapor that hung in the atmosphere until the next stop. My thoughts were full of gloomy psychotic imaginings fueled by the amphetamines. I portrayed as a lonely troubled, mumbling person, caught up in a frenzied battle with him-self. Fifty-five minutes later I eventually reached the end of the line again, where my despair, dejection and feelings of hopelessness dragged me down even further to an all-time catastrophic low.

Chapter 71

Stephen age 16

Stephen was sixteen and felt free to be what he was and do what he wanted. He did not go back to school, refusing, by leaving 'Glenallen' in the morning and then making his way by bus into the middle of Edinburgh where he discovered the Royal Terrace. His school days were over anyway because of the summer recess, as was his old life.

He would hang out along Princes Street and the Park, near to the public toilets and observe the casual trade, associations and clandestine comings and goings in the City Centre. Stephen would admire the view of Edinburgh Castle that stood majestically on the hill, across the valley gardens. It was magnificent, accurately reflecting all the tourist images. He would make his way past Waverly Station, thinking that soon he would get back on a train to London.

On the second day he headed to Carlton Hill arriving during the mid-morning. He noticed a tall smartly dressed boy hanging out by the big house, who seemed to be on the lookout for something or someone, before moving off walking in the direction of the hill. By early afternoon the boy had returned and was sitting by the Edinburgh Nelson Monument. Stephen walked towards him feeling a connection and kinship to this boy, who seemed to hold an attraction, as he glanced in Stephen's direction. Stephen found that his new bold persona was able to take the lead, by introducing himself.

He sat near and then offered him a ciggy. Craig smiled and took the cigarette, nodding with an accepting gesture, "I saw you here yesterday, Carlton Hill's a nice place to hang out in the summer".

Craig was a loner but seemed happy to acknowledge Stephen. This was one of Edinburgh's pick-up places and was a short walk from The Royal Terrace and Regents Terrace, which was where local rent boys hung out. Stephen was curious and quickly established that Craig was an experienced rent boy in Edinburgh and that they had this in common. Stephen told him that he had been to London and spoke to him about Dougie, 'Centrepoint', and the boys in Piccadilly Circus. Craig was a young 19-year-old and nodded knowingly at what Stephen was saying but seemed less than impressed. Craig talked about trade here, pointing in the direction of the terrace, saying, "I feel safer here in Edinburgh, with what I know and those I can trust".

Stephen waited a while, but Craig had very little to add, before walking over to a grass area where he laid down, seemingly to sleep. Stephen made his way back to the road and started to walk along the Terrace. He was surprised to find a car slowing down close to him. A male in his mid-forties rolled down the window and asked Stephen if he wanted a ride. Stephen was curious and asked where he was going. The man said anywhere you want if the price is right. Stephen was taken back by the directness of the offer but thinking fast replied by stating his charge and what he was prepared to do for the cash. Stephen sat in the front seat with the man who drove a short distance before parking in a quiet corner of the Royal terrace. The driver pushed his reclining seat back, as did Stephen with the help of the excited punter, who unbuckled and quickly unzipped his trousers. Stephen made sure that he had his twenty pounds before he placed his hand on the excited punters erect cock and started to manipulate his piece. Stephen tentatively moved his face and mouth closer to his willing customer who placed his left hand on Stephen's head in an attempt to push him onto his phallic. Stephen closed his mind to the faint smell of stale urine as he allowed his mouth to move over this engorged headpiece moving as fast as he could hoping that his ejaculate would come quickly and that it would all be over. He wanked him hard and long and had to offer more head, but the male held back for what seemed to be the longest time. Eventually the man took his own cock in his hand, insisting that Stephen held his face close as he brought himself off, spunking over part of Stephen's cheek and on his own trousers that were ravelled around his thigh and groin. He thanked Stephen while searching along his car door compartment for tissues.

  Stephen walked the Royal Terrace most days and found that he was getting returning trade as well as some odd balls who struggled to do anything other than talk, declare their despair of life, mentioning suicide, some would masturbate themselves next to him sometimes expecting a helping hand. Stephen did not like what he was doing but did like the cash he had in his pocket

Chapter 72

Stephen was surprised at discovering celebrity status in Edinburgh, when a driver had pulled over and invited him to attend a party at a Royal Mansion house. The driver asked Stephen if he liked 'The Bay City Rollers 'and Stephen said, "yes I used to, are they going to be at the party"? The driver said, "they might be, I will make it worth your time". The party was in a smart 2nd floor, Edinburgh apartment, close to the High Street Royal Mile. When they arrived, the driver took Stephen into the kitchen, and at first glance Stephen could see that there was one other younger boy, moving between the kitchen, and a large comfortable lounge. Unfamiliar music was playing and two older men stood drinking and talking. While a third appeared from a stairway, followed by a pale freckled faced child of about 10 or 11 years old, who was dressed in a matching tartan Pyjama set.

He welcomed Barney, by asking, "what do we have here, he's a pretty thing". Barney smiled back at Tam, pleasingly bearing his acquisition, like the displaying of a trophy and said, "A good find Tam, this wee chicken is Stephen, and I picked him up along the Royal Terrace".

Stephen could see a picture of the Bay City Rollers on the hallway wall that featured the band and this older man standing in the middle holding a gold disc. As Stephen looked at the picture, he realised that this was the same man who had just come down the stairs. Tam asked if Stephen, liked that shower of shit, adding "they have had their day, time to move on", and said, "the next big thing will be Bilbo Baggins' my new band, they will be coming later", and waving around a single record sleeve said, "this is their new track, She's Gonna Win".

He moved to the lounge and placed the record on the playing deck, and the upbeat track started. He clumsily moved to the beat, and said, "the kids will love it, what do you think Stephen". Stephen felt nervous and a touch self-conscious at being put on the spot without even hearing the whole song, but said, "sounds nice, it has a good beat".

Tam smiled with a degree of distain, as he turned away from Stephen, muttering "nice". He approached the other two males, who were holding drinks and laughed as he informed them that he needed something stronger than that to keep him going. He took something from a sideboard draw and emptied a small plastic bag containing cocaine onto a tabletop and proceeded to arrange it into small piles of four lines, two of which were quickly snorted. He grunted as the full effects of the inhalation hit him, then facing his guests he invited them to what was left while also pointing to the glass bowl full of assorted packets of pills.

Tam was centre stage, and pointed at Stephen, as though he was an object of servitude, to be used at will, then, looking at his guests, he said, "Chris this one is your type, Barney just picked him up from the Royal Mile". Stephen instantly recognised him as the man who had approach Dougie and himself at 'Top of the Pops'. He had his business card back in his bag at Glenallen, but it was the other man who seemed the most interested in Stephen and asked him if he was a local lad. Chris Denning walked toward Tam Paton and talked about Bilbo Baggins, and that Derek and Lightning Records would promote and make this a big hit. He asked about the band, and Tam informed Denning that they were a mature bunch not like Nobby, Nob head, and the Rollers. Stephen realised that Denning did not seem to remember him, and showed little interest other than, later in the evening, offered him a drink and something from the glass bowl that resembled tablets in gold and silver wrappers, which Stephen turned down.

Chapter 73

It was early evening and there was still plenty of Northern light in late August, though the nights were starting to slowly draw in. Stephen could hear the sound of bag pipes echoing across the way, from the kitchen window, which prompted him to look out of the casement, where he could clearly see Edinburgh Castle, lit up and to the left, finding that he had a good view of Princess Street gardens straight in front, and Waverly Station directly to the right.

Shortly afterwards the band arrived as a group of four. They awkwardly stood around drinking and interacting with Denning, Paton and Derek, inwardly questioning the presence of the children and Stephen. They talked about the new record, and Tam held a toast 'to success'. After an hour the band looked and felt uncomfortable and awkward before thanking their hosts and making a hasty exit. Stephen was aware that he was going to break his Glenallen curfew but was more concerned that he hadn't been paid yet and asked Barney "how long will this party be going on for", and Barney replied, "as long as Tam wants it to". He handed Stephen a £10.00 note and reminded him that he would get another £20.00 in the morning. The younger boys disappeared upstairs, and Stephen felt vulnerable and alone as Derek made an obvious play for him, sitting close with his arm across his shoulder. Stephen sensed a growing discomfort in the presence of these four men, deciding to cut and run at his first opportunity. Derek had made his way back to the other men who were drinking and toasting success.

Stephen pretended that he needed the toilet and found a back door leading from the rear part of the kitchen and exited down the fire escape stairs as quickly as he could. With great relief found him-self back out onto North Bridge Road, where he knew his way to Waverly Station and his bus back to Glenallen. He was late but arrived at a time that raised few eyebrows.

Chapter 74

Stephen had learnt and now knew that renting in Edinburgh was how he could earn enough money to get himself back to London by early September, and that if he could do it here, he could do it in London.

It was Saturday, September 2nd and he planned his departure by saving enough money to get him a train ticket, and maybe a place to stay in London. He decided not to tell anyone at Glenallen that he was leaving, even though the boys kept asking. To his surprise, Spanner seemed the most vociferous, almost badgering Stephen with questions insisting that he could come with him.

Stephen knew that Spanner was a liability and pacified him by saying you need to be sixteen, with which Spanner replied, 'you were 15 when you went, I need to get out of this place, I will go soon". He then spiraled off around the room, as was his want, banging on walls, touching and prodding other residents, until he was thumped hard on the shoulder by Greg who told him to, "fuck off, you little pervert". Spanner reeled back in pain, holding his right arm, shouting "you cunt, that fucking hurt". He moved to the door scowling with anger, and punched it, and then opened it with his left arm, only to find Stringer standing on the other side looking menacingly in the direction of the boy. He took Spanner firmly by his uninjured arm and escorted him to the office reminding him to calm down. Spanner angrily screamed that

Greg had punched him and that he should be the one to get into trouble. Spanner became hysterical, as his anxiety around Stringer was greater than his fear of Greg. He resisted for a short time, before Stringer dragged him away, while threats were obviously being spoken, directly and quietly, into Spanners right ear. This confirmed Stephen's need to get away, and he decided that it would be tomorrow, where he would take his stuff and catch an early morning train to Kings Cross.

Chapter 75

The sun was shining most of the way, with short heavy bursts of rain that trickled beaded long lines down the window forced back by the motion of the fast train.

1978 had been an inconsistent summer in Scotland. Wet and cool with odd days where the sun, was covered by clouds, that had hung on for days. When Stephen arrived in London it was a warm early September afternoon. He sensed the same excitement as he had in May when he made his first visit, but had more cash in his pocket this time, and felt an added confidence knowing where he was headed.

Stephen's first thought was to get to the Dilly and maybe find Dougie, but this time he used the underground train from Kings Cross on the Piccadilly Line to the Circus. He arrived on the concourse outside of the Criterion Theatre close to Eros and looked across the road to see if there was anyone he might remember along the 'meat rack'. Then onto the 'Playland' arcade, where he hoped he might find Dougie, but not Andy, wondering if the conflict had now been resolved.

Stephen made his way to the railings outside of the Wimpy Bar and recognised Lance who was chatting and laughing with a boy, that Stephen had seen before but did not know his name. Lance saw Stephen and invited him over, saying "hi man, long time no see, how yer going". Stephen explained that he had just got in and asked where Keith was.

Lance explained that he went home to his mum's, after being threatened and smacked about a bit by Andy's crew, "that bastard". "Dougie has been keeping his head down, he is around, but not sure where, are you here to stay?" Stephen said, "is he OK" meaning Keith, but Lance looked puzzled and answered "not sure, Dougie is a law unto himself", Stephen laughed at the confusion and told Lance that he had money and needed somewhere to stay, hoping that Lance might offer, but Lance was not in a position to invite or offer accommodation as he had lost his bedsit flat now that he was on his own again.

They talked about trying 'Centrepoint' and Lance was up for that, as he had not tried to get in there for some time. Stephen felt happy that he had met Lance and the two of them seemed to get along, so they decided to make their way off and around, laughing at jokes and banter that easily flowed and filled the space. They walked towards Covent Garden, stopping off at a café for a Coca Cola and sausage sandwich. Lance had some pills and offered Stephen a couple, saying, "they will keep you going", and as the night drew on they moved onto Sundowners at Charing Cross. Lance had told Stephen about 'Bang" a Monday Gay Night, night Club that was the best place to get out of your head and end up with someone and somewhere to stay. But that it would be difficult, as they had tightened their entry policy to 21 only, so they had to rely on sneaking in with someone influential, or they would not stand a chance.

Later when they arrived Lance was confident enough to approach several single males waiting to get in and asked if they could get them past the bouncers. Most walked on by, but some of the groups, who were clearly already high, flirty and looking for fun, crowded around the boys saying, "stay close and follow our lead". They brazenly cocooned the boys in the heart of their group, while paying the entrance fee for themselves and the boys.

The audacious approach worked and got them in, until an eagle-eyed bouncer noticed the boys move away from the group and onto the main dance floor where D.J. Gary London was introducing the next track 'Play that Funky Music' by Wild Cherry, and the vibe took hold of Stephen as he remembered his evening with Dougie at 'Glades'. He instantly found easy movement, as the mood took hold of him. Lance went along with him, impressed by his freedom and style of dance as he shifted from bump and grove, arms raised with a shift of hip rotation. The balance and panache of the pair drew the attention of the other gay men in the room. It also drew the attention of the security men who waited their time, until they were able to quietly but firmly escort the boys outside where they asked them for some form of identification, which they obviously did not have.

It was late evening, and all the theatergoers had long gone home. Lance and Stephen were ready to take their chance at 'Centrepoint' and decided to make up some false names and identities before ringing the bell. Two staff members appeared and listened to the boy's stories, but they struggled to swing their tales without reinforcing a point while striving to keep a straight face. After some discussion, and deliberation the 'Centrepoint' staff brought them in. They knew that their stories were on the whole bogus, but decided to let them in anyway, as they recognised that they were young, vulnerable, and it was important to get them off the streets, so that they could better make a judgment in the morning.

Stephen and Lance were shown to a bunk bed and allowed to stay the night.

Centrepoint log : Stevie Clements. DOB 01-06-1959. 04-09-1976.

Stevie arrived last night, late with his friend Desmond Johnson. They both said that they were 17 years old and that they had missed their last train home. Desmond was the most talkative explaining that they had come to the West End for a night out, and someone had told them about this place. Stevie clearly followed his lead and was carrying a small haversack. I felt that they knew their way around the West End and also knew where they were going once in the 'night shelter'. Will talk some more in the morning.

Centre point log: Desmond Johnson. DOB 21-08-1959. 04-9-1976.

Desmond arrived late last night with Stevie Clements. They both said that they were 17 years old and that they had missed their last train home. Desmond seemed familiar, talkative and friendly and we suspect he has stayed here before but felt it was important to get them both off the streets. Will follow this up in the morning.

Centre point log : Lance Johnson. DOB 21-08-1958
05-09-1976. Morning:

Once up and eating breakfast, Jean informed me that Desmond is Lance, who is aged 18 and has stayed here before at various times. She remembers him from 9 months ago. She talked to him this morning and he recognised that he had been found out but said that Stevie was new to the West End, and was 16 years old, and that he was looking after him. I talked to them both and explained that they should go to 'Alone in London Service' (ALS), for some advice and accommodation, as that was where Lance had gone for support before, and what is more important, he trusts and likes them. Lance was happy to do this and thanked me for the travel vouchers. I explained that we would be in contact with ALS, and they would feed back to us later in the day, and that if you both need another stay at the night shelter, we would follow their lead. Neither had any ID and both seemed happy and supportive towards each other. Lance has used us on three separate periods in the past, staying for various lengths of time, and in general he got himself sorted with accommodation.

Sharon.

Stephen and Lance made their way to 'Playland' and hung out on a favourite pinball machine and later spent the day cruising the Dilly where punters or their representatives, approached agreed terms, fully appreciating the services on offer.

Lance was a pretty, popular boy, and was in demand by punters because he was different to the regular boys; his Afro Caribbean ethnicity offered the mainly White and Arabic male punters something different.

Stephen was of interest because he looked young, and with the help of some of Lance's pills, found that he could nullify and suppress how this all made him feel by taking the pills to help him get through it, knowing that he was able to add to his stash of cash with every encounter.

Later in the day they were fortunate to be offered a sharing apartment with another Dilly boy called Stanley, who had access to a flat that had been left to him to look after, by an 'old boy' actor boyfriend who was working in the States for several months. Trusting Stan enough to take care of it while he was gone, while always expecting the worst.

They found that paying their way was possible, but money came and went easily, particularly when drugs and other necessities were needed. Stephen grew in confidence with Lance on the meat rack but was also on the constant lookout for Dougie.

Chapter 76

In time Stephen became dependent to the rent boy existence. Obsessed by the excitement of being wanted and desired. Payment for services provided him with the means to carry on but in general he hated the physical demands of what he was expected to do, often informing punters and friends that he was not queer.

However, he wanted to keep face with Lance and the other boys. Money was the driving force, along with the thrill and exposure to the many differing punters lifestyles who used their flats, some with humble ordinary homes, rooms in friends houses, and others who had the finances to afford hotels, private apartment, cars, Turkish baths, and saunas. There were clandestine, surreptitiously organised meetings, or single casual connections when time and opportunity became available to the individual. Parties, social gatherings in posh houses in the country and around the city were sometimes available, and he heard of some boys being invited onto yachts. Again, usually organised by a third party like Andy, who would recruit with specific requirements or by a particular age range that was required for the influential paying customer.

The Police had picked up Stephen for minor crimes, which included shoplifting, stealing drinks from small shops and possession of pills, mostly poppers. He was issued a warning, reports were raised but there was no attempt to repatriate him back to Scotland without his consent now that he was sixteen.

As Stephen got to know more of the regulars, some bore witness about Jimmy Savile, along with conversations concerning other famous important and rich people. He heard stories about renters who had known boys that had been taken onto boats and yachts from a Jersey Children's home.

Some were never seen again. It was also said, as part of the rumours and gossip among the rent boys who had been in care that "one day it will all come to the surface, and they will find the bodies. Hopefully those rich bastards will be found out".

Chapter 77

Dougie aged 15 had been home for six weeks and he was finding it hard living within his own mother's rules. He had visited Graeme, but his mother informed Dougie that Graeme had returned home, way back in the Spring, with a friend from London, and had gone travelling to Thailand with him in late May.

The police had taken Dougie home on his birthday. It was late and his sisters were concerned and welcoming, while his mother was distanced, almost reluctant to engage with Dougie other than to remind him that his bedroom was as he left it, and that he had to go back to school and be home by six o'clock. His sisters asked questions about where he had been and prepared him some food. Dougie eventually fell back in his room and for a while, enjoyed the familiarity and security his home offered.

He met up with William who had matured in some ways, with a visible dark moustache line across his top lip. He also had fluffy sideburns, longer hair and a noticeably deeper voice. He no longer sang in the church choir. The young teen had grown slightly taller and was losing some of that puppy fat, but Dougie still viewed him as a nice friendly lardy lump. William was surprised and excited that Dougie had returned, anticipating his special bond with Dougie would continue, knowing that they had shared a moment together, which William was sure, Dougie would remember. However,

Dougie wanted to distance himself from William, as he desired more, and found, when walking about in between bunking school that he was attracted to older men or the biker builder types.

An older lady, from the church visited Dougie. A do-gooder who wanted to talk to him about where he had been and what had happened, but she struggled to move past saying, "my name is Celestine, and I am here to talk, and be here for you". Then she spoke about how nice his mum and sisters were, that Father Ball had said a prayer for him, and wanted to know that he was safe, and carried on saying "I bet you are happy to be back home and at school, you seem to be fine, how are your friends, and we are all missing you at church". He hated the hypocrisy of his Catholic school, which promoted obedience to the church, its leaders and family. He refused to go to church, which added to the chasm that had built up and continued to develop between himself and his mother. Even if she only knew what had happened between Greame and himself she would have condemned his actions as a sin let alone what he had done with all those older men. His battle of wills with her were unflinching, and they rarely talked to each other, avoiding contact in the kitchen, and they hardly ever spent any time together in the same room.

What he had experienced with Father O'Brian, Andy and the older men was buried away in the recesses of his mind, somewhere deep inside the confusion of his abused adolescence. He could not deny his newfound sexual and sexualised knowledge, experience and understanding, which would require him to seek out more.

He found himself hanging out in Elder Park where he had first met Graeme. Very soon he made money from what he had learnt to do and was good at. He established regulars and was able to save enough money to be able to make his way back to London and the Dilly, craving the excitement he felt that he deserved.

Chapter 78

On arrival at Piccadilly Circus in November he quickly realised that the winter experience was harder than the Summer. He soon made associations with other renters and some older adults who would allow and take risks with longer stays in their homes. Dougie tried his hand at 'Centrepoint' a couple of times, giving a false name and age. At one time he carried off a two-night stay, which was challenged by the worker in charge on the third night where he was found out. He was offered support from the Soho Project, but Dougie had no intention of going back home.

During this time, he met up with Andy at numerous occasions, who invited Dougie and others to earn some cash through his contacts, which Dougie did, hating many, if not all of the situations he had found himself in, but wanted to earn and liked to have money in his pocket.

The secrecy of the liaisons with prominent people, involved surreptitious arrangements linked to clandestine groups, who were protected by a higher force. Those males who used Andy's services wanted exclusivity and privacy and exploited places like Dolphin House, Cedra Court, Elm Guest House, Central West End Hotels and other Private Apartments, with the attitude that they paid their money, expecting and deserving their rewards. Supposing that those little rent boys knew what they were doing and loved it.

Police Officers referred to the boys as being 'Street Rats' knowing that their own police procedures for looking after these children, found on the streets, were rudimentary at best and that underlying factors were never really tackled by Scotland Yard. Sexual exploitative activity in Piccadilly and around Playland was rife and investigating officers felt that all they could do was to 'firefight 'the problem. This meant that abused children were either returned to where they had runaway from or ignored by the Authorities.

Dougie had learnt that these associations paid well, but there were added perks, and other ways of making even more from the encounters.

Dougie grew adept at gathering up any and all drugs that were made available throughout the parties. Which as a consequence allowed him to build up his own supply, some of which he used to help himself endure some of the personal services he was asked to perform. He found that the head rush of Amyl nitrate (Poppers) produced and assisted some of his punter's erectile issues. Subsequently promoting a rapid outcome, so that he could get it over with quickly and then play it nice and easy until he could make his exit.

He became well known for supplying other renters, who also needed the masking qualities the drugs provided and the 'pick you up' to play the game. The street value also turned over a few extra bob, which allowed Dougie to play the clever rent boy game, on his own terms and in his own way.

The ever-present supply and demand for substances, not only for renters but also punters was constant. He learnt from other users how to mix and match, crushing cheaper tablets and mixing with some of the good stuff, or even adding other powders to bulk it out a bit, using cling film to package it up into smaller saleable portions

Chapter 79

The following Springtime Dougie was picked up by the police again in London and held in custody until he gave them details that could be verified. The police followed procedure and returned him to Clydeside, where they were surprised to find that his mother had not registered him as missing, and was ambivalent about him being returned to her. She took him back but informed social services and Dougie that she was not prepared to go through this again, distancing herself even more from her son. His sisters tried to find out where he had been, privately guessing about his sexuality, naively not really knowing what to think.

Chapter 80

Dougie soon returned to London and was as confident and resourceful as ever. When he turned sixteen, in early September 1975, he felt an independent freedom that allowed him to be more focused, seeking out a direction, as he wanted to do something with his life.

It was late summer, and Dougie was enterprising enough to persuade Andy to pay him more, if he supplied other younger renters, as and when they were needed. He also had his drug sideline.

Dougie used 'Centrepoint' a couple of times, and even went back to the Soho Project, during some low points, or when he thought that he should try to get a job, find somewhere to live, and be more normal. He had also met up with Lawrence on the Dilly, an understanding older punter civil servant, who liked the company of willing teenage boys. He liked them to be pretty and particularly those who could satisfy his sexual fantasies and needs.

Dougie stayed with him through the worst part of the winter, knowing that he was liked. Lawrence allowed him to remain at his apartment, giving him a key, so that he could come and go freely, up to a point, as long as he did not bring anyone else back. Dougie was more than happy with this arrangement, as the apartment was in Brewer Street, just around the corner from the Dilly. Allowing him to take selected, good paying punters, back during the day, while giving him enough time to clear up before Lawrence returned from work.

Lawrence was happy for a while, until Dougie messed it up more than once, by turning up drunk, and a little high. The relationship changed when Lawrence returned home early to find Dougie crushing some pills in his pestle and mortar, then splitting and dividing his stash with cocaine. Dougie became angry and abusive when Lawrence challenged and chastised him about splitting the drugs, in his flat, which brought back memories of his mother and Frankie. In the morning Lawrence informed Dougie that it was time to give the key back, as he could not be associated with dealing and the sale of drugs.

Chapter 81

Dougie spent the springtime of '1976' flat and room sharing with other renters, punters, and casual friends. He loved the pub, disco and club scene, feeling that it was made for him. Growing in confidence he had fun in mixed gender clubs and could draw a crowd when he made his moves, loving an upbeat dance session, progressing with girls, while also enjoying the exhibitionism and attention he received when dancing with male friends. He could be more provocative in a dance situation feeling it could be viewed as performance, an artistic interpretation in movement.

The gay scene in London was starting to develop with small hidden bars in cellars or pub discos. There had always been members clubs providing dinner, dance, cabaret and some dressing and camping up, but mostly within monied circles, who had the financial wherewithal to run and keep what they were doing private. When Dougie found him-self in these small venues, he could let go and share his fun-loving dance interactions with other men. He could steal the dance floor, put on a show, by being as provocative as he wanted or needed to be.

Chapter 82

Dougie dreamed that one day he would control and run his own venue, for his own community. His entrepreneurial instinct knew exactly what it would look like inside, the furnishings, colours, size, lighting, kind of music he would play, and the client group he would aim for. Very early on in his life he understood that gay men were marginalised and ostracised outside of their own groupings. That they were desperately seeking to find a way to meet each other and freely express themselves, particularly younger men, and teenagers who were stifled and closeted by society and the law.

    Dougie was able to display his dance moves and make acquaintances when attending the one-night private venues for gay men but knew that these places were restrictive and depended on a wealthy individual to organise and make it work. Older gay men like Lawrence were always anxious about being seen out for fear of being found out. The tabloids were always looking for the next political scandal. There were some who were prepared to flaunt it, and challenge how gay men and women were perceived, particularly with a growing number of actors, and musicians who were successful enough to be able to declared themselves as gay, bisexual or lesbian knowing that it would have little financial imprint on their professional lives, and willing to deal with the positive impact that coming out might have for the wider gay fraternity.

While others refused to 'come out' for fear of the repercussion and the impact it might have on their career.

Chapter 83

During 1977 Dougie established a reputation as a West Ender, who had his hands in most things, he was smart, likable, popular and a natural winner. He had used 'Centrepoint' again, a couple of times, stating that he wanted to sort himself out and find a proper place to live. The Soho Project had set him up with a short-term, supportive hostel based in Kensington, which he liked for a while. During his time in the hostel, he met other young homeless people who had struggled at home or in care. He was gaining a better understanding of how important it was that young people could gain back a life and security, while still enjoying being young and discovering all that can be positive about life.

Dougie enjoyed the contact with the staff at the hostel, but found it difficult when the questions and conversations became too painful to manage, knowing that he was only able to disclose questions from some of the issues that had affected him from his home life, let alone Father O Brian, Elm House and all the other escapades he had been involved in. They were helping him to find something more permanent, but before his accommodation was established he found himself drifting back to the Dilly for money, friendship, drugs and a need to be part of the immersive lifestyle that both repulsed and excited him. Dougie liked the company and the banter that he had developed with many of the boys who hung out on the meat rack, sustained by the hustle and drama of feeling that he was recognised as someone who had experience, and knew how to make the right moves, make money and have fun.

Chapter 84

Once again winter was drawing in and while hanging out at the Dilly, he recognised the guy he had been with at Jonathan Kings house and at 'The Hop'. Norman was having a stroll, cruising through Piccadilly, hoping to pick up a willing rent boy and was pleasantly surprised to meet up with Dougie again. They went for a drink and Dougie ended up back at Norman's place on a strict business arrangement at first. Norman lived in South Camden, which gained him easier access to the West End and where Decca Records office was based. He owned a ground floor flat on Drummond Street, which allowed him his own access through a front basement door, where he could move freely in his self-contained private space.

Norman commented on how Dougie had developed and grown since they last met four years ago. Norman liked the idea of spending more time with one person but was acutely attracted to young teenagers and had found it difficult forming lasting relationships with men of his own age. Dougie liked the idea of being under a roof, particularly during the winter, but was also happy with older male friends, and the benefits that could be gained from these associations, that usually involved some pocket money and gifts. He was not interested in being kept and hated those situations where the older man became controlling, demanding monogamy and love. Norman gave Dougie a key, but as with Lawrence, was clear about how and whom he used it with.

Dougie knew that this would suit him through the winter, and allow him to carry on working for Andy, while providing him with the time to hone and develop his interest in dealing in substances. Dougie would turn up and meet Norman at his Decca office, in Great Marlborough Street W1, which was a laugh and fine at first, but Norman found the whole thing a massive distraction and would try to find a way of moving Dougie on and out of the office as quickly as possible. It had stopped him from doing his job and was particularly difficult when he was dealing with some of his pop star clients.

The relationship endured into the following year to the point where Dougie was spending less time with Norman, who eventually asked for the key back, but insisted that they should remain friends, as he had really liked and in lots of ways loved his seven months with the young enigmatic Scotsman.

Chapter 85

Dougie occasionally, and for fun, had met and slept with some younger gay men who knew what they were, and what they wanted. One of them called 'Chris' had told him that there was a whole world of bold, young gay men who were desperately seeking to be recognised for who they were. They both accepted that it was difficult to be bold, loud and 'proud to be gay' aged under 21 years, when the law and society prevented you from being a couple, walking out in public, hold hands and hug, let alone kiss in the street.

Dougie occasionally met up with Chris, who was in his early 20's, and found himself attracted and interested in his unflinching attitude to 'Gay Rights'. Chris wanted to do something real about changing the law.

He took Dougie back to his 'Brixton squat' in Railton Road, where Dougie met up with Chris's friends who were similarly political and prepared to challenge the public's narrative and negative perception of homosexuals. They used the medium of social activism to share their thoughts and had set up 'Gay News' in 1972. Then the 'Gay Centre' followed by 'Gay Switchboard'. These places then provided gay Men and Women with a rallying point and a place to explore, argue and voice their civil rights interests.

Chapter 86

Dougie met the 15-year-old Stephen during late May 1978, in Soho Square, he was 18 years old and 19 in September. A fellow Scot that Dougie understood and could relate to. Stephen was young, pretty, and a good asset, particularly with Andy and his client wish list. He knew he could make money from him and with him. Knowing that he was a sitting duck ready to be picked up and consumed by the ever artful, Dougie. This was something he had learnt and done many times with other young people, becoming well practiced at the gentle grooming process.

Dougie introduced Stephen to his friends, in the coffee shop, who he knew would add the fun factor. He needed to work out what this younger boy was all about. Was he suitable for what he had in mind? What were his experiences, and would he be able to fit in with what would be asked of him. He soon realised that Stephen was a survivor, liked to smoke, had experienced taking pills and enjoyed the sensation it gave him. Dougie quickly established that Stephen had already picked up some of the skills necessary to endure the rent scene. He wanted to know him better would set him up at 'Centrepoint' tonight while he fulfilled a work commitment to Andy.

Two days later Andy threatened Dougie in Playland about the Rolex watch. Dougie argued and demanded his earnings then angrily walked off with Stephen and the Rolex.

They spent a day and evening together having fun at 'Top of The Pops' and the Arches 'Glades', Wednesday night gay party.

During this time, Dougie was anxious that Andy was after him and could do some serious harm knowing that the real issue was the Rolex watch. He had heard of the hard men that Andy employed to sort out any problems and did not want to get beaten up and threatened. Deep down he always felt that he could handle Andy because of their previous history. But he was also not prepared to give up something that he felt he had earned and deserved to have, from that fat pig politician, as he knew it was worth a lot of money. So, he decided to stay hidden and keep his head down low for a while by joining up with Chris again in the Brixton Squat.

Chapter 87

Chris was a strong-minded but loving individual, who liked the idea of having relationships, rather than casual sexual associations. The squat was daubed in slogans and statements that unapologetically claimed gay rights action; Pride, Equality, Lesbian and Gay Rights, Human Rights, Gay News, and The Gay Liberation Front'. There was a buzz about the various squats that met up in a large back garden, where fences had been removed, and all the gardens had become one. Dougie smoked dope, danced at will, and enjoyed a security with Chris and the group, that felt like an accepting family, who looked out for each other, providing support, education and a sense of community. He found himself listening to gay rights arguments, old blues music, smoking dope and becoming angry with the issues affecting his friends and his own life. He started to understand why some of his punters might have been driven to using male prostitutes through the security of private places and wealth.

Dougie stayed with Chris all year, and through to summer 1979, and felt a real affection for him. He had enjoyed the friendship, love and community that the Brixton squat scene had given him, while helping to sort him-self out, and manage the many angry thoughts that had been gestating in his head. A feeling of growth and maturity allowed Dougie to gather his views while formally being able to accept and like who he was. With the help of Chris, he was able to find a personal approval that verged on a positive form of self-esteem, knowing that he had much more to give and learn, always feeling that something good was coming.

Dougie had helped to run the weekly disco dance nights, enjoying the freedom to express himself and show off his knowledge of dance music. However, it was clear that he joined the squat at a time, when the many fractions of political groups that occupied the squats, were evolving, as their struggle and knowledge progressed.

People became more organised within the groups and buildings they occupied. Squatted offices and shops were raided by the police and closed down, but the reasoning and argument went on, as finance and newly squatted premises were found.

The community was scattering. The Brixton Gay Centre had shutters fixed many times against doors and windows, and that building was finally closed down by the local authority and police with permanent boarding in 1979. Long-term stable residents were moving on and the community diverted across south London. 'The London Gay Liberation Front' changed its identity to 'Brixton Faires', which became a theatre group promoting social change, addressing a range of issues about being gay, black and gay, lesbian, coming out, young and gay. Dougie liked this group the best but found the arguments about subject matter and objectives were divisive, too close to home and challenging, as it touched on his real-life experiences, something that he was not ready to share.

Dougie made some extra cash, buying and selling drugs within the communal and surrounding groups. He found that dope and grass were the preferred social highs in Railton Road. There were differing attitudes and views within the community towards heroin, poppers and cocaine, as many found themselves at a dichotomy of belief about drug practice and habit, arguing the hippy merits of self-perception through the use and control of some substances, but those who were in need of something stronger, were in general, frowned upon by the collective group, some of whom had taken harder drugs in the 60's and early 70's, and had witnessed many of the problems lysergic acid diethylamide (LSD) and heroin had caused to their friends, who became addicted to substances that consequently effected their personalities, and there was a general recognition that heroin in particular was a destructive force, particularly in this community, prompting some to become involved in drug advise and prevention work.

Chapter 88

Dougie still craved the hedonism of the West End. In general, the groups of activists at Brixton were older, militant and more serious in their effort to bring about a lasting change. Chris had become embroiled in the politics and the cause, unaware of losing sight of his relationship with Dougie.

Dougie was finding him too serious and got bored with the relationship. The thought and excitement of the Dilly was drawing him back, bit by bit with each visit.

He had taken trips in the vicinity at various times, to shop and be around Central London, still liking to look good, but was always aware that he might be spotted by Andy or associates, but if truth was told, he found it somewhat exciting, and after all this time, wondered if Andy would even still be interested in him anyway. Paradoxically he still had the Rolex watch, a constant reminder of his deviance, which he kept in his pocket or a safe place. The strap was too large to fit his wrist, and he had never got it adjusted to fit himself. He always thought of it as his insurance and would one day get it properly valued.

Chapter 89

On one of Dougie's excursions to the West End, during a late summer evening, while making his way along Oxford Street to Oxford Circus, he was drawn to turn left and tread his way down Regent's Street, and onto the Dilly, where he spotted Stephen and Lance playfully interacting outside of Lilywhites around the so-called Eros statue.

He decided to move closer before standing between the two of them, and with a big smile asked how they both were. Stephen was taken back by Dougies change of appearance, as he was sporting a dark moustache in the style of 'Freddie Mercury' and had cut his hair short and looked like a grown man. His usual confidence shone through, looking good in a tight black T-Shirt, studded leather jacket and charcoal straight jeans. He radiated a sexualised self-assurance and coolness that the 17-Year-old, Stephen had fantasised about.

The boys were happy and welcoming, continually asking questions, and doing everything they could to catch up with each other. Dougie inquired if Lance and Stephen were together, but Stephen laughed it off saying, "work and play have made us good friends". Dougie asked after Keith, and how was business? They replied by informing him 'that it was what it was, the usual'. Lance told Dougie that Keith had gone home, and that they were between places at the moment, and might give 'Centrepoint' a go tonight. Stephen then asked

Dougie what he was doing tonight. Dougie replied, "I have somewhere, but was thinking of hanging around, it would be a laugh to see if we could all still get into Centrepoint". Dougie asked about Andy, wondering if he was still around, and Lance quickly explained that Keith had been frightened and beaten up by Andy's crew last year when they were looking for you, and that yes, he was still about.

Dougie's mature appearance made him seem older than most on the Dilly, but he was still a young looking 20-year-old. He knew that his change of life had removed him from renting and wondered if he could still pull a punter, or if he even wanted all of that again.

Stephen, Lance and Dougie moved onto the 'Centrepoint' gates at 8.00pm, it was still light, and for a laugh; they queued up and waited in line to be interviewed. Paul was the worker that evening and his experience told him that these three had good previous knowledge of the West End, and quickly established that Alex, alias Dougie in particular, but probably all of them, had stayed at 'Centrepoint' before, suspecting a history. All three had spun a good story, but the boys quickly came clean as they laughed, realising that Paul was not going to let them in, even though he had not ever met them before. Paul was concerned for their safety, particularly the younger looking ones.

Their presence at the gate was provisionally recorded in a separate book, as most Centrepoint's guests were only logged in and out as individuals, with information, about their residency, support, ongoing housing, health and social wellbeing. This encounter would have been viewed as triers, with question marks about who they really were, and would sometimes get mentioned and picked up during a team meeting.

Chapter 90

Stephen, Lance, and Dougie moved back to Playland where Dougie felt safer with his boys, and if an encounter with Andy was apparent. They played the machines as the lights flashed, clackers flipped and lightening reverb smashed the steel ball about the many objects, ringing hit after hit, until it fell silent as the ball dropped to oblivion

'Playland' was full of lights and sound, as The Bee Gee's 'Tragedy' played across the loudspeakers. The Arcade was inhabited by the usual lost boys, some still not 16, available and aware of the predatory stances taken by the users. Punters stood around, playing the machines, looking to meet up with a young taker, offering free goes, while the older men often simply got pleasure from by being close, and watching the boys amuse themselves, intently trying to beat the pin ball or space invader machine.

Dougie was intent on having a good time, and wanted company, sharing quick snorts of the white stuff he had put aside for himself. The three of them made their way to 'The Sundowner' a new, increasingly popular London gay venue night club, in Charing Cross Road, that had been drawing in large numbers of gay men, who were seeking a bit of what was happening in New York's 'Studio 54'.

Some gay men in London were discovering and demanding newfound freedoms, which had been fought for through the Stonewall riots, and gay pride celebrations in

New York, through the early 70's, impacting on the gay movement, and politics of the day in the United Kingdom.

Dougie, Stephen, and Lance had managed to get in with the help of other partygoers. It was a hot, late September Friday night, and the gig was throbbing with a varying array of gay men, some of whom had come dressed to impress, with leather jackets and trousers, peaked caps necks adorned in silver chain and studs, mimicking the images viewed through the gay press and other underground publishing. While others had a more traditional suited look or wore tight fitting trousers and a statement shirt that enhanced muscles and torso, 'Boogie Wonderland' was bouncing out its rhythmic beats, Cuban heels moved and danced, denim and leather clad legs and groins interlocking, as the song slowed down to Donna Summer, 'Enough is Enough' followed by leather cowboy booted men, who rejoiced to 'In The Navy' , a gay anthem that required dancing in sequence, adding all the movements promoted by the song. The Village People's song recognised a statement of intent and power, that gay men were here, proud and nothing was going to stop them.

Stephen danced with Dougie again, and it felt natural, happy, and safe. The music continued with the best dance tunes of the year; Chic, 'Good times', Sister Sledge, 'He's the Greatest Dancer' and Funkadelic, 'Knee Deep'. Dougie helped to keep things going, for him-self and his friends, with some amphetamines laced with cocaine.

They carried it through to closing time at 1.00am and ended up meeting with a group who invited them back to a flat in Battersea, to continue the partying with as much self-indulgence as could be had.

Stephen was drunk, happy, and high, falling into bed with Dougie while the owners of the property, Simon and Daniel watched. They were both able to show off their well acquired skills, as Dougie and Stephen, standing on chairs, performed a spontaneous strip tease for their hosts, waving their dicks around, bending exposing their bum cheeks followed by a mutual fondled sex show. They then moved between their two onlookers, in an orgy of debauched drunken passion, demonstrating all that they had learnt and were good at.

Following the party, Stephen and Lance had hung around, in the building, for as long as they could, until finally recognised that they had outstayed their welcome. Dougie's cuckoo instincts calculated that he needed to move them on, if he was to stand any chance of affecting a continued stay, through the tryst he had developed with Simon in particular. Dougie arranged to return later.

Dougie made his way back to the Dilly with Stephen and Lance with the clear objective of finally confronting Andy in the hope of striking up a deal and working arrangement.

When they arrived at Playland Andy was there. Word had come to him that Dougie was around yesterday. Dougie used all his charisma and guile when approaching Andy, making sure his boys were with him, if only for safety in numbers.

Andy could see that he still had pulling power. He quickly recognised that Dougie had moved on, had grown up, and was not of the same value he had been some years before. Dougie was quick to inform him that he wanted to help him with his business again and was still able to procure boys for him. Andy invited Dougie to follow him for a coffee, knowing that he had some value as he was experienced and knew the scene. The Rolex wristwatch never got mentioned, but Andy did inform Dougie that he had cost him money and customers, and that if he let him down again, he would not be forgiven.

Dougie had made his mind up that he wanted to move away from the squat with Chris, demanding and expecting a better standard of living, and had the good fortune to be able to stay at the impressive Battersea tower block, with a glimpse of the River Thames from the balcony window, with the party guys, from The Sundowner. Dougie used his charm and due diligence to etch out as much time as he could with Simon and Daniel, who shared this impressive two bedded new build apartment. Dougie needed time to work out his finances and make things up with Andy, so it was very convenient in the short term.

Chapter 91

Several days later, Dougie made his way back to Chris and the squat, where after some soul searching, informed Chris that he was going to leave, to stay with some friends, and when Chris questioned him about going back to the lifestyle, Dougie told Chris "I am just 20 years old, and want more from life, I had fun with my friends last week, and have sorted the main problem I used to have". He then told Chris, that he needed to earn some money, make his own way and have a laugh, but wanted to stay in contact and friends. Chris tried to talk him around, siting the dangers, informing him that he needed to be aware of the health risks with what he was doing, that it was illegal, and the Police were becoming more active within this new government.

It was too late, Dougie was ready to move on, and to work for himself and Andy in the short term, at whatever brought in an income. He was ambitious and ready to find his own way and secretly harboured the notion of working in the club world, where he knew he would need money and contacts.

Chapter 92

Stephen was aware that he had limited time with Dougie and often had to take advantage of those occasions when they spent real individual periods together. Stephen would seek out the intimacy that he craved with Dougie by taking full advantage of those special times together. One of which was when Dougie gave Stephen a Sony Walkman as a present for his 18th Birthday and also supplied him with various music cassette tapes that he thought Stephen might like, with tracks that were personal to Dougie, one of which was 'Fire' by the Ohio Players, a deep funkadelic sound that oozed sexuality.

This was a complete surprise and made Stephen feel that Dougie really did think about him. It reinforced Stephen's affection for Dougie strengthening his understanding that he knew what it meant to feel love. Although he had never said those words to anyone let alone Dougie. He sensed that Dougie knew how he felt about him, that they both recognised each other as being special to one another, particularly when they were good, comfortable and at one.

Dougie always had cocaine and was generous with his friends, knowing that this dependency paid rewards, when future favours were needed. During those rare intimate times cocaine was the best relaxant, Stephen would kiss Dougies shoulders, as he knew that he liked that, on the soft spot between his neck and shoulder joint while running his hands down each side of his back, feeling little gasps of approval as he licked and kissed his spine, while helping Dougie to lube up. Positioning him facedown to enable Stephen to eagerly push his stiff cock into Dougie, entering him as deeply and fully as he could from behind, holding that position in readiness, for a quicker reciprocating motion, that allowed Stephen to fully feel his hard pulsating erection gyrate on top of his most precious friend and lover, making that primal connection with the man he had romanticised about for so long.

Stephen was awe-struck by Dougie, viewing him as a friend and lover knowing that everyone loves a winner, and everyone seemed to love Dougie. He would do anything for the man, always thinking that Dougie felt the same about him.

Dougie liked to have sex with Stephen knowing that he had an emotional hold on the boy, who now declared himself as bi-sexual.

Dougie recognised that Stephen was confused about his homosexual feelings but also knew that Stephen's homoerotic instincts allowed the boy to fully enjoy the physical contact generated between the two of them.

Dougie's Machiavellian approach to his boys allowed him to get the most from them. He understood that to be able to keep some sort of power and control over his key renters that he would use both emotional and drug dependency as his key manipulative force.

Dougie came and went like the wind, always seeming to be busy and into one thing or another. He would supply the boys and Stephen with whatever drugs were on offer, usually at a good price. Stephen, Lance and the younger ones, were recruited by Dougie at various times, and taken to addresses, where they would be expected to perform as a double act, or participate fully with individuals who were clear about what they wanted and had paid for, much of which the boys had been forewarned about, and had been given enough downers, to be able to sufficiently nullify physical feeling, while still being able to satisfy their client's needs.

Stephen would 'fuck, suck, wank, and be sucked and wanked', but was not prepared to take it, as he had always considered himself as an acting homo, not gay, but maybe bisexual, and just doing it for the money. He was clear that he did not consider himself as a total queer, because he wanted to feel like he still fancied girls.

Other requests would range from punters choosing to be treated roughly and have genitals slapped, tied, and manipulated. They would also want renters to dress up as girls and children, while other patrons had the desire to wear nappies and be tended to appropriately, and spanked with a range of items on various parts of their body, which Stephen could do, and it paid well. There was one important person, who liked the feel of rubber on skin, gloves, and gimp masks, balloons and latex strappings, and would like it rubbed and pulled across him until it, or he, screeched with delight and came. But Stephen drew the line at what he considered dirty, extreme kinky stuff, involving bodily fluids, and defecation, even though he was offered more money to do that stuff.

At one celebrity party, a very famous well-healed singer, who had expensive needs, liked well-lubricated

Champagne bottles, to be used as solid dildos. Which was a desperate drug fuel act for the punter who wanted it all.

Chapter 93

Stephen felt like he could do anything in Dougie's presence and wanted to serve him and keep him happy. Stephen was living in a derelict squat with several other younger boys that worked for Andy and Dougie. Dougie had found the building on the other side of Euston Road, leading to Camden Lock. It was an old house that had been repossessed by the council in preparation to clearing the site, but it was still pretty habitable for a while, despite the fact that it was going to be demolished to create a new housing estate. At the start they had electricity, until it got permanently cut off, but for a while it still provided them with a place to get their heads down in-between jobs, dance and have parties. Stephen felt that it never really felt like a home, but like the Dilly it became a focus and hub to meet up. Dougie spent very little time there, particularly when more renters started to use it. It was called the 'chicken house' because of the number of 14- to 16-year-olds who were frequenting it, until eventually during 1982 it was demolished.

Chapter 94

Stephen drifted between the squat and various stays with older punters. Dougie had introduced Stephen to Lawrence, and they had become friendly companions as long as Stephen did not bring drugs into the apartment it worked for short stays, particularly when Stephen was in need of a place where he wanted to feel safe for a while and use less. Lawrence liked the company of youths and still had a close affection for Dougie, conveniently finding that he was able to enjoy both of them at times, or one, knowing that trust was a slippery path that could be navigated in fair weather. Stephen would use whatever drugs he could get hold of, being happy to experiment trying to hide those times when he was particularly out of it. He knew that Lawrence had forebode it but hoped that he would put up with it as long as Stephen kept it under control.

This living arrangement suited Lawrence for a while, until too much advantage was made of the convenience of being in such close proximity to the West End and Piccadilly Circus, when Lawrence started to feel like he was, a free bed and breakfast, without the financial or physical rewards as host.

Stephen came and went throughout 1981. Lawrence turned a blind eye to lots of the drug taking, which he felt he could control by persuading and advising his young stud to be aware of how it could damage his health and their relationship. He had loved the emotional and physical connection he had developed with Stephen particularly during their more intimate times together where he had told Stephen that he would always be there for him.

During August a get together organised by Stephen and Dougie, turned into a party that attracted the attention of neighbours, the police and the 'News of the World', who were asking personal questions about this prominent civil servant.

Lawrence was in constant fear that his private life would be exposed, and as much as he had loved their company, and viewed his time with both Dougie and Stephen as 'the most fun filled, wonderful connection that he had ever had' but realised that he had to cut off all immediate bonds with the boys for the foreseeable future, in an effort to hide it all away, to avoid publicity and media exposure.

Chapter 95

During an early Autumn evening in 1981, in front of the glittering neon lights of Piccadilly Circus stood a group of three skin head youths, dressed in the 'hate' uniform of Dr. Martin boots, checked shirt, red and black braces, jeans turned up at the ankles and short shaved hair cuts.

They were standing by the 'Eros Statue' in the Circus, and looked across to the Wimpy bar, where they pointed and jeered at the boys along the railings for several minutes, calling out abusive homophobic rhetoric, 'fucking poofs, arse-lickers'. One youth, who appeared to be leading the charge, gestured to his fellow comrades in arms to follow him. They dodged and walked through the traffic, making their way across the busy thoroughfare circus junction, stopping cars and vans from getting through, following a direct line towards the boys on the railings.

They spot Stephen and taunt him and his friends from the road, holding up the traffic in the near lane of the junction. Cars and buses edged their way around the group, sounding their car horns, followed by timid gesturing to the youths to get out of the road. The skins keep walking to the railings while making loud jeering comments, about queer bastards. The leading one directs his venom at Stephen and makes direct eye contact. He moves forward in an aggressive pointing action saying "poofs, arse hole fuckers" slightly foaming at the mouth as he spat out his anger and hate.

Stephen was a confidant 19-year-old, a bit pissed and had taken 3 amphetamines. His peers and some other people, outside Boots the Chemist on the Circus, surrounded him. He felt reasonably safe on the other side of the barriers, in the open view of the public and was in no mood to take this crap from their anti-gay way of life.

Staying calm, he beckoned the main skin forward, getting into his best and bravest acting mode, and said, in his well-rehearsed, campest voice "Hi, do you want some fun you handsome cunt". The skin pushed forward, to get closer, gesturing with a full stretch of the neck, veins fully bulging, saying loudly, "are you calling me a cunt you fucking Scotch bender, poof". He stood transfixed, when Stephen said "well, I am looking straight at you darling, so it must be you I am talking to, but I did say handsome cunt, I could have called you a thick prick, but you already know that, so I called you a handsome cunt, which is a bit of a compliment, don't you think". The skin was visibly musing about this response, and bemused by his reply, Stephen stood his ground in a slightly drunken melee, taking one step back from the railing, smiling, half wishing Bernie was around to protect him, waiting for the attack to commence.

The assailant advanced in an aggressive manner with the two others. Stephen stood his ground in anticipation of an attack, and five renters moved forward to surround him, making the skins pause for a moment. Then in a total act of defiance Stephen informed the skins that he could take them all if they had two balls between them. Again, they pondered to consider the answer and their options wondering how the first blow could be made and to who. But just as they had decided to attack, they could feel a murmur running through the onlookers, as the renters turned their heads to see that help was at hand.

Two large Policemen walking from the corner of Shaftsbury Avenue towards the melee were easing their way forward from the side of the group of rent boys, which allowed Stephen to spot them to the left of his peripheral vision with a glance. Stephen then smiled at the lead skin, feeling for once, the welcomed presence and protection of the fuzz, and informed the neo-Nazi, that the 'skin head look 'was a good earner in the Dilly, and if he wanted to make some real money, to come back later and he could be introduced to a game old Judge who had a fetish for his kind. The skins carried on acting aggressive pointing and gesticulating with their fingers and forearms while directed to walk up Shaftsbury Avenue followed by the two policemen. They did not return that day and it felt like a small victory for the Dilly boys and Stephen.

Stephen and the other rent boys knew the dangers of queer bashing. He remembered that his friends had been brutally kicked and beaten during the summer, by some thugs, maybe the same skinheads, who came to the West End for some easy sport. Danny and Kieron were walking arm in arm, happy, and a little drunk, after coming out of 'The Sundowner night club 'during a warm summer evening in

1981. They were walking down Charing Cross Road and cut along a side street, making their way to the Circus, when some itinerant males jumped them, pushing, and punching the boys to the floor, while shouting abuse and anti-gay profanities.

Danny fought back but was brutally hit on the head, face, and torso, by fists that randomly struck out at any part of his body that they could make contact with and then kicked him brutally while on the floor. His left eye socket cracked from one of the kicks, and he received a broken collarbone from another, he ended up with a fracture to the skull, gashes to the face, a clavicle fracture and multiple bruising all about his body. Kieron was kicked and punched, but because they were focusing on Danny, Kieron was able to run back onto Charing Cross Road to gain some assistance for himself and call the police and an ambulance. When they found Danny, he was curled up, crying and in agony, with a small group of people trying to give him some assistance. The perpetrators had run away when spotted and were never caught.

It was an ever-present threat to the Dilly boys who learnt to support each other and move around in groups whenever they could. Regular boys who had been at it for years knew that it could be dangerous, particularly going off with a punter in a car, and they used all their experience and intuition when being taken outside of their comfort zone in the West End. Stories had become folk law in the Dilly scene, from the gangsters, 'Kray Brother' days, when boys disappeared after organised orgies at Cedra Court, a residential block in Hackney, or the posh pickup from a well to do punter in a Rolls Royce or Bentley. The rent boys got little sympathy from the Courts or the Police who viewed them as drug taking law breaking perverts, 'Street Rats' who drew the worst kind into the West End.

The local police had a different view as they got to know many boys over time and had heard the stories about those in higher positions who took full advantage of what the Dilly boys were able to offer.

Stories about Politicians, Judges, Celebrities, Businessmen, and high-ranking Police officers had been coming out in the News of the World, and other tabloids for years. The local officers talked to some of the boys and came to their own conclusions about fact and fiction.

During this time a Central London Police Station formed operational squads to investigate missing and dead children. Scotland Yard was carrying out inquiries. Latterly Operation Circus was set up by the metropolitan police to follow up on a paedophile ring, where several convictions were made from collecting hundreds of inappropriate criminal pictures and images of babies, children and teenagers from the homes of the perpetrators.

Children were found dead within and around the capitals, suburbs and in other towns and cities throughout the country. Investigation stretched as far as the Channel Islands but failed to be properly followed up. There were stories in London, expressed by rent boys, of a dangerous man who might have been responsible for some of the missing individuals who hung out on the Dilly. One renter of Jamaican descent, talked about a man who tried to strangle him along St Ann's church park railings, but he fought him off, describing him as a sleazy Scotsman who hung about the concourse and 'Playland'. There was no point in reporting the incident to the police, as he knew that they would not take seriously the story of a gay, young black male homosexual, rent boy.

Chapter 96

The 80's brought in a whole new fashion with the new romantic's wave of hedonism. Punk was out and young people wanted to express themselves creatively using second hand and new clothes that had been redesigned to reflect a more decorative style of dressing that for males hooked into an androgynous, sometimes effeminate dynamic appearance where eye makeup, face colouring, eye liner, lipstick, hair pigments and hats were the given trend.

New clubs were opening that blurred the lines between a given gender stereotype, where cross-dressing was seen as the new trendy youth revolution.

Music and popular bands promoted a look that had been influenced by student fashion statements coming from Central Saint Martin's College. Picked up by aspiring teens, exploring a new look and identity, which was found in the New Romantic subculture movement. Young people pushing gender boundaries wearing foundation cream and eyeliner.

Dougie was very quick to catch on and became a regular at the Covent Garden, Tuesday Club night at 'Blitz', where he successfully negotiated a job working behind the bar, by knowing Disc Jockey (DJ) Rusty Egan, who hosted these exclusive nights along with Steve Strange. Which was Dougies ticket to watching and learning how these events were put together.

He was also able to develop his pharmaceutical enterprise by supplying amphetamines and poppers, packaged in small plastic bags that could be exchanged for a five-pound note. Word soon got around that the charming Scottish barman had the goods, and a quick and easy sale could be made, with a handshake to transfer the cash, followed by the goods.

Dougie reluctantly continued to work for Andy and was also able to set up some of his own parties where he would arrange the entertainment and organise his own boys. He liked the money but was finding it harder to manage his conscience. The boys seemed to get younger as the years went by, reminding him of his own difficult experiences at Elm Guest House. He knew that he was using his power in the same way that Andy had manipulated and groomed him and loathed who he had become.

Chapter 97

Stephen was not into dressing up and hated the idea of wearing makeup. He found that he was being left behind by Dougie, who was socialising with new friendship groups, and did not seem as interested in hanging out with the boys and him-self anymore.

Stephen felt rejected by his friend and lover, feeling used and abused when it had suited Dougie. He experimented with different drugs and found that heroin gave him the best high. He was aware of the addictive nature of the drug but was feeling depressed and trapped by his rent boy lifestyle and felt he needed something to make him feel better. Dougie had always warned him off from using heroin because of the over addictive nature of the drug.

Stephen had missed a job that Dougie had arranged because he had fallen asleep after an episode of smoking heroin. When Dougie next met up with Stephen, he angrily informed him that he had fucked up the deal and had let him down. He furiously reminded Stephen that heroin was an expensive and addictive habit that can kill you. Repeating to him that we earn our money from what we do and can get from punters who expect at a minimum, boys to turn up when arrangements have been made. He reinforced his point by stating that it impacts on me when they don't get what they have paid for. Stephen knew he had let Dougie down but was caught up in the highs of his opium, smiling as he told Dougie that he didn't care about the fucking punters and wanted to be left alone. This was the biggest fall out they had ever had. Dougie hated what Stephen was becoming, knowing what the darker side of a heroin base addiction could lead to, and shouted at Stephen to sort himself out.

Stephen's dependency on heroine was relatively short lived as he tried shoplifting from Selfridges in an attempt to make some easy money to support his burgeoning craving for the real stuff. He was caught by one of the store detectives and handed over to the West End Police who kept him in custody for two days, where it was found that he needed medical support for his addiction. He was fortunate enough not to be sent to prison but instead was sent to a Psychiatric Youth Offending Centre in Shepherds Bush, where he stayed for 4 weeks. His stay in custody though difficult, allowed Stephen to somewhat free himself from the physical pangs of heroin addiction for a while. Once free and back on the streets Stephen stayed with Lance and the other boys most of the time, always wondering if and when Dougie might show his head.

When Stephen finally met up with Dougie he tried to explain and say sorry and that he had been through a rough time. Dougie was in a better place and brushed the whole thing off as one of those things informing Stephen not to use that stuff again. They patched things up and Dougie took Stephen to a party where Stephen borrowed Dougies leather jacket with the silver studs for the night. The next day Stephen did another job for Dougie, but it paid less and he quickly found himself back on the meat rack trying to earn again.

Chapter 98

Dougie was struggling with the notion of the male sex worker child exploitation stuff and wanted out. He hated dealing with Andy and his contacts, pimping and sending young boys to those men to be used and abused for money. He was finding that he was able to earn enough from his bar work and other gay venues to be able to start distancing himself from the street trade. He had also met someone who he felt particularly close to and wanted to dissociate himself from his previous life, keeping it secret from his new lover.

Weeks on Stephen still had Dougie's leather-studded jacket from when they were last together. Stephen had decided that it should be his because the jacket symbolized the bond, he thought he had with Dougie. He had also been trying to keep it secret that he had used heroine again.

Dougie liked the Jacket and wanted it back, thinking it would have been returned after the last job. They did not meet again until just before Christmas 1982. Dougie instantly knew that Stephen was using 'H' again, which made him angry and concerned for his wellbeing. He challenged Stephen about being out of his head and when he saw that he was wearing his jacket he became irate and accused Stephen of stealing his property. Stephen tried to joke by saying he had earned it, after all the money he had made for Dougie over the years. Dougie took offence to this statement insisting that it was Stephen's choice, arguing that after all, he was a rent boy prossie "what else are you going to do for money", calling him a smack head loser.

    Stephen hated arguing with Dougie and tried to laugh it off by removing the jacket and holding the collar catch while he dangled it in front of his friend, challenging him to "take it if you can." Dougie informed Stephen and Lance that he had enough of all the shit involved organising liaisons for ungrateful pricks. "You people need to find out for yourselves what it is like having to meet up with the wankers who I have to deal with. Punters who expect and think, that we the low life of the Dilly will do anything for money. I do not expect gratitude and respect from those cunts, but I do from you. My advice is to sort yourselves out, go to 'Centrepoint' and get a proper place to live and a job".

Chapter 99

During this time, Dougie was less driven, by sexualized renting notions to make money. He found himself determined to make his own way, fantasising about running his own club, loving the gay nighttime economy of fun and pleasure, while understanding that he needed to move away from facilitating young boys into compromising encounters and prostitution.

Knowing that he could find work in clubs allowed Dougie to continue with his more lucrative side of the business, that was now mostly paying the bills. He eventually found his way into working at the premier gay club in London, 'Heaven' firstly as a doorman/coat handler, and then barman, always learning and searching his way around a business with burgeoning opportunities, particularly for someone with vision and ideas.

Chapter 100

Stephen struggled to understand what had gone on. He knew that Dougie could be restless and vain, but not cruel. He was convinced that Dougie would eventually come about to find him, but he never did.

His life revolved around hanging out on the Dilly to earn money, growing more and more despondent at the aimlessness of his world, finding that he used too many amphetamines to keep him awake and pain killers to numb his reality.

His lowest point was when he was thrown out of an elderly punters home after he had caught Stephen stealing his medication in the bathroom. Stephen found himself on the streets racked with guilt and depression, hating who he was. He used a penknife that he had taken from one of his punters to pick away at his left forearm cutting little slashes until blood would stream out. This made him feel like he was punishing himself for not being a good son, person or friend. He wanted to find Dougie to give him back his jacket but knew that Dougie could be anywhere and questioned why he would want to spend any time with a loser like him.

Chapter 101

During late 1982 Dougie had found that he could afford to share and rent a flat with his new friend and lover called Simon. They both worked at Heaven, but Simon was the accountant who Dougie met while prepping the Bar during the day. Simon was like nobody else he had ever met before. He was organised, clean, and methodical and had an obvious head for figures. Simon smoked but refused to take pills and cocaine and as a consequence helped Dougie to stop what he was doing with pills and eventually convinced him about the addictive nature of cocaine, which Dougie always insisted was recreational, and that he could do without it if he had to.

Simon hooked into Dougie's ambition to run and own his own club and together they found a venue in a vacated warehouse that had once housed the rag trade, and they called it 'Kissarse'.

The disused factory warehouse in Curtain Road, near Old Street station was leased to Simon in 1983, and registered as a licensed premises up until 1.00am and was developed into a late night Gay dance venue open three nights a week, Thursday, Friday and Saturday, that stayed open until 5.00am on Friday and Saturday, which was something new to clubbing world.

Dougie sold the Rolex wristwatch to help finance the club, bringing in enough money to be able to purchase decks, and a substantial sound system. Together, they set up a club with a bar, security entry system, and with an interior design imagined by Dougie. The Club challenged some of the best gay nightspots in London. The word soon got around that this new venue was able to stay open later, while some of the more, well known venues had to close.

Chapter 102

Dougie wanted to disassociate himself as far away from his memories of abuse and his rent boy days as he could and only told Simon about parts of his previous life. They questioned how he had somehow avoided the Human Immunodeficiency Virus (HIV) the silent epidemic that was now running through life in Britain, a virus that seemed to be impacting significantly on the Gay community and killing indiscriminately.

Simon had always insisted on 'safe sex 'and Dougie was eventually persuaded to take the test, mainly by the incessant arguments about acquired immunodeficiency syndrome (AIDS) propagated through the main media outlets and the gay community, that they both should be tested. The realism that this virus was a killer was becoming an ever-present reality, and they were both relieved when tested as negative. Dougie felt like he had been given a second chance at life fuelled by the excitement of developing 'Kissarse'.

Dougie wondered what had happened to Stephen but wanted to keep that part of his previous life separated from Simon and his new wave friends, and as a consequence cut off all contact with Stephen, Andy and the Dilly.

He often doubted how he had survived those years, questioning what he had put himself through wondering if a broken child can ever be fixed. He knew that Andy and himself had exploited many children who had presented themselves in and around the West End of London, knowing he was part of the problem. But he also knew that it was a consequence of the abuse that he had suffered while being alone, young and naive with nobody to understand or support him.

Over the years Dougie learnt that his guilt belonged somewhere else and should be laid squarely on the shoulders of the perpetrators, punters, pimps and abusers who had used their wealth, power, position in total disregard for those young people's human rights and dignity. It was they who had manipulated and bought the favours of damaged children and innocent adolescents. It was they who should suffer the shame associated. However, he could never shake off the guilt-ridden feelings, worry and remorse when recalling his part played in the procurement of his renters. He had always questioned if they survived the virus, drugs and psychological turmoil that inevitably left scars deep within the victims of the abuse. He wondered if they had not come to London would their everyday lives have been better. West End rent boys looking for a fulfilled life. Free of prejudice, if that was truly possible in the 1980's and years to come.

Chapter 103

Stephen 1 day ago. Tuesday 25-01-1983

I spent the last five hours in the all-night café, along Northumberland Avenue, and felt like shit. Most of my money was used yesterday on buses, trains, some food, more pills, and booze. I was playing 'Mad World' on my Walkman, as I entered Leicester square from St. Martin's Street, 'all around me are familiar faces, worn out places, worn out faces', and I realised how this was me, 'bright and early for the daily races, going nowhere'…. I had to stop playing the song, as these crushing thoughts moved through me, like the heaviest weights pulling me down. My legs buckled and I could hardly hold myself up. I fell to the ground on the grass, in the square and could hear the prophecy relating to a lyric informing me that, 'the dreams in which I'm dying are the best I ever had'. What was I. How did I get to where I am, a homeless nothing, worthless, not wanted by anyone, my mum, punters and my friend Dougie. The busy people going nowhere, in this mad world, ignored my collapse, and I felt utterly alone.

Chapter 104

Stephen sat in a quiet shivering heap, head bowed, before grappling into his pockets to find his supply of mixed amphetamines and codeine, and took two, followed by two more of each. He began to shake as the cold and wetness from the winter morning grass soaked into his fragile body.

He managed to scramble to his feet, in preparation to walk his well-furrowed route to the Dilly, but because it was still early, with the main morning incumbent commuters determinedly making their way to individual respective destinations, he did not find any of his usual group, in their customary places around the railings.

He decided to walk on up Shaftsbury Avenue, turning left into Dean Street at 8.00am just as the Centrepoint alliance of homeless youths, were loudly leaving through the side door.

They did not notice the disheveled young man across the road, looking earnestly at the determined group filled with hope and the promise of a future, which he had once been part of. They were heading in the direction of their respective destinations, which had been carefully and painstakingly organised by 'Centrepoint'. Appointments confirmed and fully discussed with the most appropriate advice or accommodation agencies available in the West End and brokered by the Centrepoint worker on duty that evening, night, and through to the morning.

Stephen walked aimlessly along Dean Street until he arrived at Carlisle Street and into the familiarity of Soho Square. Instantly being reminded of his first meeting with Dougie. But he knew that he was not going to come. He was following his dreams and leaving his old life and friends behind, no more needy rent boys, or selling himself cheaply for financial reward. Everybody loves a winner and that person was Dougie. Stephen knew that he had made a new life for himself and had moved into another phase in his existence with the new wave of exciting social groups he admired, had fun with, worked besides, and was drawn to. Those with novel, original, and progressive ideas that afforded a confidence and determination that Stephen lacked. Stephen had never come to terms with who he was or might have been, never fully understanding or accepting the new androgynous notions of men trying to look like a glamorous she male.

Stephen arrived in Oxford Street with the headphones on and turned his Walkman to play, listening to Bowie screaming out 'Jean Genie'. Stephen started to move in a dance step to the melodic guitar riff that falls quietly into Bowie singing, 'sits like a man but smiles like a reptile 'gaining some looks from those around him as he sang out loud, danced and took some more of his pills. His Walkman slowly wound down and stopped. The batteries had finally discharged themselves and Stephen felt totally alone.

The shops were starting to open in preparation for the day. Stephen cautiously sat himself outside of the central window of Selfridge's overhang, to gain some protection from the blowing cold sleet that was drifting along Oxford Street. The light rain prompted the opening of umbrellas, encouraging the public to start to move quickly along the Street and into shops and doorways in an attempt to get organised before the main flurry took hold.

There was some shelter by the windows of the great store and Stephen found that odd passersby put money on his bag that was placed by his folded legs and feet, while others offered a hot drink or packets of takeaway food.

The morning progressed into afternoon. Stephen fell in and out of sleep, sporadically standing up and moving around, to feel some sense of movement and sensation through his tired joints, that had stiffened with the cold numbness of muscle on stone, that could be endured no more. He felt suspended in a complete disinclination to move on from this spot, deducing that at least some people had noticed him and were marginally willing to perceive him as a person.

It was late in the afternoon, his wrists were throbbing from the tight dressings bound to his forearms, and he took the remaining pills from his pocket and swallowed them with the help of a donated Coca Cola drink. The dampness from the cold wet day had seeped into his clothing and bones. He ached as he pulled himself to his feet once again, and tried to gain some feeling in his legs, stamping his feet to encourage his circulation. People were walking by, but they all blurred into one another, before Stephen looked to his right.

Further along the 'Selfridge' windows there was a person gazing straight at him. Stephen recognised him as the man from the 'Golden Lion' pub. After a pause of recognition, he walked up to Stephen and asked if he wanted a cigarette. Stephen was content to see a familiar face, and lighting up, took a long slow drag from the tobacco stick, which offered an instant relaxant. The man asked him if he wanted to go to the café for a bite to eat and a drink, and introduced himself as Dennis, reminding Stephen that they had met in the Golden Lion Pub.

Once in the Café, Stephen gave in, as he listened to this man's intense conversation that encouraged and convinced him to leave the café with him and take a taxi ride to Dennis's home in North London, Cranley Gardens, near Muswell Hill.

Dennis Nilsen lived in a top floor flat, where on their arrival, a small brown dog, jumped, barked, and greeted them as it leapt around with excitement.

There was a stench much greater than the stink of canine and urine that contaminated this space, but Stephen found himself giving into his previous good sense when assessing punters.

Exhaustion, the pills he had taken, and his depressive tiredness had totally consumed every part of him.

The evening progressed and Stephen found himself struggling to stay awake searching through his pockets for any loose pills and found a couple buried in the lining of his trouser pocket. He was offered whisky to drink and found him-self having to move about in an attempt to stay cognisant.

Nilsen talked and tried to engage Stephen in some kind of conversation through to the early hours of Wednesday the 26th, stimulated at having a friend to stay, while making it clear that he could sleep on the spare mattress.

Nilsen played 'Under Pressure' on his record player, with Bowie and Mercury competing to out-sing the other. Nilsen angrily shook and prodded Stephen as he tried to engage him into some kind of interaction, becoming outraged at being ignored as Stephen fell off to sleep.

He then played, The Who's 'Tommy' see me, feel me…

Stephen felt himself fall in and out of a hopeless consciousness, with thoughts of his mother in the morning, making him that first cup of tea and toast and Dougie smiling and dancing as he rhythmically swept around, moving close, bumping hips, while holding an arm and pulling him into a full embrace.

Stephen drifted into oblivion at the hands of Dennis Nilsen, serial killer, becoming 'just another lost boy'.

Epilogue

Dennis Nilsen was a predator who sought out and befriended young vulnerable males in and around the West End of London for over five years. His first victim was a 14-year-old boy, murdered on the 30th of December 1978. His final victim was 20-year-old Stephen Sinclair murdered on the 26th of January 1983.

Throughout his killing spree, he had strangled, drowned and dismembered 12 to 15 different males with another three who reported that they had just escaped Nilsen's attempt to finish them off.

Nilsen had started his serial killings and butchery when he first lived in a downstairs ground floor flat at Melrose Avenue in Cricklewood, London. He burned, mutilated and buried most of his carved-up victims in the back garden.

The full extent of his serial slaughtering's had been uncovered five years later at a new address. A drain attendant found parts of human bodies, fleshy parts, finger and toe bones, in the feeder drain, emanating from Nilsen's top floor North London home in Cranley Gardens, Hornsey, London.

The Police were waiting for Nilsen outside of his building, as he arrived home from work, on a cold snowy February evening. He led the police into the top floor loft room, and the arresting officer described a smell of death as he asked Nilsen where the bodies are. Nilsen replied by informing the inspector that parts of two were in the wardrobe cupboard, while others body bits were in boxes and a drawer located beneath the bathtub.

The black plastic bin liners containing the remains of Stephen Sinclair were tied with the crepe bandages that had been wrapped around Stephen's wrists from his stay in hospital two days earlier.

References

Centrepoint Soho.
The chairman of 'Centrepoint' Gerald Reddington, in 1977, wrote in the Shelter's report headed 'Ordinary People', that 'Perhaps above all we have failed to change attitudes towards homeless people. They are still stigmatised and blamed for their homelessness. I fear that if we have failed to change our attitudes there can be no change in our present conditions. The problem is so large it is not for the faint hearted, but for those with courage and vision, there is work to be done. Please help us in our aim to increase public awareness and understanding about homeless young people in whatever way you can'.

Progress has been made since the early 1980's, where 'Centrepoint' and various West End agencies, worked with the Children's Society, who funded and set up the 'Central London Teenage Project ' (CLTP), which opened in June 1985. CLTP supported and provided a 'Safe House' advise, advocacy and accommodation to underage young people who were picked up in the West End of London for five years.

They negotiated a system of trust with the Metropolitan Police, London Transport Police and Central London Social Service Departments, who before had struggled to find appropriate emergency accommodation, and manage the process of dealing with underage young runaways picked up in their areas by the police, putting an enormous strain on their services.

CLTP would take underage referrals directly from Centrepoint, The Soho Project, Westminster and Camden Social Services Departments, and the West End Police. They provided young people with a 'Safe House 'where the address was confidential,

Parents and Social Workers were only given a telephone number, to allow the young people coming into the project to feel safe and for trust to be built up with the workers.

In recent years Centrepoint has further developed its services, for 16- to 21-year-olds, to include pathways to accommodation. Firstly, in London opening Centrepoint House, Flats and bedsits. Funding was supported by the Princes Trust, Princess Diana's Patronage and from the year 2000 Prince William's Patronage and ongoing support.

It now provides a range of housing services in London, Greater Manchester, Yorkshire and the Northeast (Sunderland) to include Independent Living Homes, Independent Living Cottages, Flats and Shared Housing. Funding is varied where donations are made through, legacies, charitable trusts, rent, and fundraising activities.

Mental health issues, like depression and anxiety, often caused by being homeless, sleeping outside, the risk of life alone, poor family, and emotional conditions cause an ever-increasing crisis for young people moving from childhood to adulthood, who should in any normal sense of family always need to be supported through this difficult transition.

Children who have been sexually abused, and have experienced abnormal underage, sexualised behaviors, continue to be particularly vulnerable. Those with the knowledge and experience of working with sexually abused young people argue that child sexual abuse is widespread and that the perpetrators are mainly men. It is clear that sexual abuse can have a long lasting and traumatic effect on its victims for the rest of their lives.

While working with Children at Centrepoint and at the Central London Teenage Project in the 80's, it was evidently clear that we were trying to provide a service to Children with very complex needs. Many were sharing horrendous stories that had profoundly impacted on their lives. It was clear that some important people in their lives had let them down leaving unscrupulous adults and peers in the West End of London to pray upon naivety, teenage hope, innocence and gullibility.

During my time working at 'Centrepoint', as a Night Shelter Worker, I was interviewed by a young reporter from 'Time Out', which was then a prestigious London magazine, about the work we were doing with youth homelessness in The West End of London during the early 1980's. I remember speaking at length about how hard it was to categorize all the different children, youths and young adults that we supported and looked after. Providing emergency short-term care, day by day to distressed, unhappy, confused and more often abused kids, in the centre of London, during their short stays at the night shelter. The issues that affected their lives were set against an inhospitable political and social climate in the 1980's that had very little knowledge or sympathy for youths who found themselves on the streets, desperate and vulnerable.

When the article was published, I privately questioned the category and phrase she decided to use to describe our residents, as 'Street Vagabonds', which for me evoked, something more in the nature of, a happy traveller or homeless wanderer, which was very different to what I had tried to explain. That each person had a very individual story to tell, many of whom were distressed, frightened, and had a desperation that was relieved by finding kindness in a London sanctuary with advice and support called 'Centrepoint'.

Most were dealing with a sadness and pain that was a consequence of a disturbed and unhappy home life, be that in care, or in dysfunctional households, where abuse, as it appears in many forms, was perpetrated on children by adults, siblings, relatives and extended groups connected to the family.

The Perpetrators:

The 2020 Crown Independent Inquiry into Child sexual Abuse linked to Westminster concludes by stating; 'There is ample evidence that individual perpetrators of child sexual abuse have been linked to Westminster, that there have been significant failures by Westminster institutions in their dealing with, and confrontation of, allegations of child sexual abuse'. The report suggests that the whips offices were concerned above all with protecting the image of their party. There was a consistent culture for years of playing down rumours and protecting politicians from gossip or scandal at all costs. Moreover, it was done without ever considering the interest of the potential victims.

The Inquiry acknowledges the various claims made concerning Elm Guest
House, described as a tawdry establishment where child sexual abuse took place were apparent. The Metropolitan Police Service evidence goes some way to clarify the allegations relating to child sexual abuse at the Guest House involved persons of public prominence.

The report informs the reader that there was a direct deference by police towards powerful people, such as a conscious decision not to arrest or investigate someone because of their profile or position. A second form of deference being, an internal kind, where junior police officers did not challenge senior officers, for fear of harming their own career prospects.

The difference in treatment due to socio-economic status provided striking evidence. The inquiry found proof of how wealth and social status insulated perpetrators of child sexual abuse from being brought to justice to the detriment of the victims of their alleged abuse. Poverty and disadvantage were cited as a reason why allegations of child sexual abuse, were not taken seriously.

Point 20 of the conclusions and recommendations argues that insufficient consideration of the needs of the child victims and survivors was a failure by almost every institution to put the needs and safety of the children who have survived sexual abuse first.

It was recommended that Government, political parties and other Westminster institutions must have whistleblowing policies and procedures, which cover child sexual abuse and exploitation. That all government departments should ensure that they have a comprehensive safeguarding policy and that they have procedures to accompany their policies. It makes clear that all political parties must update their policies and procedures regularly, obtaining expert safeguarding advice, when doing this.

The report suggests that it is clear that during 1970's and 1980's there were profound social changes occurring relating to socially acceptable sexual behavior and the age of consent. The law was slow to change causing great mistrust within the gay community. As the century progressed boundaries of sexual activity were being challenged. The age range, in which the term 'boy 'was being used when describing 18- to 21-year-old young men changed with the notion that boys would be better characterised as those below the age of 18 or school age.

After Thoughts:

Stephen is one example of so many children running from abuse, drawn into sexual exploitation. My story is taken from a composite of children who I worked with during the 1980's, some of whom still haunt me, particularly when I think of what could have been.

I am confident that the great teams that I worked with did provide a safe house, with warmth and care during this time, and I am happy that the organisations that I was involved with 'did their best 'and continue to do so.

During 1984 'Centrepoint 'was asked to share any information we might have about the activities of the boys and males connected to the procurement of children on the rent scene at the time. The policeman who was running the investigation explained the issues, which were that of an organised peadophile ring/gang in the West End of London were being investigated. They had seized lots of indecent images and photographs of children from the homes of various male offenders some of who were high profile individuals.

He explained that they had called the investigation 'Operation Circus 'and did I recognise anyone in the pictures or know anything about what they had uncovered.

I was shown a sample of some pictures that had been taken from these perpetrators. Shock is an understatement as I was completely unaware and unprepared for what they allowed me to look at (and as disgusting as it was, I feel it needs to be known) images of babies and small children with distended anus and virginal openings, naked children of all ages photographed in various sexualised positions. It was appalling and I know the police officer was clearly sickened having to show me these few images, knowing that they had boxes full of them.

I had very little to offer in the way of information other than that 'Centrepoint', continually came into contact with underage young people and that we were faced with the dilemma of how best to manage and support them within the eyes of the law. I was able to share some of the observations about older men who were clearly on the prowl seeking out young vulnerable children and teenagers on Shaftsbury Avenue, sometimes outside of the Night Shelter. That some of the boys that we see regularly were renting and had developed survival mechanisms but were incredibly vulnerable and it was immensely disheartening when we had so little to offer them other than to return to where they had run from. I was able to share that most of these children had complicated and challenging stories and on the whole were victims of sexual abuse, unhappiness and exploitation.

Very little had changed during my time, with underfunded social services, struggling to protect society's most vulnerable.

They were labelled street rats, rent boys, chickens, and male prostitutes. Susceptible children caught up in the world of pimps, abusers and paedophiles, who would seek out every angle, to make money, and to procure a profit on their property.

In an effort to change the law and provide a different model of provision for young child runaways, 'The Children's Society 'in 1985 funded a new youth work initiative in response to under aged young people needing support in the West End of London. A specialised Runaway Project which we called 'The Central London Teenage Project', that provided a 'Safe House' concept, modeled on existing examples run in Amsterdam and America.

During my time at 'The Central London Teenage Project', working with young runaways we found that a great majority of young people ran away because they suffered various forms of sexual abuse, at home, in care and within their communities and needed to 'get away 'from a troubled life.

Very few options were available for these under aged children at the time, other than to make the decision to take the great risk and runaway, in the hope that something would work out. It was clear that if one asked young people why they come to London, we found that they might reply, that it was where the railway ended.

When I eventually found out that the Stephen that I had worked with at Centrepoint Night Shelter was the same Stephen and last victim of Nilsen in 1983 I was truly shaken and have always wanted to talk about this story.

Rest in peace Stephen (and all the other lost boys), I still remember you.

Stewart Brown

I often find myself questioning what had happened to all those abused individual survivors, whose indecent images were stolen for sexual gratification?

References:

Centrepoint Soho. 50th Anniversary Staff Past and Present: Annual report statement in 1977 by Gerald Reddington.

Daily Express 'I saw boys of 8 abused by music mogul Tam Paton' By Robert James. Sunday 17 Aug 2014. (Deceased)

Ex-BBC DJ Chris Denning Jailed for 'Child Sex Offences' BBC News and The Guardian News and Media Ltd. 7 Oct 2016. (Deceased)

Independent Inquiry Report, Child Sexual Abuse: Allegation of Child Sexual Abuse Linked to Westminster. Investigation Report February 2020. Crown Copy.

Independent News Paper: Jonathan King found guilty of abuse. Wednesday 21 Nov 2001.

Newman C. Young runaways. Findings from Britain's first Safe House for Young Run aways. The Children's Society 1989.

Daniel Boffey. The Guardian: (Elm House) Reference to a Child Brothel, a Politician and Suspicion over the death of Carole Kasir. 2014.

What happened to the 114 documents relating to organised child abuse that the Home Office admits it has either destroyed or lost?

Reed J. THE DILLY: A Secret History of Piccadilly Rent Boys. Peter Owen Publishers in 2014.

The Daily Herald: North Sea Storms/Floods. Feb 1954.

The Glasgow Times: Jimmy Reid speech, No hooliganism, vandalism and bevvying. 28 July 2011.

The SCOTSMAN: They say Leith got off lightly....they're wrong. Newsroom article 13 July 2005.

The SCOTSMAN. Disgraced Scots Cardinal Keith O'Brian. 12 July 2020 (deceased)

Music Credits in chronological order as they appear in the book :
Save your Love.   Renee and Renato

You can't Hurry Love.   Phil Collins

Staying Alive.   Bee Gees

Three Times a Lady.   The Commodores

Two Little Boys.   Rolf Harris

Love Grows.   Edison Lighthouse

The Moon Belongs to Everyone (but the best things in life are free). Frank Sinatra

Wonderful, Wonderful, Copenhagen.   Danny Kaye

Shake Rattle and Roll.   Bill Haley and the Comets

How much is that Doggie in the Window.   Patti Page

Que Sera-Sera.   Doris Day

Hound Dog.   Elvis Presley

Are you Lonesome Tonight.   Elvis Presley

Scottish Soldier.   Andy Stewart

Rubber Ball.   Bobby Vee

Calendar Girl.   Neil Sedaka

Take Good Care of my Baby.   Bobby Vee

Shang-a-lang.   Bay City Rollers

Hold Back the Night.   The Tramps

Love is the Drug.   Roxy Music

Space Oddity.   David Bowie

Bohemian Rhapsody.   Queen

Yes Sir I can Boogie.   Baccara

Do You Really Want to Hurt Me.   Culture Club

Baker Street.   Gerry Rafferty

Wuthering Heights.   Kate Bush

The Young Ones.   Cliff Richards

Satisfy my Soul.   Bob Marley and the Wailers

Night Fever.   Bee Gees

I'm Always Touched by your Presence Dear.   Blonde

Lets Go Disco. The Real Thing
Everybody Dance.   Chic
More than a Woman.   Tavares
Mind Blowing Decisions.   Heatwave
What a Waste'   Ian Dury
Love is in the Air.   John Paul Jones

You're the One that I Want.   Greese

If I Can't have You. Yvonne Ellerman
Rivers of Babylon.   Boney M
On Nation Under a Groove.   Funkadelic
Uptight.   Stevie Wonder
Baby love.   The Supremes
Coral works: O Sacrum Convivium, Jusu Salvator Mundi, Holy God We Praise They Name
Ziggy Stardust.   David Bowie
Day Dreamer.   David Cassidy
Life on Mars.   David Bowie
Silent Night.   Christmas Song
Street Life.   Roxy Music/Brian Ferry
Virginia Plain.   Roxy Music
Rock and Roll Suicide.   David Bowie
Jesus Christ Superstar.   Lloyd and Webber
Make me Smile.   Steve Harley and The Cockney Rebels
Bridge over Troubled Water.   Simon and Garfunkel
Rock Your Baby.   George McCrae
Kung Fu Fighting.   Carl Douglas
Spirit in the Sky.   Norman Greenbaum
Sugar Baby Love.   Rubettes
Waterloo.   Abba
Band on the Run.   Wings

She's Gonna Win.   Bilbo Baggins
Play that Funky Music.   Wild Cherry

Tragedy.   Bee Gees
Boogie Wonderland.   Earth Wind and Fire
Enough is Enough   Donna Summer
In the Navy.   The Village People
Good Times.   Chic

He's the Greatest Dancer.   Sister Sledge

Knee Deep.   Funkadelic
Fire.   The Ohio Players
Mad World.   Tears for Fears
Jean Genie.   David Bowie
Under Pressure.   Bowie and Mercury
Tommy (see me, feel me, touch me, feel me).   The Who

General references:

BBC 'Housewives choice' music played.

BBC 'Top of The Pops '(TOTP). Jimmy Savile. (deceased) Stewart Brown personal experience.
Decca Records Office. 15 Great Marlborough Street W1. The Surrey House. Chis Denning and Jonathan King. Personal experience Stewart Brown 1970 from visit to TOTP studio to Decca Records Offices.

'Gay Times': Identity, Locality, Memory, and the Brixton Squats in 1970's London. 12 Nov 2011.

Hare Krishna Govinda's Pure Vegetarian Restaurant 9-10 Soho Square.
Luke Howard (Testimonies) Sundowners, Charring Cross. Global Village Club. The Glades Gay Club. Chris Lucas DJ. 7 May 2013
'Mayfair 'Magazine, mentioned within text.
The Clash, Sex Pistols, Jonny Rotten, Sid Vicious mentioned in relation to Punks.
The Guardian. Spandau Ballet, the Blitz Kids, and the birth of the New Romantics. Blitz Club. David Johnson 4 Oct 2009.

Tony Manero (John Travolta) from the Movie 'Saturday Night Fever'

ABOUT THE AUTHOR

Stewart Brown is a retired teacher and qualified youth worker whose career began in the 1970s and 80s in London's West End, supporting young runaways at Centrepoint Night Shelter during its earliest days. He later managed children's homes and observation centres, drawing on his deep commitment to vulnerable young people. With a degree in Psychology from Goldsmiths, a Youth Work qualification from Bulmershe College, and a teaching certificate, Stewart has dedicated his life to education, care, and safeguarding. A father of two and proud grandfather of six, he has carried this story in his heart for many years — and only in retirement found the time to give it the justice it deserves

www.ingramcontent.com/pod-product-compliance
Lightning Source LLC
LaVergne TN
LVHW041537070426
835507LV00011B/812